The Erotics of Passage

Modern French Writers

General Editor
EDMUND SMYTH
University of Liverpool

Consultant Editors

MICHAEL SHERINGHAM   DAVID WALKER
Royal Holloway, University of London   *University of Sheffield*

This series aims to provide a forum for new research on modern and contemporary French and Francophone writing. The volumes to be published in *Modern French Writers* will offer new readings of already widely-known writers in addition to those whose work is beginning to command attention. The contributions to the series reflect a wide variety of critical practices and theoretical approaches, in harmony with the developments which have taken place over the past few decades. modern French writing will be considered in all its manifestations: novel, poetry, drama, autobiography, cinema, popular culture, theory. In keeping with the erosion of contours which characterises the moden period, 'canonical' and 'non-canonical' writers will be examined, both within France and the French-speaking world more generally. The volumes in the series will participate in the wider debate on key aspects of contemporary culture.

Future volumes will include:

Jean Duffy, *Reading Between the Lines: Claude Simon and the Visual Arts*

Jean-Pierre Boulé, *Hervé Guibert: Voices of the Self*

THE EROTICS
OF PASSAGE

*Pleasure, Politics, and Form
in the Later Work of Marguerite Duras*

James S. Williams
University of Kent at Canterbury

LIVERPOOL UNIVERSITY PRESS

First published 1997 by
LIVERPOOL UNIVERSITY PRESS
Senate House
Abercromby Square
Liverpool
L69 3BX

British Library Cataloguing-in-Publication Data
A British Library CIP Record is available
ISBN 0–85323–990–8 *cased*
    0–85323–501–5 *paper*

Set in Linotron 202 Sabon by
Wilmaset Ltd, Birkenhead, Wirral
Printed and bound in the European Union by
Bell & Bain Ltd, Glasgow

Frontispiece: Marguerite Duras and Yann Andréa, photograph by Dominique Issermann, reproduced by kind permission of the photographer (copyright © Dominique Issermann)

In Memoriam

This book was already in production when Marguerite Duras died in early March 1996. In response, I have simply changed the present tense to the past where necessary and omitted instances of the future tense which would now make no sense. This study does not offer itself, therefore, as a retrospective appraisal of a complete oeuvre. It remains firmly in the critical present and engages with a uniquely vital and constantly evolving corpus. I dedicate it to the living memory of Marguerite Duras.

Contents

Acknowledgements

This project began life as a doctoral thesis for the University of London and was aided by a three-year Major State Studentship from the British Academy. I would like to thank my supervisor, Malcolm Bowie, for his unwavering support, Michael Sheringham for his generosity and always constructive advice, and, in the production of the book itself, Ed Smyth and Robin Bloxsidge for their calm efficiency and flexibility. I thank also the staffs of The University of London Library; The British Library; The British Film Institute; The New York Public Library; Rutgers University-New Brunswick Library; La Bibliothèque Marguerite Durand, Paris; La Bibliothèque Nationale, Paris; and The Widener Library, Harvard University. Early versions of parts of chapters 2, 3, and 7 have appeared as articles: 'Le système D.—le malheur merveilleux. Duras and the erotic crimes of montage in Le Camion and Aurélia Steiner', Paragraph, No. 15 (March 1992), pp. 38–72, and, 'A Beast of a Closet: The sexual differences of literary collaboration in the work of Marguerite Duras and Yann Andréa', Modern Language Review, Vol. 87, No. 3 (July 1992), pp. 576–84. I am grateful to the publishers concerned for granting me permission to use this material. Finally, I would like to express my deep thanks to Joan and Stuart Williams for their help in dealing with some of the practicalities of the project, and to Alfred Thomas for his great patience and understanding.

List of Abbreviations

(All editions of Duras's literary work are published by Editions de Minuit unless otherwise stated.)

Un barrage contre le Pacifique [1950], Paris, Gallimard, 'Folio', 1981 (*Barrage*).
Le marin de Gibraltar, Paris, Gallimard, 'Folio', 1952 (*Gibraltar*).
Moderato cantabile (1958) (*Moderato*).
Hiroshima mon amour (scénario et dialogues) [1960], Paris, Gallimard, 'Folio', 1984 (*Hiroshima*).
L'après-midi de Monsieur Andesmas [1962], Paris, Gallimard, 1979 (*Andesmas*).
Le ravissement de Lol V. Stein [1964], Paris, Gallimard, 'Folio', 1986 (*Ravissement*).
Le vice-consul, Paris, Gallimard, 1966 (*Vice-consul*).
L'amante anglaise (roman), Paris, Gallimard, 1967 (*Amante*).
Détruire, dit-elle (1969) (*Détruire*).
L'amour, Paris, Gallimard, 1971 (*Amour*).
La femme du Gange (film) (1972–73) (*Gange*).
Nathalie Granger, suivi de La Femme du Gange, Paris, Gallimard, 1973 (*Granger*).
Les parleuses (1974) (*Parleuses*).
Son nom de Venise dans Calcutta désert (film) (1976) (*Son nom de Venise*).
Baxter, Véra Baxter (film) (1976–77) (*Baxter*).
Le camion (text and film) (1977) (*Camion*).
Les lieux de Marguerite Duras (1977) (*Lieux*).
Le navire Night, suivi de Césarée, Les mains négatives, Aurélia Steiner, Aurélia Steiner, Aurélia Steiner, Paris, Mercure de France, 1979 (*Night*).
Le navire Night (film) (1979) (*Night*).
Les mains négatives (film) (1979) (*Mains*).
Aurélia Steiner (Melbourne) (film) (1979) (*Melbourne*).
Aurélia Steiner (Vancouver) (film) (1979) (*Vancouver*).

Véra Baxter ou les plages de l'Atlantique, Paris, Albatros, 1980 (*Véra Baxter*).

L'homme assis dans le couloir (1980) (*Homme assis*).

L'été 80 (1980) (*Eté*).

Outside. Papiers d'un jour, Paris, Albin Michel, 1981 (*Outside*).

Agatha et les lectures illimitées (film) (1981) (*Agatha*).

L'homme atlantique (film 1981) (text 1982) (*Atlantique*).

La maladie de la mort (1982) (text and film) (*Maladie*).

Savannah Bay (nouvelle édition augmentée) (1983) (*Savannah*).

Les Oeuvres Cinématographiques de Marguerite Duras. Edition Vidéographique Critique, Paris, Ministère des Relations extérieures, 1983 (*EVC*).

L'amant (1984) (*Amant*).

La douleur, Paris, POL, 1985 (*Douleur*).

Les enfants (1985) (*Enfants*).

La mouette de Tchékov, Paris, Gallimard, 1985 (*Mouette*).

Les yeux bleus cheveux noirs (roman) (1986) (*Yeux bleus*).

La pute de la côte normande (1986) (*Pute*).

La Vie matérielle, Paris, POL, 1987 (*Vie mat.*).

Les yeux verts (nouvelle édition augmentée), Paris, Gallimard, 1987 (*Yeux*).

Emily L. (roman) (1987) (*Emily*).

La pluie d'été, Paris, POL, 1990 (*Pluie*).

L'amant de la Chine du Nord, Paris, Gallimard, 1991 (*Chine*).

Yann Andréa Steiner, Paris, POL, 1992 (*Yann*).

Le Monde extérieur. Outside II, Paris, POL, 1993 (*Monde*).

C'est tout, Paris, POL, 1995 (*Tout*).

CHAPTER 1

The Daisy Chain

J'étais déjà dans le cinéma, j'étais dans un film . . . j'étais quelque part ailleurs en étant là. C'était déjà transporté quelque part ailleurs voyez. On dit sublimé, je crois, les autres.

(M. Duras)

Nothing could be tougher than Duras. *Dur dur*! That is the implication of Danielle Bajomée's 1989 study, *Duras ou la douleur*,[1] and it underlies most of the major criticism on Duras's work, from Maurice Blanchot and 'the solitude of an authentic dialogue'[2] to Jacques Lacan and 'the silent nuptials of empty life with the indescribable object';[3] from Carol Murphy and absence and forgetting as alienation and disjunction,[4] to Julia Kristeva and the melancholia of non-catharsis.[5] It has even been proposed that *La douleur* (1985) represents the fundamental truth of a corpus of aporia and aphasia that had lain dormant since the publication of Duras's first novel, *Les impudents* (1943), written in Paris during the dark days of the Occupation.[6] Each of the above critics defines pain differently, of course, yet the question must be asked: how could a corpus of such sustained energy and consistently diverse range—over ninety books, plays and films between 1940 and 1995[7]—have generated this almost uniform response? Moreover, how could such an ominous sounding thematics account for the current, unprecedented popularity of Duras, once a 'difficult' writer for a chosen few but now one of France's most widely translated authors, in danger even of not being taken seriously enough? Not only has she been comprehensively pastiched by (among others) Patrick Rambaud,[8] but in 1992 a journalist sought to expose what he considered her over-inflated worth by sending a sample of the 1962 novel, *L'après-midi de Monsieur Andesmas*, to her main publishers, Editions de Minuit, Gallimard and POL (it was unanimously rejected as 'not of the highest literary quality'[9]).

For many critics of the later corpus, however, to write on Duras simply means offering a fascinated meditation on the veracity of autobiographically charged texts.[10] It is as if these critics have been

1

bewitched both by Duras's prodigious rate of production and by her immediate gloss on each new work in the media, resulting in what Michel de Certeau has termed a 'double discourse'.[11] Perhaps, too, they have been stunned by the legendary status of Duras's life encompassing, for example, a childhood spent in the jungles of French Indochina speaking fluent Vietnamese, her experience in the French Resistance alongside François Mitterrand, her script for Alain Resnais's epoch-making film, *Hiroshima mon amour* (1959), her appearance on the barricades in Paris during the events of May 1968, the record-breaking sales of *L'amant*, winner of the Prix Goncourt in 1984 (more than two million French copies now sold), and her survival in 1988–89 of a protracted and nearly fatal coma. So closely identified, in fact, has been Duras's corpus with her actual body that it has often seemed that the only safe critical approach is to repeat Duras on Duras:[12] Duras as self-proclaimed writer of silence,[13] trans-gression,[14] madness,[15] undifferentiation,[16] rarefaction,[17] dispos-session,[18] and passion. Why? Because Duras has said so: 'the films which I make are made in the same place as my books. It's what I call the place of passion. Where one is deaf and blind. Well, I try to be there as much as possible.'[19] This is the offical line: Duras goes bravely to where no other writer dares, to the heart of things, the unsayable. Hers is an heroic, often thankless, encounter with the absolute and the impossible, and pain is the sign of her success: '[t]hese books are painful to write and read', she explains, adding: 'this pain ought to lead us towards a field of experimentation. It's painful, because it's a kind of work which bears perhaps on an area still untapped' (*Parleuses*, p. 40).[20] A text like *Ecrire* (1993) is typical of the way Duras's work constantly thematises self-sacrifice in the face of the solitude and sickness of writing, or 'the writing of the terror of writing' (p. 50). In an interview in 1983, Duras even remarked there would be nothing left for her to die from since each text extracted yet more life from her body.[21]

Fundamental to the predominant view of Duras as a purveyor of lack and unsatisfied desire has been her unique status as a 'Lacanian' writer. While this is certainly not an identity that she actively encouraged, Lacan's 'homage' to Duras inspired by his reading of the 1964 novel, *Le ravissement de Lol V. Stein* (his only article on a contemporary writer), together with her own uninhibited use of such terms as *le leurre*, have clinched her reputation as a writer of 'clinically perfect madness'.[22] It has even been suggested that she marks the third point of a triangle comprising Freud and Lacan.[23] What is so remarkable about Lacan's influence on Duras studies is that in 'Hommage' he was playing a very personal and teasing game of masochistic desire, identifying with the other Jacques (the narrator of *Ravissement*, Jacques Hold) in the passive, 'held' position of obsessed and ravished interpreter of literature, so as to keep Duras, like Jacques with Lol, always one step ahead. While it does not serve our purpose here to rehearse Lacan's characteristically involved argument on the nature of the gaze and the origin of the work of art, it is worth pointing out that the preponderance of sibillant *s* sounds stirring around the signifier 'Dura*s*' in the much quoted line, 'Marguerite Dura*s* *s*'avère *s*avoir *s*ans moi *ce* que j'en*s*eigne' (emphasis added) ('Marguerite Duras proves to know without my help what I teach'), already gives a hint of the self-conscious way in which Lacan wilfully submits himself to the word of Duras.[24] Yet this has not prevented most Lacanians from earnestly falling in line to give masterful readings, à la lettre, of the Durasian unconscious. Indeed, Duras's work has become a testing ground for the Lacanian method, whether Jean-Louis Sous writing on the 'immoderation of the real' in *Moderato cantabile* (1958),[25] Michèle Montrelay on Lol as the necessary 'zero-Real' for Jacques and Tatiana in *Ravissement*,[26] Patricia Fedkiw on the feminine field of hysteria in *L'amante anglaise* (1967),[27] Mary Lydon on the subversion of the signifier in the short, so-called 'erotic texts', *L'homme assis dans le couloir* (1980) and *La maladie de la mort* (1982),[28] or, finally, Bernard Alazet and others on the formation of subjectivity in the *Aurélia Steiner* trilogy (1979).[29]

The transferential cord spun by Lacan has proved, in fact, remarkably firm. It has withstood Michèle Druon's attempt to promote the idea of Lol's successful self-catharsis,[30] Alice Jardine's blunt anti-Lacanianism,[31] Marie-Claire Ropars-Wuilleumier's defiantly Derridean reading of the 1975 film, *India Song*,[32] and Sharon Willis's strategy in *Marguerite Duras: Writing on the Body* (1987)[33] of simply flooding key Duras texts with all available theory in the hope of defining *écriture féminine* as the constant putting into question of the relation between the discursive and the non-discursive. Other critics such as Marcelle Marini have tried to read 'with' Duras, charting, for instance, the territories of silence in *Le vice-consul* (1965) that 'resonate with', and 'speak', the 'feminine'.[34] According to Marini, this novel is to be celebrated for its 'stemming' of the flood of male-dominated language, and, with its narration of a wandering

beggar-woman and her child, for offering models of female identification which sidestep the Name of the Father. Susan Cohen has gone
even further and uncovered in Duras a radical feminist poetics of
'creative ignorance', one which offers the potential for liberation from
discursive (i.e. patriarchal) domination and repression.[35] A few
critics, of course, attack both Lacan and Duras at the same time. For
example, in her book, *The Other Woman: Feminism and Femininity
in the Work of Marguerite Duras* (1988), Trista Selous argues that
Duras is a merely conventional and, like Lacan, 'monolithic' writer of
masochistically-inclined 'femmes fatales'.[36] For Selous, the reader of
Duras, faced with a seamless discourse of unexplained narrative
lacunae, or 'Blanks', is obliged to accept a masculine-encoded
position and then fantasise possible explanations for the 'other' desire
of the female protagonists according to the clichéd rules of romantic
fiction.[37] Again, however, so great has been the pull of Lacan that
oppositional critics such as Selous have done little to loosen the
enduring fixation with the ravished, zero state of a Lacanised L-o-l.
Even Susan Suleiman, not a noted Lacanian, has concluded that
Duras shares with the Lacan of the last part of *Encore* (1975) a
'pessimistic, inspired and inspiring, magnificently romantic, totally
modern vision of love and of *écriture*'.[38] After all, did not Duras
herself credit Lacan as the person who brought Lol back from the
grave (*Parleuses*, p. 161)?

How, then, to approach Duras's work from a fresh perspective
and so break the chain of identification between Duras studies and
Lacanian psychoanalysis? Kristeva's 'La maladie de la douleur', a
chapter from her 1987 study on depression, *Soleil noir: dépression et
mélancolie*, represents perhaps the best attempt at a new direction. To
account for how Duras's narcissistically depressed heroines absorb
political and historical horror into stories of personal pain, Kristeva
draws primarily on Klein's theory of object-relations and Freud's
1915 essay, 'Mourning and Melancholia', where melancholia, like
mourning, is rooted in the loss of a loved object with a sexual origin
and complicated by a sadistic resentment turned against the ego in the
form of self-denigration and self-hatred. The idea of the Duras text
being at the mercy of an arrested act of mourning is not in itself new (it
had already been suggested in the mid-1970s by Hélène Cixous[39]),
but Kristeva formalises the melancholic real as *la Chose*, or 'the real
rebellious to signification' (p. 22). She argues that Duras's female
characters experience an impossible grief for the maternal object,

resulting in the phenomenon of blocked repetition (*réduplication*), i.e. inaccessible female doubles who grow fat on melancholia to the point of violence and delirium. Without its 'jubilatory assumption' by a Third (p. 263), this 'criminal secret' of subterranean passion creates an imaginary aura of complicity which ruins in its narcissistic fluidity any sexual object or sublime ideal, offering not pleasure but 'covert rapture' (p. 253). According to Kristeva, Duras's society of doomed women unable to sustain erotic bonds corresponds to the bleaching of sense that takes place on the textual level in the form of a sparse and paratactic style. This general 'aesthetics of clumsiness', devoid of even the odd moment of narrative synthesis, constitutes in her view the apotheosis of the post-War crisis of modernist literature.

Unlike Lacan's 'Hommage', 'La maladie de la douleur' allows Duras's work to speak for itself and is decisive in its linking of form with content. Nevertheless, Kristeva's analysis still subscribes to the critical topos of a corpus driven internally by pain or the death-drive. In addition, although it declares the screen-play of *Hiroshima* to be the prototype for all Duras's subsequent texts of female melancholy and depression (p. 241), it ignores her almost exclusive interest in cinema during the 1970s prior to her return to literature in 1980 with *L'homme assis dans le couloir* and *L'été 80*. By recommending, albeit in jest, that every Duras book carry with it a health warning ('not to be read by anyone suffering from depression'!), Kristeva's study precludes yet again the chance for a proper discussion of why so many people evidently take pleasure in Duras's work. It has also led to an unfortunate rash of pro- and anti-Kristeva articles.[40] Marianne Hirsch, for example, has remarked that Kristeva's Freudian approach to the trauma of maternal abandonment depoliticises and dehistoricises Duras because it eclipses the voice of the mother in her historical specificity, thus conflating the political dimensions of women's lives with the purely psychological (something, she notes, that *Amant* already partly invites us to do).[41] Kathleen Hulley argues a little differently that by treating depression in Duras as a pathology rather than as a trope which opens up 'the holes [that] representational constructions of the subject would elide', Kristeva reads manifestations of 'shredded subjectivity' as transhistorical.[42] The psychoanalyst Daniel Sibony reveals further the limitations of Kristeva's argument when he emphasises the female relation between text and author, stating that Duras, a 'Woman-crucible of writing' and 'giver of written life', functions as 'The Other Woman' (*L'Autre-Femme*) who gradually saps her female characters of life.[43] For Sibony, Duras's writing is a self-image in which she envelops, doubles and finally surpasses her heroines, all of them depressed because prisoners of another woman's fantasy. Duras herself admits as much in *La Vie matérielle* (1987) when she remarks: 'all the women in my books whatever their age, derive from Lol V. Stein. Derive, that is, from a kind of self-forgetting. They can all see things clearly, but they're careless and lack foresight. They all make a disaster of their lives' (p. 32).[44]

It is Duras, in fact, who offers the sharpest rebuttal of Kristeva's article by calling into question one of its central propositions, namely that the roots of female frigidity are maternal. Characterising the mother as *'the strangest, maddest person we have ever met*, us, their [sic] children' (*Vie mat.*, p. 56) (original emphasis), she defines female frigidity in exclusively heterosexual terms as the result of women not having met their 'one' male lover. Paradoxically, this frigidity is also the most fertile source of the female imaginary since it results from a 'woman's desire for a man who has not not yet [sic] come to her, whom she does not yet know . . . Frigidity is the lack of desire for whatever is not him' (*Vie mat.*, p. 40).[45] Such highly motivated passivity, expressed in the apparent form of a double negative ('not not yet') as if Duras were hedging her bets, is crucially important to any discussion of Duras's later work because it draws attention to something which Kristeva's assertion of a 'white rhetoric of the apocalypse' effectively denies, i.e. the libidinal energies and drives operating at the level of the text. This is partly because Kristeva does not consider the implications of Duras's own statement that her 1980s work constitutes a new poetics of cursive writing, or *écriture courante* (literally, 'running writing'), one which writes over, and through, the maternal figure. The narrator of *Amant* is categorical on the matter, declaring that she can write with such ease about her mother precisely because the latter has become 'running writing' (p. 38). For Duras, only women who are intimately connected through history to silence can accede to *écriture courante*,[46] which is founded on contingency and metonymy and records anything personal, social, or political that 'passes' during the moment of writing. Not only is *écriture courante* open and all-inclusive but it also 'sweeps up' what it encounters, 'without discrimination, almost without choice', thus rendering everything 'innocent'.[47] If, as Duras herself admits, her writing possesses a poor, 'painful' syntax,[48] *écriture courante* endows it with a definite beauty. Here is Duras again in tantalising form:

> Are they difficult, my books, is that what you want to know? Yes, they are difficult. And easy. *L'amant* is very difficult. *La maladie de la mort* is difficult, very difficult. *L'homme atlantique* is very difficult but it's so beautiful that it is not difficult. (*Vie mat.*, p. 119)[49]

Yet *écriture courante* is not just a question of style; it also carries with it a sexual charge. According to Duras, writers are 'sexual objects par excellence', and, like all people of talent and genius, they incite rape (*Vie mat.*, p. 77). Hence, while her own work may not be expressly designed for such a purpose, it can, she casually acknowledged in a later interview, perform a specifically sexual role and so produce pleasure.[50] In addition, *écriture courante* has an ethical dimension, as the narrator of *Amant* again makes clear when she states: 'Sometimes I know that: that the moment it is not, all things confounded, a quest for vanity and the void, then writing is nothing. That as soon as it not, each time, all things confounded into a single one, essentially unqualifiable, then writing is nothing but self-promotion' (p. 15).[51] This statement has been taken by many as the key to Duras's philosophy and has precipitated a rush for authentic Durasian 'otherness'. For instance, in her 1988 study of Duras's theatre entitled *L'Autre Scène*, Liliane Papin argues, like Cohen, that Duras crosses over to the Other in a passionate expression of love.[52] In addition, key texts such as *Vice-consul*, which depict the encroaching presence of lepers and beggars on White India, have been celebrated as laying the foundations for a new 'poetics of marginalisation'.[53] One critic has even linked *Vice-consul* with the presentation of the Holocaust in *Aurélia Steiner* to argue that Duras is an écrivain engagé committed to sharing her pain with others and thus uniting the private and 'exterior' worlds.[54]

Duras's overt concern with the Other was initially formalised, in fact, not in her fiction but in her first published collection of journalism, *Outside. Papiers d'un jour* (1981), which ranges from commentary on assorted faits divers to book reviews and interviews dealing with the 'outsiders' of French society (e.g. working-class Algerian immigrants, disaffected youths, even criminals). At one point in the volume she declares that not to see the Other is not to see 'that shadow next to you', that 'common materiality' (*Outside*, p. 284). A little later in 1983, in her only public, and rather hesitant, use of the term 'alterity', she talked of 'something greater than oneself'.[55]

Such thoughts clearly connect her work with that of Emmanuel Levinas, currently the most influential French theorist of alterity, who argues that the foundation of ethics is the 'shock of the meeting between the Same and Other', a shock which opens up the self to the irreducibly Other. For Levinas, alterity is a form of externality which exerts itself outside, and unforeseen by, human consciousness, the limits of which are thereby fully exposed.[56]

In the light of such thinking it would seem highly appropriate to discuss Duras's later work in the context of *écriture féminine*, to which the term *écriture courante* clearly responds. Using *Vice-consul* as her preferred example, Judith Still has argued that the corpus overall can be claimed for *écriture féminine* 'because of its seemingly uncensored relation to the body, to sexuality, and to pleasure, its representation of desire which *"va jusqu'au bout"* (goes to the limit), which is not held back by "economic considerations", which imposes itself as necessary'.[57] She adds that the superabundant generosity of Duras's female characters, who give themselves and yet always have more to give, is reminiscent of Cixous's feminine economy. Yet those studies of Duras taking *écriture féminine* as their critical point of departure have not, it must be said, been particularly successful. Janine Ricouart's *Ecriture féminine et violence* (1991), for instance, while it may emphasise the generative energy of the violence, both thematic and formal in the corpus, suffers for being based on the never properly defined—and perhaps indefinable—concept of *écriture féminine*.[58] Duras herself already renders such approaches prohibitively difficult, for just as she once broke all ties with the 'masculine' ideology of communism (she officially left the Communist Party in 1950), so she missed no occasion during the 1980s to distance herself from those *femmes-écrivains* (unspecified) who know 'nothing' of sexual desire.[59] To study the later corpus through such a fixed, oppositional prism as *écriture féminine* would probably prove as difficult as trying to read it anti-canonically as the work of a marginal writer. To give just two examples of Duras's present mainstream status: *Moderato* is studied in France as a classic modern text for the baccalauréat, and the boxed video-set of eight of her films lavishly produced in 1984 by the Ministère des Relations extérieures—*Les oeuvres cinématographiques de Marguerite Duras. Edition Vidéo-graphique Critique (EVC)*[60]—officially established her as a major French artist.

We could opt, of course, to confine ourselves to a purely formal approach to Duras's literary work by comparing her experiments in autobiographical fiction with those of other ex-*nouveaux romanciers* like Nathalie Sarraute and Alain Robbe-Grillet. Yet a comparative analysis of authenticity and selfhood in *Amant*, Sarraute's *Enfance* (1983) and Robbe-Grillet's *Le miroir qui revient* (1984) has already been attempted[61] and still does not address the question of how Duras's texts can be simultaneously difficult, painful, beautiful, violent, erotic and pleasurable, while still being committed to the Other. Still less does it take into account all the formal and thematic developments in Duras's fictional writing after 1980, which thereby runs the risk of being regarded merely as a series of codas to the earlier corpus, in particular the long novels such as *Ravissement* and *Vice-consul*. Before we proceed any further, then, let us establish exactly what makes the later corpus so different.

Although a slim volume, *Homme assis* heralded the arrival in Duras's work of a first person 'narrator-voyeuse' operating within a recognisable linear form. The text employs the vocative address, a feature initiated in *Les yeux verts* (1980) with its intermittent dialogical format (*je/tu*, *je/vous*) and brought to full fruition in *Maladie*, where both the female narrator and the unnamed *elle* interrogate *lui* in the second person. Invited to take up the *vous* position of addressee and narratee, the reader is propelled, often aggressively, into a transferential and countertransferential encounter, what Duras refers to as a 'private affair' between text and reader (*Vie mat.*, pp. 119–20). Meanwhile, on the thematic level, the reader is now made a direct witness to sometimes graphic scenes of illicit sexual desire, incestuous in the case of *La pluie d'été* (1990) and *L'amant de la Chine du Nord* (1991), sadomasochistic in the case of *Homme assis* and *Amant*. Indeed, the previously impossible sexual event which had always taken place either just before or just after, and which, as in *Hiroshima*, could only be imitated or chanted poetically ('Tu me tues, tu me fais du bien', etc.), now occurs in the full immediacy of the textual present, the result being that by the mid-1980s Duras's novels—or what she started to call 'poems'—acquire an almost uniform length of 140–50 pages. It is as if the corpus had finally caught up with itself and were realising what one critic has termed, referring to the female protagonist in *Dix heures et demie du soir en été* (1960), the 'sadomasochistic dialectics' of its characters' willed projections.[62] In addition, if first-person male narrators such as Jacques in *Ravissement* were once exposed and 'deconstructed' in order to be returned, like Anne-Marie Stretter's train of male suitors in *India Song* or the travelling salesman in the film *Nathalie Granger* (1972), to a 'feminine' sort of *jouissance* from which they had been exiled (Montrelay),[63] now they are actively manipulated by first-person female subjects who can both enact and narrate their own desires.[64] One effect of this is that the ambiguous or impossible relationship between mother and child, explored at length in *Nathalie Granger* for example, is superseded by the sexual relationship between a young girl or woman and an older man who performs a paternal function. In fact, the father who seemed fated never to reappear after his complete exhaustion in *Andesmas* finally returns, both in the anonymous form of fantasy (*vous* in *Aurélia Steiner*, the Chinese lover in *Amant*, etc.), and as a 'real' man blessed with a name (Emilio Crespi in *Pluie*).

To gain a sense of how some of these features play out in Duras's later work, we need to experience the slipperiness of *écriture courante* at first hand. A short, representative sample is the set of consecutive mini-chapters from *Vie mat.* entitled 'Vinh long' and 'Hanoï'. 'Vinh long' begins in vague and mysterious terms by stating that there was first Vinh Long, then Hanoi, about which the narrator has never spoken (p. 27). The chapter proceeds to recontextualise autobiographically the fictional figure of Anne-Marie Stretter and her special power to 'ravish' men even to the point of their death. We hear that the narrator's younger self, aged between eight and ten, was herself sent one day into mysterious raptures by the passing sight of 'Anne-Marie Striedter''s black limousine. The second chapter immediately inverts the order of events established in the first by explaining that six years before Vinh long there had been Hanoi (p. 28). The roles of ravisher and ravished are also reversed. Whereas before the infant-narrator had not possessed the cognitive power to grasp her situation, now, astonishingly in view of her age, she displays the kind of manipulative power possessed by Anne-Marie Stretter in *Vice-consul*. She obliges her mother to chase away an older Vietnamese boy, guilty, she claims, of enlisting her in a private act of masturbation. *Je* is contrasted with *lui* who, with his 'martyr-like' face visibly suffering (molested children are referred to in French as *enfants martyrs*), is totally at a loss to understand 'a pleasure still out of reach'. For her, pleasure was already 'unforgettable', her body 'light-years away from knowing what it was but already receiving its signal' (*Vie mat.*, p. 28).[65]

'Vinh long' and 'Hanoï' have thus folded over each other, with common elements such as 'that river common to the lovers' (p. 28) displaced and rearranged. This fact is relayed self-reflexively both by the title of the first chapter, with its strange modification of Vinh Long to Vinh *long*, and by the narrator's concluding remark that the scene 'shifted of its own accord' and even grew with her (p. 29). Yet despite its apparent errors and inversions, the two-part sequence is passed off as entirely logical: *je* maintained Anne-Marie Striedter as her own 'secret' (i.e. Anne-Marie Stretter) because she had learnt the hard way at the age of four in Hanoi never to divulge the whole truth to her mother, especially if it concerned the forbidden pleasures of ineffable rapture. What this account leaves out is less Kristeva's maternal secret (which is, after all, only too manifest) than the very real possibility that the boy is standing in for Duras's own father who, as was revealed earlier in *Les lieux de Marguerite Duras* (1977), died during the same period. The exact link between her father's absence and the forced dismissal of an older, foreign boy who lured her into a scene of seduction over which she gains immediate control, is, however, a question deliberately left suspended in the two chapters. Could it be that the young girl's reversal of a simulation of paternal seduction into a personal act of revenge resolves her mourning for a lost father? Even though they purport to deliver the so far unsaid, both chapters protect themselves from exploring such interrelated questions of power, fantasy and sexual desire. In this respect, they underline the nature of *Vie mat.* as a whole which all but eclipses the presence of Duras's original interlocutor, Jérôme Beaujour, so essential to the book's genesis and completion (the sub-title reads: 'Marguerite Duras speaks to Jérôme Beaujour', and the Foreword indicates that Beaujour read all the revised transcriptions).

How, then, are we to account for such strange omissions, inversions and textual violations in *Vie mat.*, forms of textual 'event' which actually provide for rare excitement and emotion in mainly unexpressive and understated prose? Clearly Duras is not producing a transparent and 'hyperreal' discourse (Selous),[66] still less is she attempting merely to restore the plenitude and 'sublimity' of words as Dominique Noguez has argued in his study of parataxis and repetition in her literary work.[67] Hulley provides a clue when she suggests that Duras's determined passivity and silence should be considered more as tropes, that is to say, as the cause of the crisis in representation rather than its effect.[68] But the question of Duras's strategy of violence towards the rhetorical figure has never really been addressed. What, for example, are the relations between a binding, authorial female figure and a rhetorical figure 'unbound'? Does the 'ravished' rhetorical figure merely represent the related pain of masochistic ravishment or does it, in fact, 'sublimate' it, if we take sublimation to mean less a process of repressive idealisation (i.e. the transformation or diversion of sexual drives into other 'cultural' or 'moral' activities) than the investment of ego interests with a floating or suspended sexual energy?[69] In short, what are the sublimatory qualities of an eroticised rhetoric, and can it ever produce the non-oppressive handling of language which Cohen claims to discover in her thematically based study of Duras's literary style?[70]

The work of Leo Bersani in the area of sexuality and aesthetics can help us to formulate these questions more clearly. In *The Freudian body. Psychoanalysis and Art* (1986), Bersani follows the lead of Laplanche and argues that fantasy, or the imaginary expression and fulfilment of a desire, is itself a sexual perturbation (*ébranlement*) intimately related in its origin to the emergence of the masochistic sexual drive.[71] This psychic disturbance is essentially an experience of pleasure *as* pain and thus already a form of masochistic sexual excitement. Indeed, pushed back beyond reversible, Freudian fantasies of being beaten, masochism becomes a tautology for sexuality itself, located now in the very erasures of artistic and narrative form. Whether in the violent, agitated and erratic formalisms of Assyrian art or in the playful negations of a Mallarmé poem, art, according to Bersani, interprets the sexual by repeating it as perceivable forms rather than elaborating repressive substitutes or symptoms of sexual desire. Hence, the unreadable sexual can be read precisely by the excessive visibility of its subversion of narrative readability.[72] If, then, as Bersani asserts, primary narcissism represents the originary sublimation (that of the masochistically enjoyed disturbance of psychic equilibrium in auto-eroticism[73]), and if irony can also act as an ambiguously formalising principle within the erotic, what is the nature and purpose of literary sublimation in writing like Duras's which, while it may 'sparkle' due to a certain 'drollery' (Foucault),[74] nevertheless trades directly in primal fantasies of seduction and sadomasochistic desire? Moreover, how 'unfixed' can textual fantasy remain if it is still to function as a stabilising mise en scène of the otherwise formless and erratic displacements of desire?[75]

By proposing such topics for discussion we are, of course,

automatically working contra Duras, for sublimation, like alterity, is not a word she cared to use herself (she declared that it belonged to the vocabulary of 'others' [*Lieux*, p. 36]). When questioned by Pierre Bergé during their 1988 'Duras est SEXY!' interview as to whether creativity is ever possible without sexuality, she replied dismissively: 'There is no *signature*'.[76] In Duras's view, the very naming of sexuality initiated by Freudian psychoanalysis had been disastrous for the development of literature and ought to be avoided at all costs. Yet if we agree in principle that there must always be some kind of authorial signature (and on another occasion Duras admits precisely this[77]), what, then, is its link with sexuality, in particular female sexuality? Furthermore, how does the female writer 'sublimate' the violence of sexual desire, particularly if it is the case, as Duras claims, that there are almost no outlets for women's pain outside art?[78]

Duras had already, in fact, begun to confront these issues directly in 1977 and the result was a turning-point in her work more significant even than her sudden 'veering' into madness during the writing of *Moderato*.[79] I am referring to the film *Le camion* which, when premièred at the 1977 Cannes film festival, created a furore. Many in the audience jeered or walked out, some stayed on to embrace Duras after the projection. Was this the same film-maker who had made such defiantly political films as the allegorical *Jaune le soleil* (1971) and the feminist-celebrated *Nathalie Granger*, yet who had also scored such a hit in 1975 with *India Song* and its lush, 'retro'-style presentation of an impossible, colonial romance? *Camion*, where a long studio conversation between Duras and Gérard Depardieu about 'a film that could have been made' is regularly intercut with outside shots of a blue lorry running back and forth across the industrial landscape to the sound of Beethoven, could just as easily, it seemed, have been made for television. The central tale of a middle-aged woman ('la dame') hitching a lift from a card-carrying, communist lorry-driver was presumed to be Duras's way of talking about her own involvement with communism, at the expense both of Depardieu's acting talents and film's natural iconic power. Otherwise the film appeared to offer only the mantra-like chant: 'Que le monde-aille-à-sa-perte, c'est-la-seule-politique' ('Let the world-go-to-rack-and-ruin, it's-the-only-politics'). Why had Duras bothered at all?

As the 'Four Projects' included in the later published text make clear, however, *Camion* had precise artistic and political aims, being conceived by Duras as a polemic against commercial cinema which had 'abused' her work with adaptations such as René Clement's *Barrage contre le Pacifique* (1958) and Peter Brook's *Moderato cantabile* (1960).[80] According to Duras, cinema is now a site of socialised dependency, both for the audience and for the average film-maker who, ipso facto, cannot write:

> S/he who does not write and the film-maker have not broached what I call 'the internal shadow' which we all carry within ourselves and which can only rise and pass to the outside by means of language. The writer has broached it. S/he has broached the integrity of the internal shadow [*l'ombre interne*]. . . It's on this defeat of writing that for me cinema is founded . . . For this massacre is precisely the bridge that leads you to the very place of all reading. And further still, to the very place where you just submit, which any existence in contemporary society entails . . . to want to make films is precisely to want to go straight to the scene of your submission: the viewer. (*Yeux*, p. 131)[81]

The landscape's 'inside-out' appearance in *Camion*, the result of intensive industrial excavation, is thus a precise metaphor for the inversion of writing which occurs in traditional cinema, where the film-maker always sees his creation from the perspective of the viewer and is positioned 'behind', as opposed to the writer who remains 'in front'. The film's intention was to reverse such institutionalised inequity and, in the process, disqualify the very notion of ideological cinema, whether that be of the left, or women, or youth, or intellectuals (*Camion*, p. 73). The invisible figure of 'la dame' was presented as Everywoman, and the spoken word proposed as an 'unforeseen meaning which depends on each viewer, what I [Duras] call image'.[82] Taken as a whole, *Camion* offered itself as a freely circulating, reversible and liberatory construct, one which could be entered at any moment due to its 'opening on to the outside' (*Camion*, p. 100).

It is certainly true that while *Camion* is typical of much of Duras's previous cinema in its extreme slowness of pace, its reliance on long takes, and its extensive use of a static or barely moving frame (an effect compounded by the effects of pleonasm whereby, for example, Depardieu is the *poids lourd*[83]), the film evades any attempt to read it through whatever strictly applied theoretical grid. It not only refuses the fetishised, 'natural' female body typical of patriarchal, Hollywood cinema, but also renders irrelevant the long-debated question of genre in Duras's work, as generated, for example, by *India Song*'s subtitle, 'texte, film, théâtre'. Nor does the film simply illustrate the operation of Lacanian fantasy, an approach which suited the more classically constructed *India Song* and its clinical deconstruction a year later in *Son nom de Venise dans Calcutta désert*, the two films creating a perfect fetish for post-Structuralist film theory.[84] Instead, *Camion* revolves around a fundamental opposition: between Duras's studio experiment with Depardieu—where the issues of female sexuality, age, sexual difference and cinematic form are all directly or indirectly addressed—and the fleeting, yet often ravishing, shots of the lorry's passage through the landscape. That is to say, between two, radically opposed kinds of movement: on the one hand, sublimation, with its dialectical binding of the bodily and intellectual, and, on the other, the sublime, that elusive, unbound, aesthetic object which, in its received Kantian sense, exceeds any finite frame and can only be represented (if at all) as a failure of representation.

On the face of it, Duras's sublime presentation of the lorry is proof both of her stated commitment to alterity and of her attraction for the types of extreme pleasure that we have been discussing. The thrilling apprehension of awesome 'otherness', which frustrates attempts to conceive it and draw it together in the form of a concept, offers an anxious, almost masochistic mingling of pleasure and unpleasure. In fact, Duras has recourse to the adjective *sublime* whenever she is unable to describe people, objects or events that move her beyond words. Yet the term 'the sublime' (from the Latin *sublimis*, literally 'up to' (*sub*) 'the lintel' [*limen*]) can also, of course, be used to signify a powerful structuring force. Without entering into a detailed analysis of all the different representations of the sublime in literary practice and philosophical theory, we can see if we turn to Thomas Weiskel's work on transcendence and romanticism that they generally conform to a set pattern.[85] According to Weiskel, this is a three-phase sequence: (i) the normative or conventional stage, before alterity has been apprehended; (ii) the traumatic phase, or the apprehension of a tremendous object which entices the subject, disrupts his/her habitual modes of consciousness, and challenges the subject's dignity by means of the drastic contrast opened up between its apparently insurmountable powers and his/her own disorientation; and (iii) the reactive phase, or the moment of poetic sublimation, where the subject experiences elevation and empowerment through the restoration of blocked or occluded power. No longer the manifestation of otherness, the other is now seen as an aspect or extension of one's internal powers (i.e. part of one's own structure). As Longinus suggests in his primarily rhetorical account of the sublime, this is partly because the

reader now identifies with, and hence mentally subsumes, the otherness in a form of defence (mimesis).

To return to *Camion*, do the intercutting shots of the lorry
correspond to the presentation of a sublime form of alterity or to the
establishment of a sublime structure? That is to say, does the lorry
maintain its radical otherness while being cross-cut with the evolving
studio performance? If it is the case that the lorry's difference is not
maintained in the film's narrative flow, then, following the scheme
just outlined, the viewer could be participating in a form of the
'countersublime', i.e. a weaker form of whatever sublime empowerment—or 'sublimity'—the supposed author attains through the struggle for authority. Such a possibility for intersubjective, aesthetic desire
clearly illustrates that the demarcation between sublime and sublimating processes in *Camion* is not as complete as it first appears.
Indeed, it is the very interplay and potential overlap between the two
that provides for much of the tension of the film, as it does in all of
Duras's subsequent, self-styled 'poetic' work where a problematics of
alterity and pleasure similarly imposes itself. To pursue the relations
between alterity, pleasure, form and sublimation more extensively,
we will need to consider all the ways in which alterity is configured in
the film. Let us begin with the image in general.

The insistent and often brutal juxtaposition of inside and outside
images in *Camion* allows inversion to attain the status of a major
trope. This rhetorical use of montage is the film's defining feature,
rather than any possible renewal of the 'grammatical' role of the
camera (Duras's own explanation for the film's power in 'La dame des
Yvelines' [*EVC*]). In fact, what has been left out of almost all accounts
of Duras's cinema, despite Ropars-Wuilleumier's insistence on montage as a mode of writing in *India Song*, is Duras's fully active and
innovative contribution to the processes of post-production, in
particular through her long association with the film-editors Dominique Auvray and Geneviève le Four. *Camion*'s orchestrated play on the
gap between image and image, as well as that between image and
sound, obliges the viewer to approach the film both 'profoundly', as a
represented scene of fantasy, and 'superficially', as a topographical
articulation of desire. For Duras's incisions into the flesh of the
printed image in *Camion* allow both the lorry and the film itself to
'pass', highlighting in the process the cut of montage as a nexus of
violence and crisis. (Compare this with Hulley's suggestion that
Duras's literary work makes a cut within language itself, and, in a

'passage' which never arrives, 'extends that cut along the textual surface.[86]) The result is a flow of sensory energy whose effect on the film's diegesis has still to be properly quantified and analysed.

It is not only the play of the image which is dramatised in *Camion*, however. The refrain of 'Que-le-monde-aille-à-sa-perte' inspired by the Book of Ecclesiastes, together with 'la dame''s obsessive naming in full of Corneille and Proust, mark the beginning in Duras's work of an overt interest in literary history. For if representation is allowed to wither away in favour of a reduced, abstract 'master-image', or *image passe-partout* (*Yeux*, p. 93), even to the point of being totally reduced to black spacing, as in the 1981 short, *L'homme atlantique*, the issue of literary and cinematic influence becomes of growing narrative importance in all areas of the later corpus. Robert Musil and Henry James figure prominently here, and Duras even talks in terms of 'Great Men': 'I write with Diderot, I'm sure of it. With Pascal, with the great men of my life, with Kierkegaard, with Rousseau, I'm sure of it. With Stendhal, not with Balzac. With the rest, but totally unbeknownst to me. It's my primary source of food which I read avidly.'[87] Such receptivity to literary forebears would once, of course, have signalled for Duras a form of plagiarism, the very antithesis of desire[88] because contrary to a female rhetoric anchored in the body and expressive of women's 'organic night'.[89] We need to ascertain, therefore, what now constitutes a nourishing Great Man and how 'he' relates to the general return of the father in Duras's work. To do this, it will clearly be important to establish whether the inevitable, internal 'ungrammaticalities' of intertextual practice (Riffaterre)[90] can be linked theoretically with the kind of textual deformation that we witnessed a little earlier in the two chapters from *Vie mat.*

The third major instance of alterity in *Camion* is connected with Depardieu. After several such artistic collaborations with women— Xavière Gauthier in *Parleuses* and Michelle Porte in the 1976 television documentary, *Les lieux de Marguerite Duras*—Duras now engages in dialogue with a male interlocutor. This process will be repeated differently in the films that follow: *Le navire Night* (1978), for example, includes a voice-over dialogue between Duras and the film-maker Benoît Jacquot, and *Les enfants* (1985) distributes its directing credits evenly between Duras, her son Jean Mascolo, and Jean-Marc Turine. By far the most significant of all Duras's creative partnerships, however, although one still lacking full critical recognition,[91] is that with Yann Andréa, a much younger gay man with whom she lived from 1980 until her death. It may, at first, seem a little misplaced to discuss their relationship in the context of literary collaboration since, despite joint interviews, they never officially co-authored a work. Yet Andréa's only published work, *M.D.* (1983), a powerful account of Duras's treatment for alcoholism in 1982, was formally acknowledged by her as a major inspiration for writing *Amant*.[92] Moreover, Andréa was already at her side during one of her first experiments in *écriture courante*, *Eté*, which she subsequently dedicated to him. He also features to varying degrees in three of her films: as a silent image in *Atlantique*, as a voice on the sound-track of *Dialogo di Roma* (1982), and as both a silent image and voice-over in *Agatha et les lectures illimitées* (1981).

Andréa is crucial to any discussion of Duras's later work because, as 'Y.A., homosexuel' (*Vie mat.*, 79), he is the central focus of its investigation into male homosexuality. If this theme was delicately inferred in earlier works such as *Détruire, dit-elle* (1969), where male doubles live their unarticulated desire through their female counter-parts, it becomes during the 1980s of explicit concern, notably in *Maladie* and *Les yeux bleus cheveux noirs* (1986) (also dedicated to Andréa), texts which examine the implications of male homosexuality for heterosexual women. Duras writes in *Vie mat.* that all men are potential homosexuals, lacking only the 'incident' or 'evidence' that will reveal this fact to them (p. 38).[93] Yet whereas in the early 1970s she linked gay men and straight women together politically as victims of the 'phallic class'—both groups live against a similar backdrop of despair and fear, she stated in *Parleuses* (p. 152)—Duras later insisted on their radical difference, claiming that due to an onanistic self-fixation gay men represent 'death', i.e. the death of sexual difference, or that 'organic and fraternal antinomy' existing between men and women (*Vie mat.*, pp. 38–39).[94] How, then, does the presence of 'Y.A., homosexuel' affect the terms of Duras's creative project, especially in texts like *Yann Andréa Steiner* (1992) and *C'est tout* (1995) which include remarkable accounts of a love taking place in the very skin of the printed page? Can their artistic involvement be fully regarded as a passionate embrace of the Other?

By already posing these questions in embryonic form through its sustained and intimate use of Depardieu, *Camion* reveals that the movement of alterity in Duras's work is part of a constant process of experimentation and negotiation. Each instance of otherness that we have earmarked—the cinematic image, intertext, and male collaborator—constitutes a specific form of enquiry into the relations between pleasure, form, and sublimation. The result is a new kind of aesthetics, an erotics of the Other, one which demands that we approach the later corpus less as the continuation—successful or otherwise—of fantasy scenarios programmed earlier in the corpus (already well documented by Madeleine Borgomano in *Duras: une lecture des fantasmes* [1985]) than as loci of affective charge and pleasure generated by what we might call a rhetorical desire of, and for, montage, whether filmic or, as in the case of *écriture courante*, textual and intertextual. The temptation, of course, is that we plunge into the details of this discrete corpus in quest of its hidden meaning and, as Cynthia Chase has warned against in her discussion of psychoanalytical transference as trope and persuasion, that we 'transfer' on to it rather than trace, precisely by means of displacements or transferences, its devices of meaning.[95] Fortunately, an additional instance of alterity formulated in *Camion* alerts us to the risks of such easy transference since the film marks the first occasion that Duras entered her work in her own name and engaged artistically with her other, public self, 'Duras'. In fact, after *Camion*, and especially during the middle to late 1980s when, as a product of the French literary star system, she suddenly found herself an expert on everything, from football to drugs, Duras transformed herself into a kind of 'media queen', offering even the furrows of her face to be 'read' by her public. This is particularly true of the self-willed 'scandal' of her television appearances, like the famous *Apostrophes* interview with Bernard Pivot in 1984,[96] and the even more stunning, four-part self-portrayal, *Au-delà des pages* (1987), where Duras repeats, as if conclusively, that she has the impression of writing 'indecently', on the 'outside'.[97]

How are we to gain a critical purchase on such performances which, if they possess an oracular power, deliberately test the limits of publicity and self-exposure? One critic, Leslie Hill, has used the twists and turns of Duras's interventions in the media and politics to ground his argument that the entire corpus records an 'apocalyptic refusal of representation'.[98] By drawing a series of parallels between, for instance, the libidinal asymmetry of object choice in Duras's narratives and that of sound and image in her films, he proposes that her transgressive writing across genre announces 'messianically' that its 'only true object of revelation is apocalypse itself and the crisis in understanding and temporality that it effects'.[99] But can it really be the case that all the different aspects of Duras's oeuvre function in the same 'catastrophic' mode? Can, that is, media events like *Au-delà des pages* simply be amalgamated with the main corpus to form one seamless discourse without first being analysed as individual texts in their own right? If the answer is no, then we will need to examine in depth the rhetorical operations of Duras's work in the media, including even the Duras 'image'. The photographs accompanying the 'Duras est SEXY!' interview which we referred to a little earlier presented the melodrama of Duras togged up in a white polo-neck and black waistcoat. This was her 1980s trade-mark until her 1988–89 coma, after which she stopped wearing her thick, 'intellectual' glasses and sported a 'softer', more conventionally feminine attire, usually purple or crimson in colour, thus drawing out the significance of her first name, Marguerite (French for daisy flower). In fact, the nom de plume 'Duras', which Duras took from a small town overlooking the Marmande valley in the Lot-et-Garonne region of France where her father bought a house and subsequently died,[100] has come to signify a public, vestimentary style, placing her in a rich, literary tradition of female dressing and cross-dressing to which belong writers as diverse as Emily Dickinson and George Sand.

The link with Sand, whose father also died when she was four and with whom Duras naturally compared herself when contemplating her rare status in France as a regularly performed female playwright (*Vie mat.*, p. 16), is important for another reason. It raises the issue of political commitment and what one does if, like Sand after the 1848 revolution, one renounces political activism while still remaining 'consumed' by the idea. Following her split with the Communist Party, and believing that real revolution is only possible through personal freedom, Duras always presented herself as a model of the post-Marxist writer in France (her strategic decision to vote communist in the 1993 government elections notwithstanding[101]). As a temporary member of the revolutionary committee of students and writers formed at the Sorbonne during May 1968,[102] she spoke in utopian terms of '*PASSAGE*', an 'empty', depersonalising period of social inversion (*Yeux*, p. 80) as potentially useful in the long term as Bersani's biological masochism in its changing of the habitual relations between means and goals.[103] Thereafter, she eschewed almost all organised or official forms of political activity other than personal endorsements of Mitterrand, with whom she had fought in the French Resistance. In fact, during the 1980s, Duras became almost an icon of the centre-left establishment of Mitterrand, whose accession to power in 1981 effectively coincided with her own return to fictional writing. (So close was their association in the eyes of the French public that in 1987 *Globe* even ran a spoof interview on her possible election as the new Minister of Culture![104]) What this privileged position meant for Duras was the chance to pursue new creative options, in her case a style of subjective journalism bringing together contemporary politics and the fait divers. Whether in the pages of *Globe*, *Libération* or *L'Autre Journal* (of which she was initially a co-editor), she chose to write on events of both national and international importance, including the American raid on Tripoli in 1986[105] and the so-called 'Affaire Grégory', which gripped the French media in 1984. In a long article on the affair published in *Libération* in 1985 and entitled 'Marguerite Duras: Sublime, forcément sublime Christine V.', Duras argued that the only possible killer of the four-year old Grégory Villemin was his mother, Christine, then awaiting trial.[106] Like all Duras's media work, this exercise in myth-making raises further questions about aesthetic sublimity, i.e. what are the risks and implications of using social and political affairs to create beautiful, literary texts? Or, to paraphrase Barthes, what are the ethical responsibilities of form?

The problem we are clearly faced with in trying to answer these questions is how to construct a general theoretical framework supple enough to incorporate Duras's public image and the instances of the Other that we have already outlined: the cinematic image, the intertext, the gay man and collaborator. How, that is, can we analyse the rhetorical construction of alterity and pleasure in Duras's literary, film and media work without subordinating it to one master paradigm? One possible approach is to work with Duras's own term of *passage* which we have encountered in every aspect of her work (formal, thematic, sexual, political). This is a highly flexible, multivalent word in French since both active and passive—the action and site of passing—and bearing the meaning of a fragment of text or music. It can also be employed in the more general sense of a 'carrying across' of meaning as found in metaphor (Greek *meta-pherein*), the verb form *passer* being used by Duras to describe the painful literary metamorphosis of the real (the way, for example, a rose glimpsed one day can pass through the writer's 'internal shadow' and suddenly reappear as a name, Anne-Marie Stretter [*Camion*, p. 124]). Furthermore, as Mary Ann Caws has demonstrated in her study of Surrealism and modern French poetry, *A Metapoetics of the Passage*,[107] *passage* can accommodate not only concepts of role-reversal and liminality such as 'rites of passage', but also notions of textual exchange and reader-response. This is exemplified in Duras's recurring question: 'How is one to pass the text to the other who will follow you, the reader?' (*Monde*, p. 20). If we turn to the *Oxford English Dictionary* and some of the definitions of the term's English equivalent—a negotiation between two persons, an interchange of communications, confidences or amorous relation—we can even extend the scope of *passage* to include the Oedipal passage into adulthood, the *passage à l'acte*, or 'acting out', of unconscious desires and fantasies, as well as the drama of transference and counter-transference.

Passage is a highly valuable term because it serves to alert us to the general rhetorical and tropological necessities of our critical approach. It describes the loose composition of elements in one rhetorical strategy of inversion increasingly favoured by Duras and already evident in the intercutting and mirroring of inside and outside in *Camion*. I am referring to the figure of the chiasmus, defined usually as the criss-cross placing (*abba*) of sentence members which correspond in either syntax or meaning, with or without word-repetition. As Paul de Man has emphasised, the chiasmus is never a pure construction and can take the form of practically any strategy of reversal or specular reflection which crosses the attributes of inside and outside.[108] An 'open' chiasmus based on difference would seem to formalise perfectly Duras's stated commitment to alterity. By tracing the evolution of this particular figure in Duras's later work, rather than attempting, say, to provide an exhaustive list of all the tropes that Duras employs, we will therefore be better able to determine the ethical 'openness' of *écriture courante*. If we bear in mind John Guillory's narrative or figural legend of the chiasmus, i.e. origin (a) divergence; (b) repetition; (b) return (a),[109] we will also be in a stronger position to establish whether Duras's rhetorical passages, in appearance so many Cixousian *sorties* out of the system toward the Other, actually beat a path out of the textual, sexual and political flux and thus provide the pleasure of some kind of return. For the moment, let us simply use 'passage' as a kind of password to structure our discussion in three parts, following the thematic order that we established above with *Camion*.

Chapters 2 and 3 concern the filmic image and Duras's techniques of montage. Chapter 2 attempts to argue that *Camion* marks the beginning of a new aesthetics of sadomasochistic violence and 'ironic' error. It takes the form of a frame-by-frame analysis of the lorry's climactic passage in the film and reveals the extent of Duras's erotic investment in cinematic form, in particular the shot/reverse shot formation. By juxtaposing *Camion* with another Duras film of the same period, *Baxter, Véra Baxter* (1976–77), and then by placing both in their proper historical, cultural and cinematic context, the chapter determines whether *Camion* is really a reversible construct open to the Other as Duras claims. Chapter 3 explores in greater depth Duras's self-reflexive and erotic practice of montage, tracing the intersticial relations of sound and image in her four-part series of shorts from 1979 comprising *Césarée, Les mains négatives, Aurélia Steiner (Melbourne)*, and *Aurélia Steiner (Vancouver)*. By concentrating on Duras's artistic 'passage' first to Auschwitz in *Vancouver*, then into the black void of *Atlantique*, the chapter establishes the rhetorical, textual and ethical limits of Durasian filmic pleasure.

Chapters 4 and 5 consider Duras's textual and intertexual erotics. Chapter 4 examines in close detail the key passages of syntactic, linguistic, rhetorical and intertextual crisis in Duras's major Minuit work of the 1980s: *Eté, Amant, Emily, Maladie* and *Homme assis*. It analyses the complex sexual nature of the 'private affair' between text, reader and Duras's so-called 'Great Men' (here Kierkegaard, Robert Musil, Jean Renoir and John Huston), and uses Kristeva's theory of primary narcissism precisely to question the notion that Duras's literary work inscribes a rhetoric of the apocalypse. Finally, the chapter tests the fluidity and openness of *écriture courante* by revealing what particular kinds of textual and sexual 'error' are allowed to 'pass' in Duras's fiction and what are not. Chapter 5 explores further the relations between gender and textuality in Duras's later work by investigating why she appears to have constructed a gay-related, external passage, or margin, of non-Minuit texts and paratexts, among them *Outside* and *Yann*. It studies the nature of Duras's involvement with contemporary male writers such as Denis Belloc, Jean-Pierre Ceton and Renaud Camus, and unravels the rhetorical strategies employed by Duras to negotiate and frame gay influence. By placing Duras's work in the context of gay and queer theories of textual and sexual difference, the chapter aims to produce the first, properly 'crosswise' reading of her work ('queer', literally 'athwart', from the Indo-European root *twerkw*).

Chapters 6 and 7 examine Duras's relations with 'real' others. In chapter 6, a detailed textual analysis of 'Sublime, forcément sublime Christine V.' develops into a rhetorical discussion of Duras's passage through the French media and politics during the 1980s, focusing in particular on *Au-delà des pages* and her articles for *Libération* and *L'Autre Journal*. By approaching Duras in the post-colonial context of French attitudes towards racial difference, the chapter both reveals the ethical implications of her public airing of personal fantasies and assesses the validity of her repeated claim that she remained an 'outsider' in French language and culture. Chapter 7 provides a comparative and speculative study of the Duras/Andréa partnership in terms of the 'final passage' of old age. It first explores why, by Duras's own admission, the novel *Yeux bleus* did not 'pass' like other Minuit texts, then retraces the complicated steps that Duras took to rewrite the novel, including the so far critically neglected short text, *La pute de la côte normande* (1986), which presumes to tell the 'truth' of Andréa. By teasing out the erotic relations between Duras's *Maladie* and Andréa's *M.D.*, the chapter seeks to prove that Duras has invented a new form of literary collaboration, the logical culmination of all her textual/sexual experiments in alterity.

It is only by reading Duras's later work in this radically heterogeneous and multi-disciplinary manner, making it a point of intersection for different critical discourses and following all the links in the chain at every level, that we can possibly hope to understand its so far untold energies and pleasures, and our own stake in them. Only then, too, will we be able to appreciate fully Duras's contribution to the more general debates currently being staged on the relations between discourse and sexuality, gender and performance, ideology and aesthetics. Her work demands that we reconsider the social, sexual and psychoanalytical forces of artistic activity in a world where the aims and values of art are becoming ever more blurred and dispersed. In such a context, she asks, should art, indeed can art, function as a curative means of pleasure and self-preservation? Or, put a little differently, is an affirmative poetics of desire ever possible?

CHAPTER 2

Le système D.: *Le camion*

Je n'ai plus envie de filmer des histoires, des romans, mais des textes soit de hasard, soit politiques, soit de hasard (de mon hasard)

(M. Duras)

Circulating between the differently lit and angled interiors of 'décor 1' and 'décor 2' in 'la chambre noire' (or 'chambre de lecture'), and, more generally, between the home-made studio 'inside' and the industrial 'outside' of Trappes and Plaisir in the Yvelines, *Camion* appears to be essentially a set of playful variations on a theme. Its rhythm conforms both to the road-movie genre, where time on the road alternates with scenes off the road (as in Nicholas Ray's *They live by night* [1948] and Dennis Hopper's *Easy Rider* [1969]), and to a modernist aesthetic which Duras herself helped to create with Resnais in *Hiroshima*, where horizontal, tracking shots of the quotidian are intercut by vertical, still-frames of action (similarly in *India Song*, the exterior 'repeat shots' are punctuated by the 'ceremonial space' of the reception scenes).[1] In fact, the recurring outside shots of *Camion* constitute a frame through which the blue Saviem lorry passes, painfully yet sensuously, like an ever virtual, French kiss (*saviem*, first-person subjunctive of the Latin verb *s(u)aviare*, to kiss). In so doing, it performs literally what the extract from Grévisse's bible of French grammar, *Le bon usage*, used as an epigraph for the text of *Camion*, claims as the defining quality of the 'preludic conditional', namely, to 'transport' the event into the field of fiction.[2] After Delphine Seyrig's naked breast in *India Song*, Duras gives us here the most neutral object of our desires, thirty-two tons of it, in a free-flow of absorption and incorporation. Sublime.

But there are dangers. The Saviem lorry is at times lost in the mouth of a landscape whose darkened hills, together with the near-shots of thick mud and urban waste, threaten to swallow it up whole. When the lorry starts to lose itself in circles on a roundabout near the ghostly neon signs of Auchan, the shot is quickly cut so that it can resume its journey on the high road. Likewise, it will do no more than

skirt the unbearable memories of the Holocaust when it skips over the
'[t]rains. Trains' (p. 57) stacked up in the marshalling yard at Trappes
in the *train-train* of its own pace. That said, apart from the first, slow,
and only partial zoom into 'la chambre noire' which results in a
temporary alteration in the light, nothing really disturbs the even flow
of *Camion* and its regulated continuum of comfort and discomfort.
The lorry's fluctuating speed always proves just out of sync with
Beethoven's *33 Variations in C on a Waltz by Diabelli*, and Duras
continues to alternate the intonation in her voice between gentle and
harsh, thus matching the film's pointed inversions of encoded gender:
Duras dressed in austere black leather, Gérard Depardieu in a light,
open-neck shirt; she adopting at times the disembodied, unlocalised
voice-over of Hollywood cinema, he consigned to the traditionally
female position of the merely reactive, synchronised image.[3]

What, then, is being 'represented' in *Camion*? From the opening
left-pan which captures a stationary Saviem, the film assails the
viewer with questions: how to conquer its lure of fascination, its truck
of conventional cinematic metaphor? How, that is, to reduce the lorry
to size and so convert a bad object—contemporary symbol of the
Hollywood machine—into a good, 'aesthetic' object? The lorry poses
even more serious problems, however, as Duras explains in her
interview with Michelle Porte which follows the printed text of
Camion. She states that the fleeting shots of the lorry constitute in
relation to 'la chambre noire' an 'inaccessible totality' of 'clear,
indecipherable writing', or the 'first enclosure' where writing is
created (p. 104). The film appears powerless to capture this moving
volume of the 'already-written' within its cinematic frame and records
only its disappearing trace. All Duras can do, it seems, is to counter
the anxiety of arriving too late by obliging Depardieu to improvise
material she has already written. Can the image of the lorry ever be
controlled? Will Duras ever be able to move authorially from behind
the image to behind the wheel? Such is the crisis and the ambition of
Camion, and it demands that we focus both on all movement within
the frame and on the precise effects of editing, made all the more
visible and significant by the film's preference for long takes. Other
aspects of *Camion* such as lighting, mise en scène, and the manipulation of sound will be important to our discussion only to the extent
that they bear directly on the film's internal struggle for dominance.
Let us catch up now with *Camion*'s final stages.

Once Duras has brought the story of the hopeless encounter

between 'la dame' and the lorry-driver to a halt by narrating 'la dame''s descent from the lorry (p. 66), the viewer is transported back outside to catch the erring lorry slowly being discharged, as though in slow-motion, into undifferentiated traffic, a symbolic end to whatever narrativity *Camion* possessed. This slip into 'non-sense' (*sens*, sense and direction) constitutes a scene of loss and dispossession more significant than all the previous shots of the disappearing lorry. It is accompanied first by a return to the conditional mode which immediately problematises the single action ('She would have spoken one last time'), and then by a bogus, three-tier argument destroyed by the self-confirming phrase, 'cry when it was necessary to cry' (p. 67). We are left at this point in a position of impotence, unable to call back the lorry and its running inscription of passage. A cut back to 'la chambre noire' and we see that even the editing of shot (Duras) and reaction-shot (Depardieu) is becoming excessive and redundant; 'la chambre noire' is undergoing its own phase of loss and waste. Inside and outside, Depardieu and the lorry, all is being, as it were, killed off. Duras even declares that the film's unique figure of availability and ever-open love, 'la dame', could only have existed *because* of the ridiculed communist driver ('they could not have existed except in relation to each other' [p. 104]). Does the relinquishment of the lorry also mean, therefore, the rejection of 'la dame'? At all events the story has stopped. In contrast to the hoax-ending announced by Duras only ten minutes into the film (p. 23), we seem now to have reached THE END.

Suddenly, however, in a subjective shot from the perspective of the lorry, the viewer descends by means of a measured forward tracking movement (shot 103) into the bright light of a clear day, passing over ground covered earlier in the film by a lateral pan (shot 43). With Duras also modifying some earlier dialogue, sound and image seem at last to be working in unison. The lorry descends into shadowed light while Duras repeats the refrain: 'The clarity of words is obscured' (p. 68). Just as the dip of the valley is reached, however, and a white car coming from the opposite direction has been passed, the movement is abruptly cut and motivated into a shot/reverse shot formation (we pick up the lorry from the other side of the valley). If this replays and compresses the earlier crossings recorded in shot 43, where another lorry passing a water-tower generated a progression from darkness to light as it crossed a car and then a small lorry, here all is happening at once, making *Camion*'s sudden recourse to classical cinema's most conventional mode of suture, rigorously denied in 'la chambre noire' until now, an event of major importance. What we think we are seeing is a dynamic, double movement of crossing between car and lorry, shot and counter-shot. Yet the two events of traversal are actually just out of sync: the first image had already staged a crossing before it, too, is crossed out for another. The edit thus reveals itself to be imperfect, having come slightly too late in relation to the lorry's crossing of the car. In addition, the second shot, at an oblique angle from the first and from much farther away, reveals that the water-tower, passed just before the cut, has mysteriously vanished! Duras declares: 'On ne voit plus rien / cut / Rien' ('We no longer see anything. Nothing').

Camion thus performs its act of suture as a fake, even if the later text tries to pass it off as natural ('And then, the lorry. It is seen on the same road' [p. 68]). Only as a viewer do we enjoy the unexpected, ironic pleasures of this 'error' which is really the film's doubled-up self-consciousness of its own fundamental absence, i.e. of its lack of an image of 'la dame'. By cutting into itself self-reflexively as though undergoing a rite of scarification, *Camion* has effectively slapped itself back into life. For the erratic moment of suture is the closing up of the film's contingency and conditionality to form a new narrative structure. The lorry-phallus is ritualistically brought back into the static frame and begins to speed up the hill towards us. It has been erotically recalled, *da*, re-identified with, and then sublimated, by being magnificently reversed. This movement replays all the film's previous shiftings between inside and outside, fixing them into an imperfect chiasmus which is, of itself, a representation of loss. As in Merleau-Ponty's final formation of the chiasmus, the sequence cuts into the carnal flesh and texture of *Camion*, and, by excising the water-tower, exposes the film's gaping wound—the open gap between 'nothing' and 'nothing'—which has sustained it, whether that be the absence of 'la dame', or the sea, or Diabelli.[4] In so doing, the sequence executes the sign of the cross, +, and tropes knowingly on 'la dame''s pseudo-Jewish erring. Hence, in contrast to earlier cinematic experiments in fragmented montage such as *Hiroshima*, where editing replaced the 'real event' (Hiroshima? Nevers?), the edit in *Camion* is the *only* event.[5]

The shot/reverse shot sequence is not quite as irreversible as it might at first appear, however, for there is no real linear motivation behind it. This Duras casually reveals in one interview where she actually reverses the sequence, claiming instead that the lorry is initially seen from the exterior (in this case, the two shots would remain discrete and unconnected moments).[6] How, then, are we to interpret this 'fault' of montage, this 'chasm' of reversibility? Suture, as Kaja Silverman has shown, is a masochistic affair, a repetition of the subject's founding cut, out of the Imaginary and into the Symbolic. It comprises:

> [a] constant fluctuation between the imaginary plenitude of the shot, and the loss of that plenitude through the agency of the cut . . . the moment of the cut can only be experienced by that subject as an integration of image into syntactic structure, as a repetition of the transition from imaginary to symbolic. The viewing subject has learned to take pleasure in the pain of imaginary loss, in the re-enactment of the traumatic dialectic of presence and absence.[7]

What *Camion* is therefore doing with its shot/reverse shot formation is to reveal theatrically the masochistic mechanism of suture precisely by blocking it. The symbolic castration of the phallic water-tower provides a heightened reflection on the defining absence of the cinematic process itself (the 'fading' image as absence of the referent of the always fading lorry). In a manner inconceivable in Hitchcockian montage, for example, where the strange Thing remains uncanny because denied both an objective shot and its own subjective shot of the person approaching it, suture directs us here to an awareness of the transcendental (M)Other (Duras) who blocks our belief in the presence of the first shot of the sequence.[8] From the site of the second reverse shot, we are at last given eye contact with a real other, the film's driver (Duras) who, absent from the image but there now in montage, draws us deeper into her field of vision.[9]

To return to the sequence: after its sudden death play-off in suture, the lorry occupies again the position it held at the start of the film when it slowly revved up and moved towards the camera. Yet in the light of what has just occurred, the penetration of the lorry rolling into the frame of our gaze must now be read as properly erotic, as the moment—long deferred—of the kiss. From its potential as '*saviem*', the lorry has been actualised as a magical object of oral pleasure, a Latin kiss, '*savium*', across the mouth of the big screen (*savium*, like *passage*, is both action [kiss] and the site of action [mouth ready for kissing]). The erotic climax, which in Hollywood cinema usually demands a flurry of editorial 'flashing', is here one clean image of controlled motion. This is an utterly concrete reworking of the vertical resurrection of Inger's dead body by a kiss in Carl T. Dreyer's *Ordet* (1954), a film which, according to Duras, exemplifies the blinding force of the 'idea' of God (*Yeux*, p. 162). Erotic, then, but to what end?

As the lorry veers bottom right out of the frame—we are not on the corresponding 180° angle of the first shot—everything is literally up in the air, open and liminal. Just before the accompanying, strident C-minor sequence of Beethoven variations (29, 30, 31) reaches the dominant note of E-flat, however, the image is again cut, provoking a forward movement back into the lorry's 'counter-image' of 'la chambre noire'. Now begins a new version of *Camion* controlled by Duras's voice alone and in which 'la chambre noire' itself is made to function as a site of passage. If, as one critic suggests, the film writes over an absent, vague profilmic event (i.e. the 'real' film that could have been made),[10] it will now itself constitute the profilmic for all that follows. This drama—let us call it *Camion 2*—falls into three acts.

ACT 1

The new forward tracking shot into 'décor 2' (shot 105) towards the white-curtained horizon of the studio backdrop offers the belated pleasure of completing a previous tracking shot arrested in mid-shot. Is what has just taken place outside about to be replayed within? The tracking shot repeats the first half of the preceding shot/reverse shot sequence, separating Duras and Depardieu just as before the lorry had carved up the landscape and the cut of montage had dissected, in turn, the crossing. This is a *re-passage*, or iron(is)ing out, of all the film's prior movements of passage and it re-marks the viewer's spectatorial positions in relation to the lorry (inside/outside, active/passive, etc.). In so doing, it also confirms hyperbolically what was already emphasised by the shot/reaction shot sequence, namely, that the viewer was constantly divided (bisexually) between practising female author and inactive male actor, between intellect and intuition. It is Duras's voice alone, however, which is now beginning to write over the white page of the image while announcing the arrival of summer.

ACT 2

The second forward tracking (shot 105) repeats the direction of the first but now in 'décor 1'. This doubling of the first forward tracking does not repeat the chiastic event of montage, however. Rather, as if deconstructing the chiastic *abba* structure, the repetition destroys the distance between the viewer (*a*) and the object (*b*) (the table) in the express interests of inversion and difference. After the bright lights of the first tracking, the second plunges us gradually into a darkness that glows with an unheralded bloom of turquoise light as though acted upon by the 'dark, yellowed green' of the voice-over, and which, like the lorry entering into the obscurity of the first part of the previous shot/reverse shot sequence, becomes progressively darker as we head towards the table. The sea, long talked about but never shown, is rendered metaphorically by this creation of a depth of field behind Duras. More than just the (M)Other (*la mère*) of montage, Duras becomes homonymically the sea (*la mer*), 'that element of annihilation, the end of the world'.[11] No sooner is this identification offered, however, than it is withdrawn, for as we begin to approach the table, we find ourselves veering down towards the left to pick up only Duras, whose eyes are flashing almost devilishly. The burden of the viewer's frustrations, of not being able to get close enough to Duras, or to the music, or to the driver of the Saviem, has at last been lifted. It is as though we were entering spellbound into a rarefied world of split personalities concealed in hidden cellars, where Duras plays self-parodically the part of the witch. As for Depardieu, he has had his life sucked out of him as though by a maternal 'monster' of abjection who rekindles the diabolic power of one of the film's absent origins, 'Diabelli'.

This second forward tracking shot, then, and not the prior accident of montage, should be considered the film's first properly irreversible movement, from intransitive to transitive, from passive to active. It excludes Depardieu almost entirely, allowing Duras to be wholly enraptured by the viewer's interpellated gaze which she alone commands by monopolising both the light of the projector lamp and the angle of the camera. The passivity and masochism represented so far in 'la chambre noire' by Depardieu has therefore been remotivated by Duras as an erotic encounter with the viewer. Once, in *India Song*, the Duras viewer was ravished by the long image of Anne-Marie Stretter walking effortlessly into frame; now, for the first time, s/he is called upon to ride the camera's movement and 'penetrate'! The umbilical cord has finally been cut and the flesh of *Camion* can now be sublimated and released, this by a film-maker rightfully regarded as austere and abstract but who still needs the concrete clarity of camera angle and shot to obtain the requisite erotic charge. In fact, a wilful desire to be tracked down is the reality of Duras's proclaimed intention to reverse the traditional spectator's passivity and make him 'see'. Unlike, for instance, the girl in Freud's account of female masochism who first assumes the homosexual position of her rival male double in the face of the father (phase one: 'I am being beaten [loved] by my father') only then to escape the demands of her erotic life altogether by becoming the mere spectator of an exterior event (phase two: 'A child is being beaten'), Duras here is both active subject and willing object of the *jouissance* produced in self-reflexive montage, acting out her multilayered, sadomasochistic fantasy with a third party—the viewer—as one *definitive* sexual event.[12]

But what exactly has the viewer become? As tired consumer of both commercial and political avant-garde cinema, our 'sick mass' (p. 77) has been reawakened and projected forwards into a sexual transference, thus to be reborn as the film's second driver, that 'dark mass' (p. 15) which, in the tale of 'la dame', remained asleep in the back of the lorry as an always potential presence. This is nothing less than a replacement of Depardieu as the new man in Duras's film! Not Deleuze's new Greek of dephallicised sexuality, of course, who is (re)born phantasmatically through the exclusive cruelty of a cold, dominant mother,[13] for *Camion*'s performances of role-reversal, disavowal, suspense and self-fetishism (Duras's theatrical flicking of her glasses, for example) only 'masqueraded' as part of a masochistic aesthetic.[14] No, on the contrary, the viewer is positioned as a masculine voyeur aggressive enough to impose the reality principle on Duras's dangerous fantasy and provide her with the possibility of release in the passive position. Moreover, in sharp contrast with Pauline Kael's account of *Camion* where the director simply suffers for having driven the audience out of the cinema through boredom,[15] Duras deliberately draws the viewer in for a shared sadomasochistic fix, her sly grin picking up our self-splitting identification with the fruits of our enforced, scopophilic violence. Paradoxically, then, this bare, minimalist film returns the viewer to the position of the traditional cinematic fetishist who, according to Christian Metz:

for the establishment of his full potency for cinematic enjoyment (*jouis-sance*) . . . must think, at every moment (and above all *simultaneously*), of the force of presence the film has and of the absence on which this force is constructed. He must constantly compare the result with the means deployed (and hence pay attention to the technique) for *his pleasure lodges in the gap between the two.*[16]

As soon as we have savoured and admired Duras frontally at a discreet distance, we are transported towards the right by a lateral tracking movement past and over Depardieu. Muted, he is now the image of that dark, subterranean, outside Natura over which Duras is at last able to score home her unique, and absolutely 'real', film. 'A lorry crosses the whole', she states. In fact, this shot intensifies the action, for the more shadowed the image of Depardieu becomes, the higher Duras's voice soars across the boundaries of the frame. Like the water-tower, Depardieu is being literally bypassed and evacuated from *Camion* in a metaphorical replay of the film he had made a year before with Marco Ferreri, *L'Ultima Donna* (The Last Woman) (1976), where, in an equally dark and secluded private apartment, he ended up sawing off his own penis. We can still just catch sight of him, though, as he smokes a cigarette with Duras, an event which completes two earlier blocked attempts in 'la chambre noire' and which assumes in the dimmed interior the proportions of a mini-orgasm, echoed in the accelerating, rhyming cadences of grouped words: 'couleur'/'chaleur', 'air'/'mer', 'craquante'/'crisser', 'soleil'/ 'sol', 'l'été'/'c'est l'été'/'l'été'. In addition, the alternating soft and hard syllables extend the verbal violence glimpsed previously in such phrases as 'tellement dur, tellement dur' (p. 27). As projector-lamps begin to light up the area behind Duras, we experience in the tracking-shot a beautifully manicured, vertical spasm, or *ébranlement*. The ecstasy which had always been slightly denied by the tense of the lorry's movement—first-person plural imperfect of the French neo-logism, the verb '*camer*', i.e. '*(nous) camion(s)*' ('we were coming')— is now being fully realised. The film has *come*!

It is clear, then, that *Camion*'s constant drive for the sublime was a prerequisite for its one properly sexual moment: the agitated 'shatter-ing' and penetration of Duras's discursive space ('le décor éclaté' [p. 69]). For once its sublime (and abject) axes of 'all' and 'nothing' have been redirected into an internal, intellectual structure, the film as a whole is desublimated by the irreversible movement of the forward trackings.[17] Certainly, masochism was always present in *Camion* but it is, at last, fully displayed, and melodramatically so, by the camera's dynamic move towards Duras, a self-reflexive displacement of the first forward tracking shot which only restated the split presentation of the film. This first tracking was, however, absolutely crucial in telling the viewer how to read the true nature of penetration in the second. Indeed, the image's eroticised consciousness, provisionally structured during the crisis of montage by a perception of the sadomasochistic relations among its terms, is a *prerequisite* for the enjoyment of heterosexual desire. It is not simply that the alternating inside/outside play between Trappes and Plaisir has now been exposed as mere, histrionic foreplay (what Duras means, perhaps, when she talks of the film's ten or so moments of flashing [p. 122]). Rather, the aggressive pleasures of Duras's erotic self-'entrapment' prove that the verbal and visual sadism displayed during the film towards Depardieu's 'rentable' body was really a manifestation of her own projected masochism, or derived sadism, one affording a pleasurable fantasy-identification with the intense pain (real or otherwise) of the victim internalised as other.[18] Without the 'error' of chiastic suture and the reasoned lure of the first self-reflexive tracking shot, this sadomasochistic pleasure might easily have destroyed Duras, and the viewer, in too close a union. Thus, calculated failure in montage—a crisis of form—has bred certain, literal success in the shot. Indeed, the second tracking-shot can now be read as the film's symbolic birth of intelligence and the overcoming of a fear that had always stalked it, namely, that the cab of the lorry, or 'la chambre noire', might at any moment be engulfed by a flood of light, '[t]he fear of catastrophe: political intelligence' (p. 42). Against all expectations, it allows Duras to achieve, yes, personal catharsis: 'I can now say that from this film on I stopped being afraid politically. You know, just as one says one has freed oneself from the faith.'[19]

But *Camion* Act II is not yet over. As Duras's monologue continues, the camera eclipses a ghostly Depardieu ('Then it [the lorry] disappears' [p. 70]), leaving behind a sibillant space of death-liness, 'a rustling of bushes of thorn'. Key lexical elements such as 'c'est l'été' are reassembled, as if to emphasise that this is an eternal, metapoetic event which has no connection with the earlier reference to tanks entering Prague during the summer of 1968 (p. 45). More-over, words used conceptually before such as 'fixed' and 'dominated' are now blessed with a concrete literalness, and it soon becomes clear that the viewer is witnessing a displacement by inversion of Duras's earlier novel *Andesmas*, which was ignited by the arrival of a dog crossing over a plateau towards the ageing Andesmas (here the 'oldish' Lady). The adjective *'caniculaire'* (literally, 'of the little dog') elucidates the accompanying enigmatic phrase, 'the memory of a passage', and drives home the point that Depardieu and the viewer are dutiful objects of Duras's mastery. For the ascending, rasping word of Duras is the good, the only lorry, passing in and out of, over and again, the highlights of her journey which is now entering the safe haven of full syntax. After all the previous fragments of attitudinising dialogue, Duras delivers an almost classical, literary description of her own personal passage. The sentence comes complete with a subject, verb, object, and dependent clause, although it turns on a 'thorny' point of grammar based, significantly, around the preposition of possession, *'de'*:

> It [the lorry] leaves behind it a rustling *of* bushes *of* thorn [*un froissement de buissons d'épineux*]. It is the force of the wind stirred by the passing of the lorry's mass which makes the dead plants of summer rustle. (p. 70, emphasis added)[20]

The technically incorrect repetition of *'de'*, which, in the interests of rhythm, transforms the adjective 'épineux' into a noun ('of thorn'), is exacerbated in the following sentence which uses the word a remarkable four times. The stressing of 'force' 'remué', 'passage', 'plantes mortes' to optimum effect highlights not only the rejuvenation of dead cinema but also Duras's unstoppable erotic and rhetorical manipulation of the viewer. Yet her fantasy has still not run its course. With the lorry having totally disappeared, Duras starts up again in apparent complicity with the viewer—'On attend'—and the image is suddenly cut into black.

ACT 3

(Or Duras's version of *film noir*, in which 'la chambre noire' becomes a *camera obscura*).

The phrase 'On attend' is developed after the cut into another full sentence: 'On attend l'accident qui va peupler la forêt' ('We await the accident that is going to people the forest'). Thus, at the interface between printed image and black spacing, the mirror of a trisyllabic rhyming scheme has been simultaneously formed and shattered: 'On-att-end / cut / l'acc-i-dent'. This is the chiastic scene of false suture replayed on a higher level: the text inverts the edit with its apparent self-contradiction (how, after all, is one to expect an accident?) and produces thereby a self-reflexive comment on montage's 'acc-idental' powers of expansion and generation which allow 'peupler' to become 'peuplier' (poplar tree). What is remarkable about this linguistic play is that it is taking place in the forest which had always been sequestered in the Durasian imaginary as a hinterland of forbidden, mad desire, but which has now been cleared away and transformed into a fertile space of filmic reproduction. However, Duras refuses to 'pass on' the secret of this mysterious birth, admitting to only the most banal of facts: 'C'est le bruit d'un passage. On ne sait pas de qui, de quoi' ('It is the noise of a passage. We don't know of whom, of what'). It is as if, during the film's only major subversion of the limits of its oral frame, Duras is speaking over and through the cut, resealing the black hole of foiled suture with the rhyming power of her own voice. The endless reversals, split-selves and punctuations of image in *Camion* have been replaced by Duras herself as the punctual source of meaning, her precise, flat modulations of tone articulating a self-sufficient passage of controlled narcissism. Such is the victory of the text, the 'indefinite bearer of images' (p. 75). If Duras had destroyed the classic Hollywood model of the remake with her *India Song/Son Nom de Venise* dyad, here, in *Camion*, she has gone even further by constructing a cycle of self-ironic remakes. The film has been cut and recut continuously into higher forms of sublimation, desublimation, and resublimation. After one last pregnant silence, one final refusal to divulge the reason for the noise of the lorry's passage, and as the credits begin to rise up in white over the black screen (the black and white film which 'would' have been made?), a diminuendo on the sound-track is abruptly reversed by the repetition of Diabelli's trite, up-beat theme, as incidental/accidental as the odd image of a passing lorry. All to be resumed with Dominique Noguez in their 1983 interview, 'La dame des Yvelines': Duras: 'Do you want to play *Le camion*?'; Noguez: 'Yes'; Duras: 'Help me, Dominique!'

We see, then, that the entire film, and not just its one shot/reverse shot sequence, is really a hoax. For rather than being a reversible and interchangeable construct open to the outside, *Camion* assumes the symbolic potency of all those cheap Hollywood vehicles which it had seemed on course to render null and void. Duras's stated empathy with the radical negativity of 'la dame''s love ('unformed, disordered, dangerous'[21]) is also a feint, since by being rendered incarnate as the flesh of Depardieu, 'la dame' serves only as an imaginary vehicle of mediation for Duras's own erotic self-penetration ('It's through her that I can see. Through her that I take in the exterior and engulf it within me' [p. 79][22]). If Depardieu can be said to function as the artist's model (his framing in 'la chambre noire' recalls that of Paul Cézanne's gardener smoking a pipe and leaning against a table in a series of portraits he painted between 1890 and 1895), 'la dame' is a purely invisible model, what Duras 'would have preferred to be' ('La dame des Yvelines'). Duras, 'M.D.', and not her inverted mirror image, 'la DaMe', is *Camion*'s true 'self-commuter' (*auto-stoppeuse*), engaged chiastically in a passion for regression which can immediately be recuperated as 'under way, in progress, fundamental' (p. 81). Duras could, like 'la dame', have been all things at once. Instead, she projects both a limitless magma of reproductivity—'la dame''s past life of bearing children—and a mad excess of undifferentiated desire—'her body was his body, inseparable, day and night, from her own body . . . Two billion men' (p. 31)—in order precisely to abject 'la dame'.

Duras may claim that her decision not to allow an actress to perform the role of 'la dame' was made in order to avoid a repetition of *India Song*, where, despite being merely 'cited' by Seyrig, the character of Anne-Marie Stretter constantly ran the risk of becoming a 'definitive statement'.[23] Our analysis of *Camion* has shown, however, that, on the contrary, Duras tropes definitively on what she purports to honour: the unpredictable and the free. Moreover, the film's relay of metaphor is secured only if we, as viewers, are willing, like Duras's caricature of the 'crippled, autistic [and] psychotic', political militant,[24] to act in the manner demanded by the French Communist Party, i.e. put ourselves in the hands of a machine which will carry us away.[25] Hence, the idealistic interpretations offered by some critics of *Camion*—for example, that it represents a vaguely Jewish and utopian, 'infinite aspiration',[26] or a benign, Winnicottian 'potential space of playful becoming' shared by writer, talker, hitch-hiker and reader,[27] or even a general, spiritual love based on an indeterminate '*dépassement de soi*'[28]—appear misplaced, if not naïve. Ultimately, it is only the film's violence to both itself and the viewer that ensures that 'it will have existed'; that the conditional perfect of indecipherable writing is transformed into the future perfect of readable cinematic fantasy.

Yet the sadomasochistic pleasures generated in *Camion* through montage also record the film's passage from abjection to the plenitude of enunciation. Such a movement, from first, through second, to third gear, and repeated in Duras's self-troping voice-over, is prefigured by that one cross-fertilisation of shot in chiastic suture. This represents the channelling of a Lyotardian 'acinema'—an ideal space of open viewing where each element is held in a state of flux and enjoyed for its own affective intensity (the rhythms of shot, the crackle of paper, etc.)—into a highly productive narrative of return.[29] Having stripped cinema down to its basics—the binary mechanics of montage—in order to allow for a free dispensation of cinematic energies, Duras then siphons off libidinal discharge into a fantasy which is finally reclaimable as *Camion* Act III. In fact, the erotic climax is made possible precisely because Duras has built up a structure of sounds and images powerful enough to record its own self-shattering. For this reason, the film does not perform a desiring fantasy understood in Bersani's terms as 'the dislocation of non-narrative representation'.[30] Rather, the floating sexual energies of auto-erotically inspired subli- mation have been put to the services of self-gratification, the *chi* of chiastic montage returning as the *ich* of narcissism. Furthermore, by committing criminal acts of differentiation through duplicitous cut- ting and recutting in the third, 'reel time', or *fort/da*, of montage, Duras, both *monteuse* and *menteuse*, 'betrays' the double fantasy operating between herself, Depardieu, and the otherwise unreadable lorry which always vanished past her during the shooting of the film (a period she refers to in 'La dame des Yvelines' as the 'scattering [*émiettement*] of the subject'). Although the de/dis-figuration of form might at first appear to herald *Camion*'s own self-cancellation as a film, it is, in fact, fertility itself, or the 'extraordinarily fecund night' of montage (*Parleuses*, p. 88).

To return to the idea of the ambition of *Camion* with which we began our discussion. The film's scansion of sadomasochistic desire tropes over the lorry's blue writing of pain, and in so doing inscribes a concrete representation of control, or 'rewriting',[31] over the very 'invasion' of writing.[32] Over cinema, too, for *Camion*'s erotic violation of cinematic form reverses the normal process whereby writing is reduced to a script expecting an 'after' (*Yeux*, p. 92). (Compare Duras's triumphant, frontal position with that of Godard in *Numéro Deux* [1975], where, while editing a collaged 'super- scription' of blown-up video images of physical and societal rape and anality, he remains caught within the frame of abjection rather than at a safe critical distance from it.) In fact, because explicitly programmed as an activity of writing, *Camion* produces finally the same painful pleasures of 'wonderful misery'—'*le malheur merveilleux*'—which Duras experiences when she is writing a novel:

> The book advances and while it does so it is nothing but life in its potential for existence, and like life it needs all the constraints of suffocation, pain, slowness, trammels of all sorts, silence and night. It passes first by way of the disgust of being born, the horror of growing up and coming into the world . . . This voyage must be suffered with the book, the hard labour, during the whole time of its writing. One acquires a taste for this wonderful misery. (*Yeux*, p. 92)[33]

Strangely, Duras denies that *Camion* creates a 'spectacle' of writing. She states: '[i]n general, there is projection on to the page and the seizing of writing by a third party. Here that doesn't happen. You don't descend towards the explosion of the text.'[34] Yet as we have seen, while the film may appear to prevent the cinematic image from destroying the force of the imaginary (one of the key points of the 'Four Projects' [p. 73]), it also requires that the viewer be projected on to a screen embodied by a third party (Depardieu) who is then totally relegated.

In her authorial confrontation with abjection in the name of pleasure, during which she initially gives herself over to *De-par-dieu* in honour of her real name, *Don(n)-à-dieu* ('gift-to-God'), it is Duras herself who plays God (indeed, a halo of light always seems to be resting just above her head).[35] Furthermore, the self-sublimating rituals of sacrifice and fertility resolve the question posed throughout the film of how to inscribe one's own personal passage if one has rejected the God of political '*PASSAGE*'. They serve as rites of passage, the necessary first step to a new, post-'68 aesthetics which crosses out, literally, all previous forms of political engagement, in particular involuntary, Communist 'self-mutilation'.[36] *Camion* may depict the physical geography of apocalyptic aftermath but it magisterially inscribes a new *rapport* across the void of sexual difference. It is, in fact, all that is possible when belief in the 'holy cow of the proletariat' has been extinguished, and it confirms Kristeva's notion that, in the absence of God, writing and style are the only remaining sites of purification.[37]

But how can we account for the extraordinary force and violence of Duras's formal refusal to identify with 'la dame', even to the point of disqualifying her? One obvious way is to try to resurrect the person on whom Duras displaced this violence, Depardieu, who also starred in another of Duras's films released earlier in 1977 entitled *Baxter, Véra Baxter*, an adaptation of her 1968 play, *Suzanna Andler*. While still at work on the post-production of *Camion*, Duras was already proclaiming *Baxter* a failure, a 'regression' no less,[38] a judgement which might seem rather premature given that the film exhibits all the by then familiar features of her technique (the alternation of static and tracking shots, repetition of musical motifs, etc.). Yet so strong was Duras's belief that *Baxter* is flawed that in 1980 she eventually rewrote it as a screenplay for another, as yet unmade, film, *Véra Baxter ou les plages de l'Atlantique*. What part does Depardieu play in these exceptional circumstances, and what does it say about the nature of his, and therefore 'la dame''s, subsequent treatment in *Camion*? In other words, what can *Baxter* reveal of the intensity of Duras's erotic reinvestment of cinematic form in *Camion*?

Before shooting *Baxter*, Duras had decided to diminish the original importance of Michel Cayre (Depardieu), the extra-conjugal lover of Véra Baxter (Claudine Gabay) to whom her husband effectively sells her for the price of a villa, by introducing a stranger who, once aroused by the mention of her name, would attempt to tell Véra her own story. This new role was intended for a man but, after allowing herself to be, as she put it, 'misled' by the dictates of feminism, Duras finally gave the part to Delphine Seyrig. The switch in sex proved 'a grave error' (*Véra Baxter*, p. 5), one that not even the considerable skills of Seyrig could correct. For Duras discovered that heterosexual desire was rendered impossible by the 'physical pseudo-community of women' comprising Véra, the Stranger and Véra's friend, Monique Combès (Noëlle Chatelet), a former lover of her husband, Jean. Here is how Duras explains the outcome:

> If there had been a man in place of the [female] visitor, the fact that they [i.e. he and Véra] avoid each other as they [i.e. the women] do would be directly inscribed in the cleaving of a future desire, a positive relationship . . . Without a man looking I am unable to see Véra Baxter's body.[39]

What actually happens in *Baxter* is that Véra becomes fixated by the Stranger with whom she can only exchange averted glances, and the film quickly becomes a tale of unsuccessfully mediated desire, of '[r]eported words. Deviated eroticism. Silence' (*Véra Baxter*, p. 70). As was the case during Elisabeth's abortive conversion in *Détruire*, where her symbolic passage through the mirror towards her female double, Alissa, was suddenly frozen, filmic desire is homosexually blocked. Duras again: 'I thought that I could transgress homosexuality, that taboo, that kind of difference. Which goes to prove that you must never go against your nature.'[40] Active transgression is not possible in *Baxter* and although a final scene of deliverance is produced, Véra appears unaware of its significance: '[i]t has happened. She leaves. Extracts herself from the Colonnades . . . The thing has happened imperceptibly, she must not have known that she was leaving' (*Véra Baxter*, p. 110).[41] In fact, the main event of the narrative—Jean's decision to rent the villa—had already taken place before the film began.

Contrary to the claims made by Judith Roof for the later *Véra Baxter*, where Duras took no chances and restored the male identity of the Stranger, the Véra of *Baxter* cannot initiate her own 'organic and subversive play' because she does not know the meaning of her own feelings which have always been unconsciously transferred on to her children.[42] Her dialogue splinters involuntarily out of despair rather than for ironic effect, as in the following example: 'I no longer love anything. Anybody. I didn't know that . . . [break]' (*Véra Baxter*, p. 61). Whereas Jean is able to 'invent' the pain of being left by his wife in order to regenerate his ebbing desire (*Véra Baxter*, p. 114), Véra, as her name indicates, is too truthful to assume *rhetorically* her own act of adultery and thus remains suffocated by her marital status, '*Baxter/Véra/Baxter*'. The greatest victim in *Baxter*, however, is the film itself, since it has remained overfaithful to the Duras style, burning itself out in an endless cycle of pans and meandering tracking shots which cross through the funereal space of the villa, past Véra and the furniture covered up in ghostly white sheets, towards the windows barring all access to the outside. Ticking by to the relentless, fluted beat of a South American tune, these shots prove as superfluous as the many lost, unnoticed events of ocean crossing in the background or the stifling close-ups of water and sand. The ironic counterforce of *Baxter*'s figuration of 'exterior turbulence', for which the prostitution economy of les Colonnades could perhaps have acted as a 'spectacular decoy' (Roof), always remains at an impossible distance from the film's visual frame. Inevitably, it is deep within the villa itself that the film's climactic moment of blockage occurs: a shot of Véra reclining naked on her bed. Here, stranded in middle long-shot, her body is clinically rather than erotically represented, lacking the ironic power of the close-up of Seyrig's sweat-coated breast in

India Song. For thirty seconds *Baxter* even appears to be supplanted
by the iconic status of painting—Véra's pose approximates that of
Manet's *Olympia* (1863), although from the opposite side and minus
the maid-servant. Durasian cinema can represent another medium
only to its cost! (We recall also that it was after his eye was caught by
the androgynous angel in Fra Angelico's *Annunciation* that the
narrator of *Gibraltar* found himself locked into an adventure of
impossible passion [p. 54].)

Baxter is not the only Duras/Depardieu collaboration, of course,
which fails to commit an act of heterosexual 'passage', whether
literally or metaphorically, through montage. As the anonymous
salesman of the earlier *Nathalie Granger*, Depardieu made anxious
crossings in, through, and out of the central axis of the corridor of the
women's home but was always unable to initiate any kind of
reciprocal or erotic contact with either them or their daughters, his
virility effectively negated by their unrelenting gaze.[43] All that could
be recorded was a conventional and often banal series of shot/reverse
shot formations: Moreau would exit left to right, Bose would then
enter right to left.[44] Upon Depardieu's departure, the viewer was left
in the women's 'pre-verbal, pre-male' domestic space (*Lieux*, p. 12),
which even a dog wandering outside was afraid to pass. A little later,
in *La femme du Gange* (1973), where Depardieu played the leader of
a moving band of young people, two female narrators (or 'wandering
voices') became immobilised by their emotion while enacting a
legendary 'model' of 'mortal desire' which they were supposed only to
relay. Their mutual declaration of love unto death provoked a deadly
encounter between 'the film of the Voices' and 'the film of the Image',
resulting in an indefinable and unreadable space of lesbian desire,
'without undulation of forms, barely differentiated'. The image, fully
synced, proved in the end redundant, an 'excess of image' (*Granger*,
p. 185).[45]

We are now in a better position to appreciate Duras's achievement
in *Camion*, which represents nothing less than her dramatic compensation for the lack of a male other in *Baxter*. The montage of signs in
the later film writes over the unforeseen homosexual traces of *Baxter*,
and, in so doing, reverses the trajectory of Depardieu who, in his role
as Michel Cayre, had expressed his faltering heterosexual desire thus:
'I am at the point where I will not be able to touch another woman'
(*Véra Baxter*, p. 27). By working the rich seams of asynchronous
montage and repeating at every edit the founding separation of

absolute heterosexual difference, *Camion* reveals that it is always, in effect, breaking out of what Kristeva has called the 'homosexual-maternal facet', i.e. the primal regression experienced by women during motherhood when, at the threshold of language and instinctual desire, in a 'whirl' of words, they reunite phantasmatically with the body of their own mother.[46] For what *Camion*'s writing over 'la dame' ensures, and what *Baxter*'s fascination with Véra prevents, is the necessary transporting of the Duras image out of the imaginary realm of the maternal figure, nowhere more dangerous than in *Barrage* where the mother is forced to play piano in a cinema without ever being able to see the screen, the latter assuming in the process the ghastly form of a white shroud.[47] When the Duras image does attempt to represent the mother, as in *Des journées entières dans les arbres* (made for television in 1976), it is fully synchronised and formally unadventurous, including even a conventionally realised flash-back to a tropical childhood.

A series of equations for Duras's cinema can now be established: the image = representation (cinematic, pictorial) = synchronisation of sound and image = unmotivated shot = close-up = female body = stasis = homosexuality. The simple conjunction of sound and image invariably signifies either the female body, homosexuality, or death. In *Night* (1978), for example, Bulle Ogier's supine body filmed in long-shot ('her bed is thus open to everyone's gaze') suspends all movement, the image of a young man, possibly a prostitute, on the Champs-Elysées coincides with a reference to the strange, male desire of 'the Cat', and Père-Lachaise cemetery is visually depicted while being simultaneously described on the sound-track. Thus, the abjecting of the still-frame image in Duras's film-work represents nothing less than the sublimation of homosexual desire, founded in Freudian theory on the principle of analogy[48] and which, according to Duras, denies the possibility of separation: '[i]t is *oneself*', she states (*Yeux*, p. 233). So crucial is this operation that the very mention of resemblance during the opening voice-over in her later film, *Agatha*— 'You would think that they [Agatha and her brother] looked alike'— is enough to provoke a sharp cut out of black into the first printed image.

We can only grasp the full sexual significance of *Camion*, however, if we place it in its proper historical and cinematic context. For the anguish caused by the lorry's fading also represents Duras's own fears of a potential loss of identity and heterosexual difference in the face of the advancing 1970s wave of lesbian-feminist film-making, a form of feminism which she herself inspired with *Nathalie Granger* but which she later dismissed as the 'naïve fascism of a new, liberatory morality'.[49] In fact, by 1974, Duras was already disavowing *Nathalie Granger* as other to her true nature since she had not been 'completely in her element' (*Parleuses*, p. 78). Nine years later, in 'La classe de la violence', she argued further that the film paved the way specifically for the work of Chantal Ackerman. Let us look finally at one of Ackerman's films, *Je Tu Il Elle* (b/w, 1974), since it is highly representative of that early period of feminist film-making and throws into clear relief the singular nature of *Camion*.

Je Tu Il Elle belongs to the newly-created genre of the European road movie which, although partly inspired by Barbara Loden's *Wanda* (1970), a low-budget American tale of drifting and impossible relationships, deliberately sought to explore new forms of same-sex relationships, as in Wim Wenders's rambling male-buddy movie, *Kings of the Road* (b/w, 1976).[50] *Je Tu Il Elle* tells the simple story of a woman (played by Ackerman herself) who is picked up by a male lorry-driver as she tries to reach her female lover. Formally, the film possesses all the qualities that *Camion* so vigorously denies: realist detail, sexual explicitness (both the lorry-driver's masturbatory desire and the women's oral and anal passion are shown), as well as the creation of a natural, 'female' time, corresponding possibly to that of a menstrual cycle.[51] By not privileging any particular movement or sound, the static Ackerman frame is rocked dangerously and mercilessly by the undifferentiated chaos passing through it, a technique later refined in the long-takes of her 1976 film, *Letters from Home*.[52] This can be directly contrasted with *Camion* which categorically forbids the cinematic apparatus from functioning as a tool of female essentialism. Indeed, Duras's erotic investment in montage effectively transcends Ackerman's always proximate, Jewish body and her white sheets of homosexual passion, figured in *Camion* by the white curtains of 'la chambre noire' which are, at the end, completely swept back.[53] Furthermore, Duras's highly original, self-editing 'passage' in *Camion* tropes precisely over *Je Tu Il Elle*'s use of the old French nursery rhyme, 'Nous n'irons plus aux bois, / Les lauriers sont coupés' ('We will go to the woods no more, / The laurel trees are cut'). If we also bear in mind Duras's bawdy joke in *Camion* that she smokes *only* Gauloises bleues (p. 27), we could even say that she is smoking the influence of lesbian-feminist cinema out of her lair in an ironic consummation of form.

But with its one, knowingly 'false' cut, *Camion* is also severing the umbilical cord which had once connected Duras with French feminist thought and culture in general. This bond had been established with Xavière Gauthier during their unedited, and often very sticky, interviews between jam-making in *Parleuses*, and it appeared cemented in 1976 by such providing acts as the filmic back-projection for the Paris production of Cixous's play, *Portrait de Dora*, and, a little later, her post-face commentary for Erika Lennard's book, *Les femmes, les soeurs*, a radical experiment in lesbian textual identity.[54] However, in her interview about *Camion* with Michelle Porte, Duras proclaimed her suspicion of a female writing of the body thus: '[writing] . . . is a sort of internal command. I don't mean of the body, because that's all over . . . Women speak of their bodies like that all the time. I don't want to hear about it any more, at all' (p. 105)[55] In *Parleuses*, Duras is adamant: the body is *not* the orgasm, and the female orgasm experienced in lesbian desire can *never* rise to the 'dizzying' heights of passion produced 'hygienically' with a man.[56] As she puts it elsewhere, a touch self-mockingly: 'I hate myself, what I love is my desire.'[57] In *Camion*, where, as we have seen, Duras privileges not so much the integrity of the female body as its capacity for change through violent, sexual contact with a male other, she is effectively recording her refusal to play the role of grand-mother for a newly founded, avant-garde tradition of feminist writing. Indeed, despite attempts by some critics to identify her as 'la dame', even *la mer*,[58] and notwithstanding the fact that the auditorium in which *Camion* was premièred is called 'La Croisette', the name of her mother's farm, Duras is purposely employing a negative projection of the maternal figure in order to preempt precisely that kind of transferential identification. The self-deconstructing chiasmus initiated in the valley (the paternal association of which we noted in Chapter 1) enables her to come to the fore very differently as a proponent of sadomasochistic, heterosexual desire, riding over the homosexual 'turns' of both writing and cinema, including her own (what she means in the film, perhaps, by the strange phrase, 'aberrations of youth' [p. 32]). It is certainly no coincidence that Duras's blanket dismissal in 1980 of militant feminists and gay men due to their equally 'depressing' need for separatism and martyrdom is accompanied by a still from her earlier *Détruire* of the sick Elisabeth driven 'mad' by the female desire of Alissa (see 'Femmes et homosexu-alité' in *Yeux*, pp. 182–83).

One thing is sure: while Duras's promotion of *Camion* as 'une forme aiguë du désespoir politique, aiguë et gaie' ('an acute form of political despair, acute and gay')[59] may allude in part to the oral form and structure of Nietzsche's *La gaya scienza* (1887),[60] and perhaps even to Godard's radical 1968 experiment in sound/image praxis, *Le gai savoir (repartir à zéro)*, which also takes place in a *camera obscura* (a deserted television studio), it certainly cannot be used to recuperate the film as a positive gay statement, as one critic has recently suggested.[61] For while it may appear to destroy the grammar of phallic mastery, Duras's dazzlingly resourceful, cinematic strategy in *Camion*, let us call it: '*le système D.*', always insists that she is the Master, even if only a 'Master non-thinker' ('La dame des Yvelines'). Indeed, despite the homonymic links in French between the words '*gai*' and 'gay', the particular use of syntax in Duras's phrase already points to *Camion*'s chiastic, *heterosexual* workings ('acute . . . / despair . . . / acute . . . / . . . gay'). The question arises of what form desire in Duras's cinema will take once all figuration of the human body, including her own, has disappeared. This we shall attempt to answer in Chapter 3 where we examine Duras's major films after *Camion*, up to, and including, her most minimalist film, *Atlantique* (1981).

CHAPTER 3

Every Which Way but Loose: Duras and the Erotic Crimes of Montage

Le rapport du texte à l'image, tout est là.
(M. Duras)

After *Camion* the Duras image continues to approach the farthest limits of the visible. In *Night* (1978), for example, where three actors are filmed in silence as Duras and Benoît Jacquot recite a story of blind telephone passion on the sound-track, abstract shots of engulfing mirrors, under-exposed wooden interiors and overgrown woods are juxtaposed with dawn views of Paris filmed in extreme long-shot as if it were an ocean. Deleuze, who talks of the Duras image in terms of the visible covering itself over or burying itself, has proposed that such natural leanings to abstraction place Duras firmly in the French school of seascape painting.[1] Yet while the image in Duras's films gradually loses its accustomed iconic status and power, the sound-track is refined to the point where it becomes a single voice, that of Duras. This is a deep and sometimes gravelly voice but which possesses an extraordinary hypnotic force, as Duras herself acknowledges. She may try to maintain as flat and neutral a vocal tone as possible, and, by means of 'undisciplined punctuation', attain that democratic 'neutral territory where words arrive on an equal basis' (*Yeux*, p. 175), yet a 'lure' operates just in the way her voice 'resounds', clearly and intimately, over the images (*Yeux*, p. 187). Can, then, a combination of Duras's unhindered voice and assorted, self-abstracting images remain fluid enough to produce, as some critics of her cinema claim, a dramatic, if not liberating, creation of spectatorial lack?[2] And what is the role and effect of montage, especially in a film like the forty-eight minute *Vancouver*, where, over an apparently random series of stark, black and white images of the French coastline near Le Havre, Duras introduces explicitly the theme

47

of the Holocaust? Do the grave images and themes of *Vancouver* counteract the seduction of Duras's voice and bar the possibility of filmic pleasure? Let us explore these different questions by analysing in close detail the interstitial relations between sound and image in Duras's most important films after *Camion*. We begin with *Vancouver*.

AURELIA STEINER (VANCOUVER)

In the first of many differences between the soundtrack and the published text, and only after we have been confronted for several long moments by the close-up of a stone unequally rent in two (a shot which is itself divided by the two-part title, *Aurélia Steiner*), Duras's voice-over begins: 'It's the middle of the day'. This anti-climactic punctuation of the silent, still-framed image defies us to read anything more into it than its most literal meaning: a split in time, space and nomination. 'Aurélia', with its Nervalian echoes of *rêve*, melancholia, mediation, and syncretism, is pitted against the hard, Germanic stone of Steiner. It is with such an uncompromising introduction to opposites that we receive Duras's first words and the opening shots of the Normandy coast near Harfleur, a sequence which Leslie Hill has described as producing a progressive loss of contact between sound and image, and a blurring of the processes of identification initiated by an unusually close matching of image and text. Hill explains:

> the shot and the spoken text . . . trace the line of the horizon (and describe it as unbridgeable), then efface it by tilting up to the clouds (and comparing the horizon to an erasure). The horizon traces a limit at the edge of both image and text. Instead of positioning a story at the fantasmatic junction of image and sound, the film disturbs and denies that junction.[3]

Such a reading, however, misses the point, and quite literally, for it ignores the presence of an edit just after the adjective 'géante' in the sentence: 'il [un large trait noir] est de la régularité d'une rature géante et sûre, de l'importance d'une différence infranchissable' (*Night*, p. 139) ('it [a large black mark] is as regular as a giant and definite erasure, and the size of an unbridgeable difference'). This edit actually reverses the direction in the image from a gentle, upwards-tilting pan across a dark-clouded sky above the horizon into a diagonally descending low-angle shot of a clearer sky broken up by small, wispy clouds. At the very moment, then, that the sound-track crystallises

into signification, the certainty of its definite and unassailable difference is dissolved by the image's own formalisation of difference. This
averts a 'double erasure' which would be caused by, on the one hand,
a perpetual blurring within the frame, and on the other, a total fusion
of text and image. The image's close mimicking of the text's
development showcases precisely their fantasmatic conjunction. A
little later, the phrase: 'at sea, but smaller, you see, a sea in the entirety
of the sea', is answered by a cut immediately after 'smaller' into a
detail shot of the same image of black rocks, thus providing the viewer
with a sensation of movement but actively depriving him/her of the
chance to experience the natural progression of the sea's colour and
shadow.

What Duras is really doing here is offering us aesthetic pleasure
where we would least expect it. For the viewer, *vous*—interpellated
variously as father, mother, sailor—is seduced into a game of
ambiguity and suspense based around the idées fixes of an abject
image, whether that be the boulders of black rock, an abandoned
blockhaus, large, uterine pipes, or sawn and numbered logs piled up
at Le Poudreux like solidified lumps of excreta. The knowing
construction of tantalisingly close, parallel flows of sound and image
is often unbearably frustrating but, through repetition, can be
anticipated like the pain of the edit and even welcomed as desirable.
The skilfully programmed touching of sound and image even provokes their magical, almost Surrealist, coincidence in sudden, exceptional circumstances. The words, 'the slow dislocation . . . between
the green and black waters of the sea', for instance, are crowned by
the advent of a new colour: 'the huge pool has become blue with the
sudden gust of wind' (*Night*, p. 147). Indeed, throughout *Vancouver*
the cut of montage falls on key words of rupture and transition:
's'entretuer', 'dislocation', 'passage', 'reconnaître', 'suivie', 'inverse'.
Editing thus becomes a self-reflexive agent of mastered irony which
provokes action, the eternal present of montage providing an immediate and more intimate replay of the textual event now made closer in
time. It marks, and re-marks, the difference between, for example 'I
closed my eyes', and: 'I have just done it' (*Night*, p. 160). It can also
simulate the 'passage' from life ('*passer*') to death (*trépasser*, to pass
away), as when it dissects the following phrase: 'It [the sea] has passed
in the space of a few seconds from life / cut / to death' (*Night*, p. 151).
The image which accompanies this statement provides no more than a
different angle of the same shaded window-pane. We are compelled to

look again, but still we see nothing, the cut bringing us closer to the
text but only, it seems, to rebuff us. Even within the frame there is
frequently an element of gentle mockery. For example, a measured,
lateral tracking-shot past the rows of numbered logs and the deserted
trains at Harfleur—images clearly evoking the Holocaust—calmly
deflates the tales of sexual vagabondage recounted by the narrator
(*Night*, p. 143).

At this point we should turn directly to the text itself, for we can
see that the film's formal erotics ironically duplicates Aurélia Steiner's
repeated fantasy of self-naming enacted with anonymous sailors who,
while assuming a paternal role, are instructed to abuse her with the
Nazi insult of '*Juden*'. In this scenario of self-inflicted pain (a twist on
the standard father-daughter plot of French cinema[4]) the forever
eighteen-year-old Aurélia acts out in reverse, and with consenting
men, what might perhaps have been her (grand-)mother's fate of
enforced prostitution at Auschwitz. In so doing—and this is a typical
Duras counterpointing of extremes—Aurélia is able to survive the
memory of a double catastrophe: her traumatic beginnings at the end
of all ends (the Holocaust). The diaspora of Aurélia's loss and exile in
Vancouver is played off cinematically at nodal points of excitation
and discharge and then remoulded into the syncopated rhythms of
filmic desire. This we can fully comprehend if we juxtapose two
parallel movements, one textual, the other filmic. In the first, during
the act of sexual penetration, Aurélia writes over the blank pages of
her solitude and pain figured in her memory by the white rectangle of
the concentration-camp compound, thus achieving symbolically what
her family could not: a crossing of the snow-white borders of
Switzerland into safety (*Yeux*, p. 178). In the second, during the slow,
three-part fade-in and fade-out of Aurélia's changing hand-written
signature—first 'Aurélia', then 'Aurélia Steiner', finally a number,
200095—the film's white screen is recuperated as something which
Aurélia's narrative will never be: a page of erotic montage and
difference. This writing in and over the frame, as calmly erotic as the
shot of the erect stems of four roses appearing and disappearing over a
description of the sea's assault of the town (p. 150), is reprised later in
the film but this time minus the number. The signature simply enters
and exits the screen in a compulsive, filmic movement of sexual desire.

These carefully planned sequences of montage result in controlled
variations of an otherwise impossible representation of *jouissance*.
Aurélia's violent sexual rituals, during which the sailor's penetration

tropes vertically on her fantasy of a nourishing, maternalised father stealing soup for his newly-born daughter in Auschwitz (a scene rightly heralded by Marini as an instance of 'paternal metonymy'[5]), are offset and decanted in the filmic present because they are mimed metaphorically in the contraction produced by the intercut. This is because, as in *Camion*, the edit here is always concretely and self-consciously pre-staged. One example occurs immediately after the phrase, 'I tell him the name', when morsels of cut paper are suddenly thrown into the frame, their moving reflection in the water a reanimating of all the white specks that had lain dormant throughout the film on the black rocks. Because of the absence of a visible agency here, this 'unnatural' violation within the so far pristine shots of nature draws our attention to the cutting of the image by the authorial hand of montage. Another example is during the period of sexual climax. The text makes ready the sailor's measured, 'inverted' entry into Aurélia's body: 'In a very slow movement, the reverse of his being transported [*inverse de celui de son emportement*], he enters the body of Aurélia Steiner' (*Night*, p. 164). Rather perversely the sky becomes at that exact moment more grey and neutral than at any time so far in the film. With 'inverse' hardly uttered, we are suddenly cut into the sky's opposite, the sea, with waves rolling gently left to right across the frame like a processed page of *écriture courante*. This formal inversion by the text performed in tandem with the image plays off in advance the sexual climax of the narrative which is thus maintained as pure seduction. Sound and image are engaged in a process of inversion as replacement and sublimation, recalling the ever-virtual deferment of Lol V. Stein's imaginary cinema of repeated rapture in *Ravissement* where, 'but for a cat's whisker', she would have been replaced by Tatiana in the eyes of Jacques in 'a rigorously parallel and reverse progression' (pp. 49–50). The deliberately prosaic end to *Vancouver* —a continuous pan across the coast-line summarising beach, port and sky in one slow sweep—is the film's final moment of self-release by means of detached understatement.

What *Vancouver* clearly illustrates is that if Duras divests the image of its unconscious, dream-like fascination, she does so for specifically erotic ends. This is how she herself describes the gap created in the film between sound and image:

> When the sound withdraws and there is talk of the sombre light of her [Aurélia's] eyes, hair, and body in the mirror, when there is talk of a veiled image and the beauty it reveals, this over the black of the great blocks of

granite against which her image can harm itself and tear itself apart, then I am no longer only at the cinema but suddenly elsewhere, further elsewhere, in the *undifferentiated zone* of myself where I recognise without comprehending. Here, everything connects and merges into one, the wound, the frozen cutting edge of the black stone and the warm softness of the threatened image. *The happy coincidence between word and image fills me here with evidence, with bliss.* (*Yeux*, pp. 114–15, emphasis added)[6]

This description of a withdrawal of sound leading to the *jouissance* of synthesis might at first appear to exemplify the story of Echo and Narcissus, which one critic has used to claim for Duras's film-work a love affair between text and image.[7] Such an account of the sound-image relation would leave business unfinished, however, as would Noguez's blithe proposal that the film be understood as a new poetic genre of '*correspondances*', the 'game of one in the other'.[8] For Duras's cinema of restless, just-out-of-sync (non)correspondences between sound and image produces, paradoxically, their magical equivalence, one which immediately inverts their roles. It is the sound-track, after all, which now provides the image ('image voilée') and the image-track onomatopoeia ('le tranchant glacé').

Perhaps the best way of grasping the full power of the Duras edit is to compare it with Roland Barthes's contemporaneous experience of the photographic *punctum*. In *La chambre claire: note sur la photographie* (1980), Barthes describes the *punctum*'s effect as 'certain but unlocatable': 'it does not find its sign, its name; it is sharp and yet lands in a vague zone of myself; it is acute yet muffled, it cries out in silence. Odd contradiction; a floating flash.'[9] The detail or 'partial object' which breaks out of the 'sufficiently large image' is already in metonymical expansion in the form of 'passage', and it offers the thrill of a mysterious, unpredictable 'tilt', 'a tiny shock, a *satori*, the passage of a void'.[10] At other moments, an 'hallucinatory fusion of body and soul' leads the spectactor via the agency of Time to the disturbing, inverted limits of photographic madness. On the other hand, in the 'undifferentiated zone' of Durasian cinema as presented by Duras in *Yeux* (and *Yeux* seems at times to be directly rewriting Barthes's study), the 'ideal image' is always 'sufficiently neutral to avoid the trouble of making a new one' (*Yeux*, p. 93). While Duras may claim that the flow of the images and the flow of the words are 'unpredictable and constantly accidental' (*Yeux*, p. 188), *Vancouver* proves the opposite: that the pleasure of Durasian cinema lies precisely in the way montage can lock word and image together into a reliable rhythm of ritualised shocks and encounters. Far from being a passage into madness caused by the viewer's incapacity to collapse two movements into a stable meaning, this process offers, in addition, the added, intellectual satisfaction of re-cognition, equivalent to Aristotle's mythical, displaceable event of *anagnorisis*, or the three-stage passage from knowledge, its absence, to final recovery.[11]

It is precisely the cyclical aspect of Durasian 'passage' which denies what Isi Beller has described, with Duras's approval, as an 'orgasmic' dark zone formed for the spectator by the unbridgeable gap separating sound and image:

> He [Beller] sees this darkness as *a passage through non-thinking*, a stage in which thought may tumble over and be obliterated. He sees this obliteration as joining *the dark of orgasm* . . . Here, in my films, he [the viewer] does not decipher; he lets himself be acted upon, and this opening inside him gives way to something new in the link which ties him to the film, something which would be of the order of desire. (*Yeux*, p. 114, emphasis added)[12]

On the contrary, in its spontaneously deliberate self-administering of a wound, Durasian montage exposes and replays with a heightened self-awareness the traumatic gap between sound and image, creating in the process a delicious, inverted mixture of pain and pleasure. We cannot anthropomorphise this gap by saying, as Pierre Fedida has done with regard to *India Song*, that the split is somehow figurable allegorically by the female sex,[13] for Duras seals the disarticulated time of unbound sound and image into the metaphorical parameters of erotic fantasy. Nor can the non-coincidence between sound and image be simply passed off as 'an impossible image of the unrepresentable, a failed representation of a catastrophe which cannot be made present' (Hill).[14] Rather, the *écart* formed at the point of the cut is the *only* possible representation of catastrophe, a *coincidentia oppositorum* which, in its very deadlock of form, locates and effectively formalises the impossible inscription of *jouissance*.[15] Duras is thus telling only half of the story when she states in *Duras Filme*, a documentary by Jean Mascolo and Jérôme Beaujour on the shooting of *Agatha*, that she shows what cannot be shown or said by deliberately cultivating lack (in this case, filming a summer tale of incest in the Loire valley during a Normandy winter).[16] For if, to take another example, the impossibility of understanding the relationship between the two lovers conversing on the sound-track of the film *Dialogo di Roma* is already metaphorised by that film's 'impossibility' of filming Rome (it shows instead, for example, mutilated statues lacking genitalia), Duras's desired intention of a 'passage through non–thinking' is always erotically reconfigured in the structures of montage.

We see now how far we have come since *Camion*. *Vancouver* replays the earlier film's one spectacular, chiastic event of shot/reverse shot at almost every junction of the cut, and as a defusing mode of controlled, sadomasochistic desire. Maurice Lemaître may attack Duras for remaining within the established boundaries of 'amorous passion' and for failing to attain his own 'Lettrist Super-love', but it is because she stages at every edit what Lemaître would like to claim as his own, namely a 'discrepant and never synchronised montage',[17] that her cinema actually avoids the dangers of emotion and affect.[18] The success of this strategy depends entirely on how much rhetorical irony can be generated through multiple processes of domination, submission, and inversion which simulate and sublimate desire. Montage performs, in fact, the same function as the transcendental image for Dreyer, a film-maker who, according to Duras, produces 'a completely anarchic kind of love, but completely controlled in its form . . . all is smooth'.[19] Indeed, the edit is the true 'ideal image' which haunts Duras's thinking on her cinema, not because it is a Deleuzian *'image-temps'* of sound and image linked together in a *'rapport indirect libre'* ('free indirect relationship'),[20] nor even because it proposes a new chiasmus of reciprocal dominance between visual language and a linguistic image,[21] but rather because it actually fashions and delimits that illusion of unbound freedom between sound and image—the nebulous *noir*—at the chiastic point of reversal. Put a little differently, the artfully 'accidental' cut acts as an ironic agent of *érotisme noir* which preempts the otherwise hallucinatory effect of a formless, aimless, and feminine *materia prima* without closure.[22] Moreover, as we have just seen in *Vancouver*, it is strangely what happens within the shot itself, representation is at its most self-evident and banal (a forward tracking shot, the pan of an incoming tide, etc.), that seals the Duras film's necessary self-release.

Madeleine Cottenet-Hage and Robert Kolker have commented on the 'quasi universality' of Duras's images and on her search for yet more abstract visual equivalents of the verbal text, a process perceivable in the way that the tracking shots of *Son nom de Venise* abstract those of *India Song* and thus pose the possibility of a hidden Platonic form.[23] Duras, they claim, 'could be seen as standing in a middle ground between a modernist rejection of transcendent meaning and a neo-platonic nostalgia for absolutes, for a perfect pre-existence to which the text points'.[24] But even Cottenet-Hage and Kolker's sexualised notion of the Duras image as a 'virgin' prostitute lying with different texts though unable to assume even a temporary meaning fails to account fully for the programming of erotic violence in Durasian montage, the third term of the *Sound/iMage* relation. For the more neutral, static and abject Duras's images become, the more ripe they are not so much for neo-Platonic inscription as for formal conversion into a site of passage, or structured fantasy. Let us call it: 'An image is being cut', for Duras never lets go of the wound of montage. Compare this with Godard's approach to montage, especially in his later video work such as the *Histoire(s) du Cinéma* project (1989–), which also relies heavily on chiastic structures at all levels. There, the positing of a 'third point'—'the invisible between the two pieces of film'—represents instead a kind of 'common ground', relief at last from the fierce struggle for 'territory' during the editing process.[25]

As for the Duras viewer, although clearly not involved in the 'totalising effort' demanded by commercial cinema, s/he is nonetheless 'had'. This is because in a film like *Vancouver* there is no possibility of creating unconsciously the space of its reception, the aim, according to Stephen Heath, of a truly avant-garde cinema where 'passage is the performance of the film [and] the movement of the spectator making the film, taken up as subject in its process'.[26] Duras admits as much when she adds the following to Beller's account of *Vancouver*'s 'dark orgasm': 'this dark would perhaps, in fact, be a space for decipherment which would entail letting oneself be taken over by this film more than by other films' (*Yeux*, p. 114). Indeed, in its sublimely self-reflexive mode, Durasian montage obliges the viewer to 'find' him/herself by exploiting his/her latent capacity to enjoy sadomasochistic desire. We can go further. Eroticism in Duras is an aesthetic expression of sexual violence designed to counter the institutionalised violence of commercial cinema, in particular that of the pornographic genre. In Duras's world of sublimation, films such as Liliana Cavani's *The Night Porter* (1973), the graphic tale of a woman resuming a sadomasochistic love affair with a man she recognises as the SS commandant of the concentration camp in which she spent the war years, are gross literalisations of sadomasochistic fantasy (what Bersani might call the 'melodramatic narrativisation' of masochism[27]) and ought only to be conducted in the controlled rapture of violent, heterosexual intercourse, better still, within the interstices of sound and image.[28] It is precisely due to the super-imposed pleasures of montage, rather than to any 'neoromanticism' inherent to the medium itself, as suggested by Kristeva,[29] that Duras's cinema transcends the otherwise unresolved stories of masochism related on the sound-track. As long as an image can be framed, there is, for Duras, always the possibility for an erotics of form.

The curative potential of erotically reinvested cinematic form is so great, in fact, in Duras's work, that it can even operate through other media. Such is the case with the controversial torture scene in *Douleur*. At one point during the prolonged torture session of 'Albert des Capitales', the narrator, Thérèse, imagines this cinematic inter-lude: 'I'm at the cinema. There she is. Once she was on the embankment of the Seine. It was two o'clock in the afternoon on a summer's day and someone kissed her and said he loved her' (*Douleur*, pp. 144–45).[30] Hill has claimed that the impossible image of torture is absorbed here into an amorous encounter, and that cinema, the cavern of images, thereby becomes the site of an impossibility of representation.[31] Yet as *je* is split into *elle*, so the impossible image of torture is transformed first into an image of seduction ('someone [*on*] kissed her'), then into amatory discourse ('and said he loved her'). In other words, the 'bad' cinema of torture has been reversed by the sudden violence of a cut from first to third person in a parade of sweet seduction. The value of the Duras edit lies precisely in this kind of formal inversion, where passivity is actively redetermined and made heterosexually gratifying. The narrator con-cludes the scene thus: 'there she was, she knows it still. There is a name for everything. That was the day she decided to live with a man' (p. 145).[32]

But let us return again to *Vancouver*, for Aurélia's inversion and transformation of her (grand-)mother's last look at her dying (grand-)father represents more than just a scene of erotic seduction. Aurélia's stunning imaginary fantasy aims to overcome not only, as in Duras's screen-play for *Hiroshima*, the 'generalisation of death' via the 'accident' of one survival (see *Yeux*, pp. 159–60), but also the very 'banality' of the Holocaust. In February 1979, the year Duras made *Vancouver*, Marvin Chomsky's nine-and-a-half-hour long colour extravaganza *Holocaust* (1978) was broadcast on French television. At totally opposite poles from the visual austerity of *Vancouver*, especially in its pandering use of spectacle, *Holocaust* was immedi-ately vilified by (among others) Elie Wiesel as Hollywood's offensive trivialisation of an indescribable, metaphysical event, one that should be described only by its survivors.[33] We can presume that, by contrast, Wiesel would find Duras's film an exemplary case of not attempting to represent the Holocaust visually and thus not interfering with oral testimony. Yet it is an inescapable fact that *Vancouver* also represents, in Duras's words, her own 'personal translation' (*Yeux*, p. 178) of Wiesel's account of the concentration camps in *Night* (1958), two scenes of which—the protracted hanging of a thirteen year old *pipel* and the brutal shooting of the narrator's father—it condenses into the impossible hanging of Aurélia's young (grand-)father.[34] This is not the place to debate whether Duras, being non-Jewish, has the legitimate right to use, and even reinvent, work on the Holocaust for artistic ends. However, it could well be argued that the overall effect of *Vancouver* is ultimately not too far removed from that of *Holocaust*, since both films perform exactly what Wiesel warns against, i.e. a romanticisation of the Holocaust. In the case of *Vancouver*, this is achieved through the use of Jewish archetypes (blue eyes, black hair) and by the staging of scenes of enforced 'passivity' (anonymous male flesh made to perform to the tune of '*Juden*'). Indeed, it would not be impossible to link Duras's film with one critic's definition of contemporary racist cinema as that where the Other is maintained as 'pure difference', an 'unnamable inhumanity'.[35]

It is not, of course, that Duras repeats what Sylvia Plath has been accused of doing in her famous poem, 'Daddy', i.e. appropriating an enormity of ready-made emotion for her own private ends (Plath portrays her father as a Nazi and herself as a Jewish victim).[36] Rather, by insisting emphatically with each new cut that art, specifically an erotics of art, is always possible after Auschwitz, her film actively refuses the possibility of a political orality which an ironic formalism can sometimes provide, as, for example, in Resnais's documentary short on the same subject, *Nuit et Brouillard* (1955). There, too, the viewer's sensory collaboration is fully required but this time in an actual repetition of the Nazi past figured by its imagery (black and white archive material of Auschwitz intercut with contemporary images in colour of the same area). As Bersani and Dutoit have convincingly argued in their analysis of the film's differential repetitions and inaccurate replications of *raccords*, by making the viewer ironically alert to the horrific reappearance of images and sounds 'that we have no reason to resist', *Nuit et Brouillard* may actually initiate 'forms of resistance no longer based on the comforting and politically defeating denial of our complicity in that which we must resist'.[37] While equally ironic, the erotic cuts and elegant abstractions of *Vancouver* offer no such political reevaluation of the Holocaust, nor even, as one critic has recently suggested, a materialist reappraisal of objects such as the blockhaus unjustly condemned by history to an abject silence.[38] Instead, Duras asks only that we acknowledge sexual and textual fantasy, however clean, as ultimately a violent, cruel and narcissistic affair of collusion and cheap thrills, as banal as that one gag holding together Duras's last film, *Enfants*, where a forty-year-old actor (Axel Bougousslavski) plays the adolescent prodigy, Ernesto.[39] She offers us no escape except to look and hear, and hear and look, through her cinematic cut.

CESAREE/MAINS/MELBOURNE/VANCOUVER

Vancouver was accompanied on its release in Paris in 1979 by three other Duras shorts commissioned by Henry Chapier on behalf of the City of Paris: *Melbourne* (35 min.), *Césarée* (11 min.) and *Mains* (18 min.). Do these three films operate along the same erotic lines as *Vancouver*? In addition, if taken together as a whole, does this four-part series perhaps constitute in itself a movement of 'inter-filmic' desire? To answer these questions, let us look briefly at each film in turn.

Melbourne is a painfully slow journey by boat along the Seine into the dark underbelly of the City of Lights, from Bercy in the west to Passy in the east. As the female narrator, another Aurélia Steiner, proceeds to mourn a lost love object (*vous*), the moving camera tries in vain to circle the Ile de la Cité, capturing the cathedral of Notre-Dame only in silhouette. The reflections of the bridge's lights in the water recall Whistler's *London Nocturnes* series of 1870, thus sealing the film in a plaque of blinding Impressionist mist already evident in the opening shot of the hinterland at Bercy. It is as if *Melbourne* were bowing to the solemn influence of cinema's anterior other, painting. Even the irony created by the uttering of the phrase, 'And then you saw me', just as a coal-barge enters the frame from left to right, is not sustained.[40] The camera is as though afraid to cross under and through the skeletal rib-cages of the bridges lined up in the distance, always turning backwards or sideways to delay the horror of entry. Only a quick cut forwards to the other side, or a repetition of the approach shot from a different angle, saves it from dissolution in the dark tunnels reverberating with the deafening noise of the boat's engine. In fact, montage soon becomes a literal reflection of the text rather than a metaphorical instance of perversion. The film's axis never rises above that of the water which ranges in colour from putrid green ('that London plague') to a bloody-red (*'saigner'*). As opposed to Jean Vigo's 1934 film, *L'Atalante*, where a barge also became the setting for a story of romantic love, the camera here is unable to follow the Seine out of Paris to the estuary at Le Havre. Instead, by passively recording all that strays into its frame ('what happened passed, what appeared returned' [*Yeux*, p. 158]), it appears to re-enact the fatal journey of French Jews deported to the camps. At the end of the film, the camera rises briefly into the sky before descending once and for all into the water ('this drowned-out town, this obscure land').

When placed alongside the formally perfect *Vancouver*, *Melbourne* appears at once blocked and hollow, like a bare and infernal doublet. This structure is repeated by the smaller pair of films, *Césarée* and *Mains*, both composed of footage of Paris originally shot for *Night*. It is tempting to link *Césarée* with Stuart Pound's short film, *Codex* (1979), a parody of tourist London which Duras discusses in *Yeux* and where she juxtaposes it with a still from *Césarée* (see 'Le cinéma différent' [pp. 107–08]). Like *Codex*, a study in manic cutting which also mixes static and tracking shots, *Césarée* inscribes itself as a tight, self-ironic construct of blue, black and white images, of front and behind, beauty and horror, pleasure and pain. Ravishing horizontal tracking-shots past statues by Aristide Maillol in the Tuileries gardens (notably La Méditerranée and the sprawled-out figure of La Rivière) are cruelly interrupted by static shots of the Obélisque and an encaged, scaffolded statue at the Place de la Concorde, as well as by odd punctuations of black spacing. However, if *Césarée* constructs in the style of *Codex* an 'axis of immobility' where any 'irregular', 'interior' movement can be clearly registered (*Yeux*, p. 108), it also denies its viewer the same intoxification of speed precisely because it precludes any 'rhythmic coincidence' between sound and image.

Paradoxically, montage in *Césarée* is most in evidence when the image best supports the possibilities of figuration, such as the tracking-shot along the Seine evoking Bérénice's last sea voyage and a still-frame of the scaffolded statue recalling her imprisonment on the Roman vessel. It is as though the concordance of image and textual motif had to be simultaneously sought and ruptured but all the time deciphered, like the hieroglyphs carved on to the Obélisque and themselves written over by the constant movement of shadow. As might be expected of a film which takes place at a former site of revolutionary decapitation, *Césarée* also undergoes its own 'caesarean section'. During a repeat tracking shot right to left past a Maillol statue (this time in long shot), we are suddenly cut off in mid-flight, rejoining the statue almost head-on many frames later. The result is a split-shot sequence which generates internal difference and which reverses in one fell swoop the film's opening, double tracking shot sequence from left to right. The apparent arbitrariness of this clearly deliberate self-incision extends the text's first and only proper rhyme recorded seconds before, 'blanche comme la craie, apparaît' ('white, like chalk, appears'), and this is developed immediately afterwards in the final shot of the film, where the camera scales the walls of the Louvre before alighting on a new female statue, yet another 'possible' metaphor for Bérénice.

Césarée dramatises the crisis of the cut as early as the credits with its repeated slippages between printed and unprinted image and between the French passive (*César-ée*) and the Latin active (*Caesare-a*).[41] By contrast, the dawn journey by car from the Bastille to the Champs-Elysées in *Mains* never provokes an ironic recognition of the places it either omits (parts of the rue de Rivoli) or obsessively repeats (e.g. the three tracking shots past the Porte Saint Denis). Its indented surface is passed off as essentially natural, the edits becoming simply a means of illustrating activity within the text. A typical case occurs after the phrase, 'slowed down by its [i.e. the sea's] force', where the violence of the cut to another part of the rue de Rivoli enacts, rather than undercuts, the force of the elements being related. Similarly, the appearance of a large statue shrouded in white scaffolding at the bottom of the Champs-Elysées is greeted by the words, 'the white spectre'. As in *Melbourne*, there is no internal, self-reflexive interplay between sound and image to create a distinctly cinematic fantasy and thus overcome the spoken theme of the grotto. The viewer simply rolls from side to side through a darkened, sinister world of tarmac and under-exposed stone, a group of black refuse-collectors coming into frame at one point like worker-ants rising out of a subterranean hole (an episode we shall come back to in Chapter 6 in the context of racial difference). Again, unlike *Césarée*, no concerted, secondary fault of montage tropes over the 'first time' of urban passage which, for all its odd elisions, *Mains* faithfully relays. A more perfect 'negative' of *Césarée* could not be found.

Césarée, *Mains*, *Vancouver* and *Melbourne* are all defined, then, by whether or not they render passage literally or metaphorically. As such, if they are returned to the order in which they were originally shown, they sketch the sublimating figure of a chiasmus: *Césarée* (sublime) / *Mains* (abject) / *Melbourne* (abject) / *Vancouver* (sublime). One way to measure Duras's achievement here is to contrast the films' key elements, notably the images of Paris and the Racinian figure of Bérénice, with similar motifs used by Louis Aragon in *Aurélien* (1944), the last in his four-part series of socialist-realist novels entitled *Le monde réel*.[42] The link is valid because Aragon is the only writer other than Duras herself to receive any substantial attention in *Yeux*. In a chapter there entitled 'Il n'y a pas d'écrivains communistes' (pp. 168–69), Duras delivered a stunning diatribe against Aragon, an inveterate 'liar' (p. 169) whose originality as a writer was ruined, she claims, due to his militant support for communism. In *Aurélien* (which Duras admits in her 'Duras est SEXY!' interview with Bergé to having read when it first appeared) the hero, Aurélien Leurtillois, finds himself doomed to an impossible love-affair with Bérénice whose desire for the absolute he can no more answer than he can his own wish for a 'true' socialism. Haunted by the images of those lying drowned or floating in the Seine, he cites and recites Antiochus's line from *Bérénice*: 'I remained a long time wandering [*errant*] in Caesarea'.[43] Duras, whose *Césarée* returns to Racine's play precisely to remythify it, effectively lifts the dead figure of Bérénice out of the Caesarean fantasy in which Aragon's Aurélien had fatally encased her. In addition, the fully active Aurélia of *Vancouver* invokes her own 'Unknown of the Seine' in order to stage efficient scenes of non-committal, sexual desire. As a figurehead of Duras's pure, erotic aesthetics, she thus offers herself as a solution to Aragon's by now archaic literary and political influence.

L'HOMME ATLANTIQUE

Yet what happens when the printed image disappears altogether? This is the question posed in 1981 by *Atlantique*, an ostensibly loose collection of shots recording Yann Andréa's movements on and around the beach at Trouville. With the need to convert the bad spectator to a rhetorical appreciation of montage now over (we are, after all, perfectly schooled by this stage in the Durasian way of seeing), the narrator delivers a brutal lesson in seeing and difference to her lover, *vous*, who has now abandoned her 'definitively'. Yet at the very moment that *vous* is summoned (in fantasy) to return and admire his 'inalienable royalty', the image of Andréa is rudely cut and black spacing takes over. A little later, just twenty minutes into the film, the black which had always encroached on the images takes over completely and continues uninterrupted until the end. Although at the beginning of *Atlantique* Duras's voice had dictated fairly efficiently the fate of the image (the mention of the sea, for example, had obediently brought forth an image of water just as 'disparition' had blocked it out), the lack now of a visible edit means that an ironic or productive play-off between sound and image is no longer possible. The narrator states: '[a]bout the film I know only, I know that not one image, not a single one more, could prolong it' (*Atlantique*, p. 28).[44]

All the previous, 'neutral', *'passe-partout'* images in Duras's films were but metaphorical approximations of this cinematic dead-end, which she presents in *Yeux* as 'the avowed murder of cinema' (p. 93). Indeed, as the film critic Alain Philippon has commented, *Atlantique* is a 'black Mass' celebrating the death of the image which has become superfluous.[45] This means that Duras's voice is now free to perform in the blackened auditorium its own private, sadistic fantasy of 'passage' with, and against, an anonymous, abandoning *vous*: '[n]o-one, no-one else in the world but you will be able to do what you are going to do now: pass here today for the second time, at my command alone, in front of God' (*Atlantique*, p. 24).[46] The traditional cinematographic poles of sexual difference have been stripped down to their basics and reversed: a female voice opposes the image of an absent man, and, paradox of paradoxes, no possibility of traditional representation can save the viewer from the awesome force of Duras's delivery. Indeed, cinema's standard visual mode of aggression has simply been replaced in *Atlantique* by that of the invocatory drive. Impelled in part to assume the occluded position of *vous* against whom Duras intones an unerotic fantasy of revenge, the viewer shares Andréa's own experience during the shooting of the film: 'She [Duras] is there at the end of the screen. She rules . . . here is the woman who writes on the black screen.'[47] What might perhaps have been justified as a gesture of love *contra* the evils of representation, i.e. the 'worshipper' of *Atlantique* being allowed to re-engage with his/her 'historical shadow' or '*magma*',[48] becomes instead something of interest only to Duras.

It is as if Duras were destroying cinema at one of its few points of resistance, the grain of a female-authored voice, an idea which has also been explored to positive effect by (among others) Chantal Ackerman, Yvonne Rainer and Sally Potter.[49] Only a critic like René Payant, who discovers in the 'pre-subjective' rhythms of Duras's 'maternal' voice a 'regressive, narcissistic satisfaction which cuts off all communication, *which cuts all communication*' (emphasis added),[50] could take real pleasure in *Atlantique*. For if the film exceeds the mirror of the cinematic screen and realises Nicole-Lise Bernheim's 'sorceress' fantasy of revenge against commercial, 'phallic' cinema (a fantasy implicitly shared by Duras during the period of *India Song*[51]), it nevertheless thrusts us right back into the relationship of need cultivated by the Hollywood system, where the viewer 'swallows up' the fare he/she is offered with child-like glee and fascination (*Parleuses*, p. 91). The black screen represents nothing less than a total inversion of the 'dark orgasm' which has until now subtended Durasian cinema and from which, and against which, were generated the intellectual thrills, or *petites morts*, of disjunctive montage. The written version of *Atlantique*, published by Minuit a little later in 1982, reveals, in fact, that chiastic, sadomasochistic desire need no longer be strictly filmic in nature. It can now take place entirely within the parameters of the text, between the first- and second-person and between the alternate, thematic movements of film and text (film: pp. 7–16; text: pp. 17–22; film: pp. 22–27; text: pp. 27–31). If the self-reflexive ironies of cinematic desire are thematised directly as 'those valleys cemented by wars and joy' (p. 26), we can see from the following extract, which preserves the original format, that the text also performs its own self-inverting play of erratic formalism in the form of typographical self-incisions and indentations, eroticised, as we would now expect, at the point of the cut:

> Of those things I
> know only this: that I have
> nothing to do now except suffer that
> exaltation on account of someone
> who once was here, someone who did not
> know that he was alive, and whom I
> knew was alive,
>   of someone who did not know

how to live, as I was saying, and
of myself who knew it and who
did not know what to do with
that, with that knowledge
of the life that he was living, and who
didn't know either what
to do with me. (*Atlantique*, pp. 29–30)[52]

In this intricate series of inversions stretched across 'I'-'him'-'you',
'who'-'whom'-'what', 'know'-'live', and finalised by one clean, final
rhyme ('quoi'/'moi') ('what'/'me'), it is a chiastic formation constructed around the first- and third-person singular to which the
reader (*vous*) is explicitly directed: 'I knew . . . [a] / . . . [he] was alive
. . . [b] / cut / . . . someone who did not know how to live . . . [b] / . . .
myself who knew it . . . [a]'. This cut allows the text to repeat
paraphrastically the double fact of *vous*'s ignorance and *je*'s knowledge of it, thereby making the narrator's original excess of 'exaltation' merely a thing of the past ('I told you'). The concluding, quasi-
authoritative paragraphs summarise matter-of-factly the theme of the
text which was always only the narrator's self. *Vous* was merely an
impenetrable, and indifferent, other: '[t]hat's how you stand facing
me, softly, in a form of constant, innocent and impenetrable provocation. You are not aware of it' (p. 31).[53]

Atlantique (text) reveals itself, therefore, to be the true, ironic,
sadomasochistic version of *Atlantique* (film), which simply cancelled
itself out in its raw ingredients of non-derived sadism and masochism.
The extensive gaps of white spacing which dot the printed text
indicate precisely that the base matter of the black screen has been
transformed, and that, as when white marks begin to appear at the
end of the first stage of the alchemical process of purification
(*nigritudo*), the erotics of Durasian sublimation is in full progress.
Hence, Duras's presumptuous claims for the dialogue of *Camion* as a
text which, of itself, can be both desire and the consummation of
desire,[54] have at last been fully realised. On her own terms alone has
she 'won forever'—cinema has become a truly 'secondary' phenomenon.[55]

Are such fantasies of textual montage as that realised in *Atlantique* (text) also possible, however, in Duras's fiction as a whole? And if
so, how? For without the clarity of binary oppositions provided by
cinema (sound/image, text/film, etc.), can Duras's novels stage the
kind of erotic and rhetorical 'errors' of inversion which we have
witnessed during this chapter? What form of eroticism is possible,

moreover, in a style such as *écriture courante*, which is designed to be fluid, open, and indiscriminate? These are the questions we must answer as we turn now to Duras's major work for Minuit during the 1980s, beginning with *Eté*. As with Duras's films, we will enter fully into the flesh of these texts by focusing on the crucial moments of crisis around which they are arranged, when all their different elements—thematic, rhetorical, syntactical, etc.—are most visibly in play. We will also explore their intertextual dimension, one which, with Duras's 'personal translation' of Wiesel in *Vancouver*, has become an increasingly important issue based around the concept of her 'Great Men'. Finally, we shall analyse the role played by the reader. Will it be the same as that reserved for the viewer in Duras's cinema? Our ultimate aim in juggling these various questions will be to establish the precise sexual valencies of *écriture courante* and the truth of its stated commitment to the Other.

CHAPTER 4

Midnight Tales of Great Men: Error, Intertextuality, and *écriture courante*

Il a fallu couper . . . Jouer Tchékov contre Tchékov . . .
jouer contre lui, c'est pour le servir, lui.
(M. Duras)

L'ETE 80

Eté would seem to be the epitome of Duras's notion of *écriture courante*. It embraces in one continuous stream of prose all that passes through Duras's mind during the summer of 1980 which she spent at Trouville. Included are meticulous observations of the changing seascape, personal thoughts on major political events then unfolding such as the shipyard strikes in Gdansk, and the account of a relationship supposedly being played out on the beach between a holiday-camp monitor and one of her young charges, a boy with grey eyes. This free-play of matters personal, social, political and fictional expands with each new chapter and appears to be taking Duras to the very limits of authorial self-dispossession and exteriority. Suddenly, however, in chapter 7, the narrator (*je*) invokes a young man (*vous*) (p. 63) who, as we learn a little later, has just arrived to stay in her apartment (p. 86). Three parallel and interrelated movements of desire are thus created: the female narrator and her male lover in 'la chambre noire' unable to consummate their 'illusory' love (p. 87), the monitor's strange and all-consuming obsession with the boy as 'witnessed' by the first couple from their window, and finally, the fantastical tale spun by the monitor about the adventures of a little boy, David, pursued by the shark, Ratekétaboum, which has just eaten his parents after the sinking of their ship named, appropriately enough in view of Gdansk, the '*Amiral Système*'.

Eté weaves in and out of these different layers of narrative until its

67

climax in chapter 10, when, as the monitor (*elle*) refuses to turn around and face the boy (*lui*) as he requests, leading him instead towards the dangerous areas of the beach, the narrator stages for herself a series of provisional moments of symbolic equivalence. Firstly, in a move that surpasses the monitor's own naming of the boy as '*ça*' (p. 84), she transforms *vous* first into Gdansk (*elle*), then the sea (*la mère*, *elle*), then 'the boy with grey eyes' (*lui*), then *ça*. She states: 'It [Gdansk] [*elle*] is mortal, it is the child with grey eyes, it is that. Like you, that' (p. 89). Secondly, having been absorbed for most of the text in a masochistic identification with what she calls the 'infinity' of the sea and the boy (p. 72), the narrator now swallows up *vous*, *lui* and *la mer* together in one magisterial act of imaginary engulfment: 'In the dark room, I have enclosed you in turn. In the unlimited space of the sea I have enclosed you with the child. It is done. This black colour of my closed eyes, these beats to the heart, your definitive similarity' (p. 95).[1] This accelerating drive into sameness, underlined by the duosyllabic '*couleur*' (colour) which is divided and extended homonymically into '*coups*' ('beats') and '*coeur*' ('heart'), is reversed shortly afterwards. The monitor has fallen down on to the sand and has instructed the boy to leave her. All is now silent in 'la chambre noire', until, '[s]uddenly, this caving in of duration, these corridors of air, this strangeness which filters impalpably across the sands, the surface of the sea, the flow of the mounting tide' (p. 102).[2] If the beginning of this sentence appears to repeat elements from the one just cited (the clipped sounds of '*tout à coup*' and '*couloirs*', for example), the formal introduction of 'otherness' into the text produces an altogether different, chiastic effect of '*f*' and '*s*' sounds, as we can see more clearly in the original French: 'cette étrangeté qui filtre, / impalpable, à travers les sables, / la surface de la mer, / le flux de la marée montante'. This major textual event, the first of its kind in *Eté*, precipitates a double movement within the narrative. *Je* and *vous* witness with bated breath the boy's solitary journey back to safety, yet, at the very moment that the latter achieves total separation from the monitor by disappearing from her view, they themselves are brought together by means of an elliptical swerve into the first person: 'You say: the child is advancing. You say: he is on the point of disappearing. You say: It is done. I say I love you' (p. 102).[3] The boy returns to his coach and makes a quick exit from Trouville. As for the monitor, she will later leave the beach under cover of night.

In crude psychoanalytical terms, it can be stated that the monitor is sacrificed as the Real in order to ensure the boy's dramatic passage into the Symbolic. By extension, the monitor and the boy, functioning together as *eux*, represent the pre-Oedipal stage of the adult desire operating between *je* and *vous*, which, if it was once as mad and unstable as Gdansk (p. 89), is now anchored firmly in fantasy. Indeed, the narrator's ritualised dialogue of love with *vous* rewrites the monitor's furious, masochistic desire linked with the 'aberrant' sea (p. 72), and, at the same time, reverses the trajectory of *je*'s precarious relationship with *vous*, who, she claims, had previously indicated his wish to die (p. 89). But what connection exactly does this narrative relay of sacrificial desire have with the textual moments of equivalence and chiastic reversal which bring *Eté* to such a dynamic close?

Let us return to the moment in the text when the monitor articulated the nature of her love for the boy. She explained to him that she wanted their relationship to remain 'completely impossible . . . completely desperate' (p. 85) so that they might experience its 'overwhelming, terrifying, definitive' pain (p. 85). The monitor is expressing herself here in the same terms that she used earlier to describe a book she had just read telling of a love that invited death without provoking it, a love 'infinitely more violent than if it had gone through the process of desire' (p. 70). This is surely the same unfinished book that the narrator also admits to having just read (p. 36), and which left her in a similar state of 'endless torture'. The book in question is not *A la recherche du temps perdu*, even though this is alluded to on page 18 in the spectacular form of Andrée and Albertine. It is in fact Robert Musil's *Der Mann ohne Eigenshaften* (1952) (*The Man Without Qualities*), in particular, the third, incomplete part which focuses on the unresolved, tragic story of incestuous desire between the protagonist, Ulrich, and his sister, Agathe. The real of *Eté* is effectively constructed out of one of the work's key episodes, the couple's holiday by the sea, where they revert to being children and playing games with each other on the beach (like and not like *lui* and *elle*), before returning to their hotel room where they eventually find themselves making love to each other (like and not like *je* and *vous*).[4]

To repeat, both the narrator and the monitor are plunged into a similar crisis of writing: they both feel the urgent need to close up the open wound of Musil's text and so rescue it from its 'frightening isolation'. Yet how can an unfinished text of incestuous desire become finally a text with an end, and thus, paradoxically, without end?

Proust serves as an anti-model here since, according to the narrator, he was already living what he was writing. At the beginning of *Eté*, she had asked rhetorically: '[w]hat has become of the slow and idle evenings of the summer dragging on until the last glimmer of light, to the point even of love's dizziness, its sobs, its tears? Written evenings, embalmed in writing, henceforth readings without end, without substance. Albertine, Andrée, were their names. Who danced in front of him who was already struck by death and yet who would look at them . . . [and] was already writing the book of their past' (p. 18).[5] In this reconfiguring of the Proustian real as lesbian, any idea of a simple inversion of reality (say, Albert) into fiction (say, Albertine) is impossible because the former is already the latter, resulting mysteriously in readings 'without substance'.[6] How, then, *Eté* asks, can a literary sublimation of consequence be assured if the real is already a text, i.e. *The Man Without Qualities*?

The textual sequences of compression and containment in 'la chambre noire', playing as they do on the idea of distance and separation, have to be read as the narrator's answer to this question, for she has restaged metaphorically the isolating impossibility of Musil's text and, in the process, reversed it. This approach stands in perfect counterpoint to that of the monitor who foolishly attempted to embody Musil's impossible passion by acting it out masochistically with the aid of the young boy, and at great risk to them both. This divergence in female interpretation is perhaps the text's main drama, and it determines how we read the narrator's story about David, evidently pure fabulation on the narrator's part and an exemplary response to her demand that one avoid the 'insanity' of theory and proceed by way of the imaginary (p. 74). In the tale's embedded and hyper-depressed narrative, David found himself in a *Candide*-like state of 'perdition', as profound as that of the narrator when faced with the challenge of Musil. He was threatened with abduction by the depressed shark to the bleeding, maternal space of a wounded whale ('the dead point of the world'), a threat which, because the shark is personified as male, could also be construed as a homosexual wish to seduce the boy (echoes here of the biblical story of David and Jonathan). If this pain were not already enough, David was also exposed to the suicidal sadness of the spring ('la source') in her Atlantic grotto (p. 52). Just prior to its act of chiastic formation, however, the text informs us that in the midst of this 'tank' of tears there suddenly appeared an illumination of spontaneous pleasure, and that 'la source' was inspired to dance the 'slow, funereal passacaglio of the wind of the dark night' (p. 100). David was subsequently rescued by a passing boat and 'la source' achieved immortality (p. 101).

This *mise en abîme* of regression overcome participates actively in the text's carefully calibrated network of inversions and reversals because it serves chronologically and thematically as a necessary pre-narrativising of the narrator's successful fantasmatics with *vous* over *eux*. In fact, the happy resolution of 'la source''s fate functions as a 'monitor screen' on which are projected and re-read the narrator's dramatic rewriting of the monitor's 'incorrect' obsession with Agatha and Ulrich's 'other' state. As for the chiasmus, it illuminates and formalises the text's various relations of difference—*je/elle*, *elle/lui*, *je/vous*—by staging a set of inversions between equivalent terms. It is precisely because the ideas of equivalence and difference can operate simultaneously in the figure of the chiasmus that it also stages a new set of relations among its terms, i.e. a new similarity between *je* and *vous*. For at the very moment that an impalpable otherness is being declared, the text is already reflecting upon it ironically and controlling it in a fixed form of desire, expressed in the simple four-part and self-folding sentence: 'Je dis vous aimer' (i.e. pronoun, verb, pronoun, verb). In the process, Musil's text is revealed as no more than a trivial tale 'without qualities', as banal even as the tune sung by the monitor entitled 'A la claire fontaine'.

One could not imagine a more utterly self-reflexive text than *Eté*. *Je*'s writing over *elle*'s maternal body—the 'dead body of the world' over which one always writes (p. 67)—mirrors perfectly the text's own self-completion as a Minuit text which had to overcome novelistically its original state of 'wandering in the real' (p. 8) (it was first serialised in *Libération*). In addition, the three calls which punctuate the boy's passage to safety and which echo the passacaglia—an instrumental composition in which a theme is constantly repeated in slow and stately triple time—represent the three stages of Duras's writing of *Eté* as outlined in the preface: day one to enter into the actuality of the real, day two to forget it, day three to 'efface' what had been written (p. 8).[7] As the narrator proudly remarks at one point: 'See how one can read through [*au travers*]' (p. 87). If there is a message in *Eté* it seems to be that desire must first of all be intertextually read if it is to be lived, and that intertextual erotics can act as a valuable filter for the immediate reading and sublimation of desire which is then reclaimable in rhetorical fantasy as love. We are informed at one point of the exemplary case of *Aurélia Steiner*, originally written by the narrator in the form of letters addressed to *vous* as a way of surviving the violent sexual desire she once felt for him. This desire would have proved 'a murderous folly' (p. 65) if acted out for real and without the aid of a third party or text.

Yet in its rough handling of Musil is *Eté* perhaps going even further and suggesting that narrative configurations of desire are already a figuration and resolution of a more urgent crisis—one of intertextual erotics? Are, that is, the ostensible family psychodramas of Duras's Minuit text no more than the visible end-result of intertextual relations? In search of a possible answer let us turn now to *Amant*.

L'AMANT

For the adolescent girl-narrator of *Amant*, the supreme moment of *jouissance* would be to make her Chinese lover do to her schoolgirl friend, Hélène Lagonelle, exactly what he does with her, and in her presence:

> I want to take Hélène Lagonelle away with me to that place where every evening, with my eyes closed, I have imparted to me the pleasure that makes you scream. I'd like to give Hélène Lagonelle to that man who does this to me, so that he may do it in turn to her. I want it to happen in my presence according to my wishes. I want her to give herself where I give myself. It's via her body, through it, that I would then experience from him ultimate pleasure. A pleasure unto death. (*Amant*, p. 92)[8]

This stunning scene of imaginary fulfilment, locus of all the sexual and racial crossings in *Amant*, has been celebrated in various ways. For some critics it shows how each participant can occupy all positions, and thus how the feminine self in particular can gain power by envisioning herself as other.[9] For others, it represents both inter-changeability and fusion, the culmination of the text's 'ethics of non-differentiation' and 'ex-centricity', i.e. its openness to the third which enriches *jouissance* and opens up the union of the couple to an absolute.[10] Even Elizabeth Meese, while recognising that the narrator refuses one unthinkable move, i.e. herself and Hélène as lovers, nevertheless argues that this configuration of desire signals a partial disruption of the usual subject/object relation and, hence, the 'perpetual un-ease of (ex)tension and change in the "subject" '.[11]

Any idea, however, that this imaginary encounter is a benign passage of giving and non-possession is contradicted somewhat by the fact that the girl-narrator would be in total control of the other participants' desire. Indeed, the scene is conceived primarily as a tribute to her own uncompromising will-power: 'She says that she wants to do it. She does it' (p. 49). More importantly, when seen in context, although the episode is presented as a formulation of ultimate heterosexual bliss between *je* and *lui*, it actually marks the resolution of an uncontrollable, murderous, female desire for Hélène expressed by *je* just moments before: 'Hélène Lagonelle makes you want to kill her. She conjures up the wonderful dream of putting her to death with your own hands . . . I am worn out with desire for Hélène Lagonelle. I am worn out with desire' (p. 91).[12] The principal reason for Hélène's attraction is the 'fabulous power' of her breasts which receive in *Amant* the kind of narrative attention never accorded to the body of the Chinese who is merely the 'motor' of *jouissance*. These impossible white objects of desire, which demand to be kneaded and retained by an other, *any* other ('She [Hélène] offers these things for hands to knead, for lips to eat' [p. 91]), inspired in *je* a masochistic desire that took the particular textual form of a chiasmus: 'Etre dévorée de ces seins / de fleur / de / farine / que sont les siens' (p. 91) ('To be devoured by those flour-white breasts of hers'). In this sequence, '*seins*' has been reversed into 'les siens', which, although in the context clearly means 'hers' (i.e. Hélène's), could also, theoretically, denote 'his' (i.e. the Chinese lover's). Masochistic desire is indiscriminate, and it is left to the differentiating structure of the chiasmus to emphasise this point.

Inspired, as it were, by this chiastic ordering of forces, the girl-narrator's controlled circuit of imaginary desire, where she positions herself both masochistically (she is excluded from the sexual act) and sadistically (she is in total control), allows her to desire Hélène narcissistically as a projection of her own desire for sexual ravishment. In the process, Hélène's 'sublime' and amorphous body (p. 89), 'incomparable' like the 'sea without form' of sexual *jouissance* (p. 50), finds itself rechannelled into the rediscovered, protective, 'lagoon' waters of formal, heterosexual desire (*[le]Lagon-elle*), there to function as no more than a mirror reflecting in the clearest of light the *jouissance* experienced between *je* and *lui*. This reorientation of sexual desire restages and reinvests all the other crossings in the novel made by *je*, in particular her crossing of the Mekong river, an event of mainly metonymical displacement since her male fedora hat was only 'displaced' (p. 15) like the vehicles doubled up against each other on the ferry, and because the ensuing sexual 'experiment' with the Chinese led simply to a repetition of her family's violence, pain, despair and dishonour (p. 92). Yet the chiastic twist on 'seins' and 'siens' also represents the culmination of the adult narrator's own sustained play on Hélène's floating, ineffable name: *elle*, *'aile'* (wing), Hélène L., Hélène Lagonelle, H.L.. For as soon as Hélène has been made formally equivalent to the Chinese—'I see her as being of the same flesh as that man from Cholon' (p. 92)—she is then dispensed with, almost indifferently, by a selectively erratic memory: 'I don't know what became of Hélène Lagonelle, or even whether she's dead' (pp. 93–94). If Hélène was presented earlier as the only one female figure to escape the 'law of error', or '[t]hat self-lacking in women brought about by themselves' (p. 28), due to her arrested mental development, she now becomes one of its victims. For this reason, *Amant* celebrates less Hélène's escaping of the 'rule of error' than its own ironic 'errors' of accelerating textual abstraction, a strategy highlighted by the ideal, 'defectless' immortality of the narrator's 'younger brother', revealed in a late correction to have been two years her senior. All the while, the text's founding 'error'—the apparent omission of an answer to the question posed on the first page: what happened at age eighteen to make the narrator's face change so dramatically?—has gone by unchecked!

But *Amant*'s dedication to Duras's long-time film cameraman, Bruno Nuytten, also hints at the possibility of another 'experiment' operating in the novel since it encourages us to consider the cinematically prolonged, 'absolute image', the Mekong crossing, in properly cinematic terms. The only overt reference to cinema in the text hinges on a detail of the young girl's hair during that momentous day, a detail linked directly to the image's 'determining ambiguity' of the fedora hat. The narrator states: 'I had never seen a film with those Indian women who wear those same flat-brimmed hats and plaits coming down in front of their body . . . I have two long plaits coming down over the front of my body like those women in the films whom I have never seen but they are children's plaits' (p. 23).[13] *Je/elle*'s precocious powers of invention here are such that they preempt cinematic influence and twist it around in the form of a double plait. If we bear in mind the chiastic nature of this process—'I had never seen a film with those Indian women . . . / . . . . plaits coming down in front of their body, / . . . two long plaits coming down over the front of my body . . . / those women in the films whom I have never seen'—we see that it actually prepares for the narrator's later eclipsing of Hélène's breasts. Could it be, in fact, that Hélène is somehow linked to Indian cinema, or at least films about India? One such film is Jean Renoir's *The River* (1950), a colour film shot in English on location near Calcutta and acknowledged by Duras as one of her favourite films precisely because it recalls her childhood spent in the bush.[14] While the case for an intertextual link with *The River* cannot be proved, the autobiographically charged nature of *Amant* and its emphasis on foreknowledge invites the viewer to speculate that at each mention of the Mekong crossing it is actually 'crossing over' to Renoir's classic. Let us therefore look briefly at the key elements of *The River*.

Like *Amant*, *The River* offers a coming-of-age story set in the colonies. It is narrated on the sound-track by the protagonist's older self. Harriet, a misguided young girl and would-be poet, loses the love of Captain John who returned home to marry one of his cousin's daughters (he remains the only character in the film to escape across the Ganges). Upon the death of her younger brother by snake-bite, Harriet finally resigns herself to a life of submission. In fact, the film is obsessed with the spiritual need for resignation (its motto is: 'Consent to everything'), to the point even that it never performs the act of metaphor and metamorphosis which it constantly invokes. And whereas *Amant* emphasises the sexual violence and pain of growing up, *The River* is content merely to evoke yearning, especially in its use of Indian actors for long sequences of festival dancing and in its creation of a general romantic mood, features which Duras admits in *Yeux* to finding highly problematic.[15]

By playing chiastically with Hélène's ravishing, formless body, *Amant* can be said to have straightened out the different threads of *The River*, in particular Harriet, who is also a symbol of abortive passage and wasted potential (a fact reinforced by the superfluous, silent *h* of 'Hélène'). Indeed, by projecting H.L. into an imaginary sexual scenario which lifts her temporarily out of regression and the destiny of her name, i.e. HomosexuaLité, *Amant* comments again self-reflexively on its own 'experiment', i.e. its correction of a classic foreign film made in English and dominated by 'those Indian women' of cinema. Just as *je/elle*'s silence in *Amant* colluded with the family's humiliation of the Chinese in a club named 'La Source', so, too, the novel elides the indigenous population of its cinematic precursor, consigning it to a space behind the shutters of the garçonnière and forcing it to function as no more than 'the volume of a film turned on too loud' (p. 52). *Amant* will continue to cross over (and cross out) *The River* in a perfect Duras marriage of form and content until *je/elle*'s first journey into sexual pleasure with her father-lover is finally replayed in reverse by her return crossing of the Pacific to the fatherland of France and the subsequent rediscovery of her mother's 'profound grace' (p. 117). Once this has taken place, the one imaginary moment of passage over Hélène's body can finally be replayed and relegated to pure conjecture, as merely a probable scene of 'domestic' penetration between the Chinese lover and his Chinese wife:

> Then the day arrived when it must have been possible. That day, precisely, when the desire for the little white girl must have been such, so impossible to control, that, as in an extreme, high fever, he could have rediscovered his complete image of her and penetrated the other woman with this desire for her, the white child. (*Amant*, p. 140)[16]

It is only through Renoir's film that we can fully appreciate the effect of the fairy-tale end to *Amant* immediately following this last, narcissistic display of erotic attraction and which has seemed to many critics so untypical of the text as a whole. The Chinese's swearing of eternal love, presented by the narrator in the controlling form of indirect speech ('[he said that] he would love her until he died' [p. 141]), is nothing less than a final ironic spin, the kind of adolescent wet-dream that Harriet may have indulged in but which the always adult narrator of *Amant* expressly forbids.

We see, then, that, as in *Eté*, the major intrigue of *Amant* is intertextual in nature, even though it involves a different medium, and that rhetorical manipulation constitutes only the most visible aspect of a long and involved process of textual sublimation. What happens, however, when Duras engages with literature and cinema simultaneously? This is the question posed and answered by *Emily*, which includes Duras's most extraordinary use of pretexts.

EMILY L.

The one spectacular moment of narrative suspense in *Emily* is clearly the unforeseen and potentially dangerous encounter between a small red ferry crossing the Seine and a white petrol-tanker coming in from the sea. It is captured by the female narrator thus:

> Out on the quay someone shouted . . . The ferry is moving towards the
> tanker. The tanker also continues to head towards the ferry . . . The ferry
> has cut across the tanker's bows [*l'avant*] and disappeared behind it. The
> tanker continues on. The ferry reappears in the wake of the tanker . . . The
> danger is over. (*Emily*, pp. 45–46)[17]

Much later, however, and just as unexpectedly, an even more
significant event of apparition and reapparition takes place, this time
on the textual level. On page 146, the primary story of the narrator
and her male interlocutor runs head-long into their own tale of the
poet, Emily L., which they had been projecting on to the screen of a
passing English couple visible in the mirror of the café at Quilleboeuf-
sur-Seine. There is no two-lined gap of white space to separate the two
moments and they simply run into each other. A crime of contamination has been committed: real fact—the conversation between the
narrator and her interlocutor—is now taken over for five pages by the
flow of the purely novelistic, thus finding itself, like the ferry ('le bac')
with the petrol-tanker, temporarily relegated to the background. This
perfectly 'superficial', typographical admixture has produced in the
real a new tranquility, however, a free-flow of water, or 'connivence'
(p. 149), between the Seine and the sea, part and whole. The story of
Emily L. also appears to have crystallised. We are told that the
caretaker, having travelled the world to reclaim, even kill, Emily L. if
ever he should find her, suddenly catches sight of her dancing on the
deck of a large Australian cargo ship. Their story of chaste love—'a
story greater than death' (p. 151)—is now able to retake its natural
course and it converts Emily L.'s most important poem, an ambiguous
statement on the nature of despair ending on the 'sight' of death
(p. 85), into a maritime vision of everlasting beauty and love. All has
been made symbolically equivalent; there is now no fore or aft.
Similarly, *vous* has repressed his need to go out cruising with other
men and lies asleep reassuringly in the room adjacent to that of the
narrator (*je*), the threat of his departure now lifted.

But can these metonymical instances of doubling up have resulted
already in literary and sexual sublimation? Not yet! 'And then I
awoke' (p. 152), the narrator declares. After allowing her narrative to
be taken over by what Duras terms the 'transcendental' powers of her
protagonist,[18] *je* now finally comes into her own. Emily L., who is
nothing more, after all, than a stock-in-trade Jamesian heroine in the
way that her mystery is only revealed at the end of the novel (this
aspect of Henry James's technique is explicitly mentioned on page

138), is effectively written over by the narrator who now rises up and crosses over to awaken *vous*. She 'pierces' him and her text erotically by inserting what we now realise remained latent throughout all their stilted discussions on writing. I am referring, of course, to the literary manifesto of the last two pages, a breathlessly intense cross-cutting of comparisons and reversals, of before and after, of too much and too little, of oxymoron and paradox, which, in its wild reference to dogs, includes a stunning anti-humanist crack, a deliberate non-sequitur of fraudulent logic played out over *ça*. With its disruptive, paradoxical use of *avant*, this revising of the notion of *écriture courante* reworks ironically all the text's previous moments of doubling, substitution and passage. The narrator states:

> . . . it was not enough either to write like that and have people believe that it was done without any thought at all, simply by following your hand; just as it was too much to write with only the mind in control, watching over the activity of madness. It's not enough: philosophy and morality and the most common examples of human existence (dogs, for instance) are not enough; they don't get through to the body which is reading the story and wants to know it from the beginning, and wants with every reading to be even more ignorant [*ignorer toujours plus avant*] than it is already. (*Emily*, p. 153)[19]

The author-narrator concludes with a knowingly false reflection on her brilliantly crafted and self-styled novel: 'I told you that one ought to write without making corrections . . . eject what one writes, mistreat it almost . . . take nothing away from its useless mass . . . leave everything in the state that it appears' (p. 154).[20]

Murphy has argued that this climax allows *Emily* to maintain as virtual the 'leap from self to the other in the act of (re)writing self as other'. It is to be opposed, she claims, to the negative *mise en abîme* of *The Beast in the Jungle*, where the narrator 'enacts a death-leap (death-to-self) in the death or absence of the other'.[21] Yet such an idea, although formally attractive, is difficult to uphold in the face of the novel's elaborate intertextual play. For as it happens, the major intertextual event in the novel does not concern James at all, but rather, through the concept of '*apparition*', Emily L.'s poem on despair, a poem, in fact, written by Emily Dickinson beginning, 'There's a certain Slant of light'.

Revealed as one of the poems stolen by Emily L.'s husband, the Captain, and thus already 'lacking', 'There's a certain Slant of light' presents Dickinson at her most uncompromising.[22] It is suspended 'like the Distance / On the look of Death', its cathedral space a locus of random and invisible winter rays that 'oppress' with the difference of 'sovereign' and 'annihilating' 'Seal Despair'. Duras quickly 're-Slants' Dickinson's poem into French prose, endowing it with a title ('Winter Afternoons') and finally closing it off with a full-stop. It is then subjected to repeated paraphrasings. For example, the line, '. . . internal difference, / Where the Meanings, are—', is rewritten as: 'la dernière différence, celle interne, au centre des significations'. When Dickinson's poem is paraphrased in full on page 85, however, it undergoes a crucial change: its plural winter afternoons are inverted and reduced into one summer night. Juxtaposed, these two ideas form a chiastic structure: Winter / Afternoons / *nuit* / *(d')* *été*, thus illustrating the degree to which *Emily* has worked rhetorically the seam of (mis)translation between English and French already laid out in the title, *Emily/eLle*. Not only does this chiasmus formalise the intersection of reflections of the English and French couples caught in the mirror of the café (and the play of projections which thus ensues), but it also emphasises the novel's graphic play of *apparitions* which synthesise the elements of Emily L./Emily Dickinson's mystical and masochistic self-sacrifice into a textual space of programmable, erotic penetration.[23]

The second part of the chiasmus, '*nuit d'été*', indicates, however, yet another intertextual story in *Emily*, and one which directly reflects the visual and projective nature of the book's structure. I am referring to John Huston's film, *The Night of the Iguana* (1964), which has so far been ignored in discussions of the text, even though Huston is a director whom Duras has recently championed and claims elsewhere to 'love'.[24] For the passing presence in *Emily* of 'fifteen or so' Korean men (*eux*) dressed uniformly in white—'the same person indefinitely multiplied' (p. 11)—which the narrator regards as a threat to natural difference (she later dismisses them as eunuchs), can be compared to the coach-load of American women tourists in Huston's film who are led by the homosexually frustrated Miss Fellowes (Grayson Hall). Similarly, the Captain's wife, the 'little iguana', drinking herself into oblivion, represents an almagamation of the film's male protagonist, the alcoholic Reverend Shannon (Richard Burton), and the live iguana which makes a brief appearance. We can go even further in this intertextual vein. In its original version as a play by Tennessee Williams, *The Night of the Iguana* included as an epigraph an excerpt from another Dickinson poem beginning: 'I died for Beauty'.[25] By incorporating its reference to Williams within the poetic framework of 'Winter Afternoons', *Emily* can thus be said to have reversed the submissive, part-to-whole relationship between female poet and male playwright. This constitutes an act of poetic will by the narrator who, by enlisting her young lover into the narrative process, reverses the trajectory of the 'kinsmen' in 'I died for Beauty' who 'met a Night—/ . . . talked between the Rooms—/ Until the Moss had reached [their] lips—/ And covered up—[their] names'. Moreover, *je* and *vous* exemplify the simple hope expressed by Nonno, the old poet in Huston's film, that human courage prevail over despair. As Nonno remarked in his rather trite lament just before he died: 'How calmly does the orange branch / Observe the sky begin to blanch / Without a cry, without a prayer / With no betrayal of despair'.

The result of this gendered cross-breeding of poem and film, in which Dickinson is played off erotically with Huston, is that the poet is reborn as a prophet of the Possible, and the film-maker, for his part, is relieved of the intense sexual ambiguities of Williams. We might consider this to be a radical recuperation by Duras of an intertextual female other but Dickinson, like Musil in *Eté*, is used here primarily to narrativise the pain of the real represented by the English couple (*eux*), in particular *elle*. Indeed, it would be very presumptuous to suppose, as one critic has done, that the multiple relays of erasure and replacement created by the text, whereby 'Emily D.''s poem is 'erased/ replaced' by that of Emily L. which is, in turn, erased/replaced by M.D.'s novel, emerge finally as an implied critique of canon formation.[26] For if, like Emily L.'s poem, the novel affirms not 'difference between' (a mark of the symbolic) but rather a feminine space of 'internal difference', this has more to do with the intricate folds of Duras's intertextual affair with Huston than with the inescapable metaphoricity of the female body, an idea which would elide the particular violence of Dickinson's shafts of directed light. In fact, Dickinson is retained, and re-retained, in an erotic *fort-da*, before being eventually inverted as a metadiscursive '*apparition*' serving to illustrate the narrator's own compositional skills. Whereas Dickinson was often engaged in a murderous, and sometimes suicidal, poetics of aggression with a God/Father/Precursor/Lover (a trauma usually denied closure),[27] in *Emily* the unending despair encapsulated in 'There's a certain Slant of light' is resolved by the facilitating Third of *The Night of the Iguana*, which, in the process, is cannibalised. Put a little differently, Huston allows Duras to Slant away from a female over-identification with both Dickinson and her own creation, Emily L.. As an imaginary construction, he also offers more real security than the flimsy white guard-rail lining the banks of the Seine and which is linked by *vous* on page 63 to the final, blue-white seascapes of Nicolas de Staël (a painter, we note, who took his life in 1955). In short, *Emily*, with its explicit subtitle, '*roman*', represents a formal triumph of authorial self-possession, or the *patria potestas*, the right to die *and* kill, which Dickinson, locked in battle with a Blakeian 'Nobodaddy', never quite pulled off for herself.[28]

Having crossed over from text to text, let us try now to formalise Duras's intertextual practice. *Eté*, *Amant* and *Emily* each stage in different ways precise, rhetorical events of ironic 'error' which are thematically, linguistically, syntactically, orthographically and even typographically extended and refined. These moments are inter-textual in nature, the text's surface functioning as a mirror to invert literary figurations of the real, or what we might call, in view of the way they crystallise the textual process, 'mutative' metaphors of textuality.[29] Yet before they become self-ironically evident, such intertextual adventures are so discreet and 'impalpable' that they almost pass us by! The just readable, and therefore still corrigible, intertext is made temporarily unreadable by being left unnamed, or misnamed, even renamed, in order to ensure not merely its own embellishment but also the successful parturition of *écriture courante*. When the intertext is too present, its potent mystery is cancelled out and performative intertextual desire is impossible. This perhaps explains why in *Vie mat.* Duras refers to Musil's text as '*L'homme sans qualité*' (p. 119) and why Montaigne's *Essais*, named as such in *Eté*, are essentially irrelevant to its internal dynamics (despite the fact that Montaigne is a self-styled 'painter of passage'[30]).

The unveiling of Duras's transfer to an inducted intertext is the very 'error' of figuration in her Minuit work. Indeed, intertextual figuration is being proposed by Duras as *the* figural, a desire at once ironic, erotic and fulfilled because it falls within the strict parameters of fantasy.[31] Moreover, the privileging of surface disorder in Duras's Minuit texts accords to chiastic displacement a power of erotic violence that even de Man, concerned only with the figure's threat to the signifying system, would not perhaps have foreseen. It is therefore impossible to promote Duras's overdetermined intertextual relations as simply the result of an 'unlimited hypertextuality' (Borgomano)[32] or a 'pluralising plurivocity' (Cohen).[33] Reformulatable concepts such as Gérard Genette's transtextuality or architextuality[34] are likewise inadequate to deal with the sexual valencies of intertextual difference in *écriture courante*. They would also ignore the subtle irony of such phrases as 'lectures illimitées' in *Agatha* which, like *Eté*, dissolves the rich complexities of Musil's magnum opus by reducing it to one core issue, incestuous passion, reconfigured as an ideal love thriving on its prohibition due to the intercession of other partners.[35] Even when she is adapting Chekhov's 'formless' and 'refractory' play, *The Seagull* (1896), Duras feels impelled to retranslate and recut her intertextual other in order to restore him as a 'discreet' proponent of sexual pudeur.[36]

For Duras, then, as for Bloom, the trope is less a figure of knowledge than a figure of poetic will, a '*cut* or *gap* made in, or into, the anteriority of language' (emphasis added).[37] And yet, if Duras's poetic crossings and counter-formations recall Bloom's ephebe poet rising sublimely against his predecessors in agonistic rivalry (they share, after all, similar ratios of contraction, expansion and appropriation), they nevertheless involve texts that are radically 'faulty'— incomplete in the case of Musil, suspended in the case of Dickinson— and which need to be 'stitched up' along the traditional seams of sexual difference. This explains why Dickinson, although a 'strong' poet for Bloom, cannot herself function as an intertextual Third in *Emily* but has to pass through the prism of Huston. Such filial, as opposed to 'feminine', writing records not just a 'will to divination' or a daughter-father relation in some literary 'daughteronomy' (although this is much emphasised by Duras in her own commentary on Dickinson[38]). It also enacts a repeatable Scene of Instruction in sadomasochistic desire and one which rivals the confrontation between sound and image in Duras's film-work, the difference being, of course, that the intertextual 'image' is already weak and so offers immediate access. One specific violation, one crime.

Duras's metaphorical 'retention' of flawed, and therefore seductive, intertexts is, in short, a fantasmatic introjection of the other and is, of itself, erotic. The fact that the intertexts are specific and delimited means that they siphon off an otherwise uncontrollable over-flow of erotic vibrations that could be generated by having too many weak intertextual others. Hence, while *écriture courante* may appear destined for collective, textual disorder, it always assures itself the pleasure of self-administered, intertextual *perturbations*.[39] This is less sadomasochism as a mode of intertextuality than intertextuality as a sublimating mode of sadomasochistic sexuality, for the rhetorical processes of intertextual fantasy serve to draw the Duras text out of a suicidal, Dickinsonian over-identification with, and imitation of, the wound of the fractured Other. By condensing the diaspora of disparate material into a fixed metaphorical representation, intertextual fantasy tropes precisely on the real of textual *jouissance* and its unconditional *hors-texte*.[40] Indeed, the more aggressive the transformation of the 'other' text, inter lingua and inter media, the more sublimely sublimated is Duras's own. The Duras narrator may be intertextually 'possessed' but her narrative can immediately recuperate this loss as an act of individuality performed with her Great Man. As Duras states in a more overtly sexual context: 'We [women] possess our lover just as he possesses us. We possess each other. The site of this possession is one of absolute subjectivity' (*Vie mat.*, p. 41).[41]

L'HOMME ASSIS DANS LE COULOIR/LA MALADIE DE LA MORT

Without a circumscribed intertext, however, there can be no intertextual perversion in Duras's work and it risks falling into abjection. To gain a full measure of what is at stake here, not only for the Duras text but also for the Duras reader, let us see what happens when Duras directly approaches the sexualised body in her so-called 'erotic' texts, *Homme assis* and *Maladie*. Duras makes clear in *Yeux* (pp. 60–61) that she never intended the first of these to be published by Minuit and we shall quickly discover why.

As in its original version as a short extract published by *L'Arc* in 1962,[42] the first-person narrator-voyeuse of *Homme assis* sets out to describe the strange and violent sexual scene taking place before her between a man and woman left unnamed as *lui* and *elle*. The sadomasochistic 'acts' (p. 24) of the couple's desire become progressively more extreme and *je* attempts to form an alliance with *elle* against *lui* and an unspecified *on*. This is not reciprocated, however, and so the narrator's ambition to enter into the scene herself and direct it (e.g.: 'What I desire is that she sees' [p. 17]) is never realised. Instead, her role is reduced to that of a passive spectator or go-between ('I speak to her and tell her what the man is doing' [p. 16]), and she eventually falls victim herself to *elle*'s unbridled masochism and wish for 'self-deformation' (p. 10). There is no intertextual 'screen' here on which to project *elle*'s intensified anal and oral regression and so negotiate the increasing semantic confusion between *elle* (the lover), *elle* (her counterpart's penis ['la pine']), and *elle* (his hand ['la main']), a confusion which runs parallel to *elle*'s fetid journey into 'that other femininity' (p. 28) of *lui*'s (ungendered) anus. From page 31 on, after the 'lovers' have experienced orgasm, *Homme assis* does no more than catalogue with silent fascination their slide into madness, leaving the narrator to conclude impotently: 'I know nothing. I do not know if she is asleep' (p. 36). The text, too, has ended up a 'dead thing' (p. 35).

Marini has celebrated *Homme assis* as a subversion of the pornographic genre on account of its moments of pronominal ambiguity and its use of the conditional perfect.[43] Yet what may initially have been a subversion of sexual identity on the level of the signifier (that a penis be 'she', for example, and thus *elle*'s desire for '*elle*' be read as a daughter's pre-Oedipal desire for the mother) is immediately nullified once the act of mechanical and 'material' consummation has taken place. An overwhelming literalness now takes over: 'lèvres' refers only to lips, not the vagina, and 'la' is linked only to one feminine noun, 'la femme'. Lacking what could be called a 'genital' process of metaphorical penetration, the text pursues its pre-Oedipal, metonymical movement of regression without offering any reformulation of *lui*'s 'criminal' penis: 'It [*elle*] [her tongue] retains it [*la*] [his penis] which is on the point of being swallowed up in one continuous sucking movement' (p. 28). Indeed, like *elle* with *lui*'s penis, 'that vulgar and brutal thing' (p. 27), *Homme assis* has choked on the punctiliously punctuated matter of its large typographical font. No poetic or rhetorical irony here, just a confirmatory repetition: 'I see that nothing equals the power of this softness except the formal prohibiting of any injury to it. Prohibited [*l'interdit formel d'y porter atteinte. Interdite*]' (p. 27). The 'dead point of the world', intertextually passed over in *Eté*, has now been fatally reached.

Maladie, published three years later, rectifies these structural faults in design and produces a very different sort of conclusion. Its formal address to *vous* corresponds to its transfer to an archetypal Great Man, Sören Kierkegaard, and his 1894 treatise, *The Sickness unto Death (A Christian psychological exposition for upbuilding and awakening)*. Kierkegaard can sometimes appear completely self-sufficient and thus bar all intertextual access.[44] This is not the case, however, in *The Sickness unto Death*. Indeed, its anatomy of the

Christian sin of despair needs to be up-dated to the present day. Accordingly, *Maladie* redefines Man's immaturity not as a lack of Christian belief but as a specifically sexual problem, that of one man's fear of the female body, so great that it leads him into a state of regression, as exemplified by his retelling of boyhood tales (p. 51) and his homosexual love of the same ('the grace of the bodies of the dead, the grace of those like yourself' [p. 37]). As we would expect by now following our analysis of *Eté*, *Amant* and *Emily*, *Maladie* stages a carefully prepared, dynamic climax. I am referring not to the moment of sexual consummation when *vous*'s initial oral desire to 'drink' *elle*'s breasts is remotivated into an act of penetration, but rather to the act of renaming whereby Kierkegaard is simultaneously capitalised and truncated. For once *elle* has delivered to *vous* her crucial instructions in heterosexual recognition and metaphor (the 'hollow' between her legs is the real 'dark night' [p. 53]), and after this process has itself been replayed on the textual level through the multiple use of the verb *reconnaître* (p. 56), the naming of *vous*'s sickness as 'la maladie de la mort' is re-executed hypervisibly, and Anti-Climacti- cally, by the narrator as: 'Maladie de la mort' (p. 56). This unexpected but calm rupture of the textual surface by the discovery and transformation of an intertext is *Maladie*'s primary erotic moment. It is rounded off self-ironically in a generalising, clichéd statement on the evanescence of love, the last part of which, significantly, is just one syllable short of becoming a perfect line of alexandrine verse: '. . . you have managed to live that love in the only way possible for you, losing it before it happened [*en le perdant avant qu'il soit advenu*]' (p. 57).

The delicate self-cutting and intertextual transmemberment in *Maladie*, which extends even to a dialogical space of narratorial doubt ('And then you do it. I couldn't say why' [p. 42]), constitutes a sublimation of the oral retention and anal fixation recorded so naïvely in *Homme assis*.[45] Through its calculated use of single and double- sized blocks of white spacing, *Maladie* also creates calligraphically an erotic play of differentiation. Yet the intertextual act in *Maladie* represents above all else a 'rebuilding' of Kierkegaard since it reinstates dialectically a true Kierkegaardian sense of the potenti- alities of mastered, vertical irony and seduction displayed in other works by Kierkegaard such as *Diary of a Seducer*.[46] The malady of homosexual non-loving, worse even than Kierkegaardian despair in the sense that there is no life left to die from ('sans vie préalable à mourir'), is played off hyperbolically as a playable and repeatable element, i.e. as simply 'the sickness of living, wickedness, the devil' (*Yeux*, p. 233). Indeed, it is the text of *Maladie* itself, rather than its male or female protagonist, which acquires the deliverance and self-reflexiveness usually accorded to Kierkegaardian consciousness and selfhood. Its textual 'accidents' allow it to transcend both the 'sickness of death' and *elle*'s body, offered as the sign of sexuality itself. *Elle*'s careful and emphatic distinction during her lesson on love between 'accident' (or 'mistake') and 'will' (p. 52) is effectively dismissed, the two concepts being fused together on a different level in a textual fantasy of formation and controlled deformation. Moreover, *elle*'s 'buried sex', which 'swallows up' and 'holds' without appearing to do so (p. 29), functions less as an object in itself than as a metaphor for the textual process, i.e. the swallowing up and holding down by *Maladie* of its intertextual filter, reflected in the 'filtered green' of '*elle*'s eyes.

   Maladie's use of its 'lacking' intertext also confronts us directly with the reality of our own position as reader. By exposing first its projective identification with, then introjection and final reprojection of, the 'bad' intertext now made magically 'good', it brings us to a stunning recognition of our own critical 'fading'.[47] This happens only after the text has energetically tapped the libidinal basis of our *Wisstrieb*,[48] daring us, like *elle*'s slender body 'crying out' to be strangled and raped, to assume the aggressive and penetrative role of interpreter. The same is equally true, of course, of *Amant*, whose ideal male readers are portrayed by Duras as having a centuries-old desire for incest and rape (*Vie mat.*, p. 43). What this means in practice is that 'he' is often 'put right' even when not 'in error'. For example, the narrator of *Amant* notifies the reader for no apparent reason that 'he' has been misled, that it was not, after all, at the cantine in Réam that she met the Chinese but two or three years later, after the concession had been abandoned (p. 36). Such gifts of surplus information demand that we read *Amant* and *Maladie* as intertextual revisions not simply of Duras's previous work but, more profoundly, of ourselves as 'faulty' readers. For if we are sollicited to take part in the telling of legendary stories ('Look at me, on the ferry' [*Amant*, p. 24], etc.), we are also quickly cut short by Duras's corrective impulse. Such a position refutes the author's view of *Amant* as a 'constant, unending metonymy . . . which never "cuts out" the reader, or takes his place', although Duras does admit elsewhere that '*Amant* is a book which acts upon [*sur*] the reader' (*Vie mat.*, p. 19).[49] We 'exist' in *écriture courante* by default, being simultaneously drawn in, drawn up, and beheaded in order for a sublime moment of intertextual re-crossing to snap the Duras text back into ironic life. That shock, at the moment of apocalyptic unveiling, when the reread intertext is finally released, is the text's 'properly' erotic moment and another tangible instance of Duras's desired 'hygienic orgasm'. We have become no more than an 'immediate' reader of 'monitor' screens, the personification of a provisional intertextual construction always to be corrected and even relegated as an inverted mirror image. 'Scandalous' the Duras Minuit text may be but only because it has chosen to market itself under the misleading label of *écriture courante*.

THE SECOND VOYAGE

If we have now fully determined the complex nature and effect of Duras's rhetorical passages of intertextual transference and translation, we have still not accounted for them theoretically. Duras herself is adamant that her writing bears no relation to Aristotelian translation, or 'the passage from potential being to actual being' (*Vie mat.*, p. 30), and instead emphasises its violent physicality, its 'appetite for freshly killed meat . . . for the consummation of strength',[50] such that death is 'mutilated' with every new poem or book (*Monde*, p. 17). Writing, in fact, for Duras, is originally an interior 'black block', and she 'tears it out' by 'transporting' and 'breaking' its mass (*Vie mat.*, p. 30). This does not mean, of course, that she is unaware of the filtering process involved in writing. As she explains:

> Writing itself, the text, passes through a filter which transforms it. It passes through a transgression which I call the filter. This definitive modification by the filter is writing. That which I call writing is the filter. The filter that transforms performs the modification. The writer is the person who performs this passage.[51]

Once again, we catch both the slipperiness and dexterity of Duras's style, for, in typical chiastic fashion, writing passes through a filter and the filter itself is writing. The final assertion of active authorial involvement ('The writer is the person who performs this passage') goes without saying.

Yet what kind of textual transgression are we dealing with in *écriture courante* if Duras's self-styled daughter-text is always made safe, just like the little girl in her commentary on a famous *fait divers* of 1961, 'Nadine d'Orange' (the only article to feature in both *Yeux* and *Outside*), where it was the very strength of the abductor's love for Nadine that allowed him to 'transgress' any thoughts he may have had of raping her? How, too, are we to explain the curious fact that, while they put *vous* under erasure, Duras's intertextual operations also ensure the reader's safe passage out of a potentially uncontrollable crisis of affect, depicted in *Vie mat.* as a 'private relation' of tears and complaint between text and reader (pp. 119–20)? It is surely not an overstatement to say that our position as a critical reader of *écriture courante* is always safeguarded intertextually. Can we at least give a name to this enabling texual Third who is paternally 'bound' in Duras's Minuit texts yet who, in marked contrast to Virginia Woolf's sublimating project, for instance, where an introjected male other also disrupts the self's unifying pattern and causes erotic *perturbation*, can never be neatly attributed to the agency of the superego?[52]

Let us turn to one last scene of paternal seduction, this time featuring an intertextual other from *Amant* who does not actually perform there as a Great Man. I am referring to Charles Laughton and his 1955 film, *The Night of the Hunter*, a classic black and white Hollywood film on the theme of human evil used in *Amant* simply to underline the fact that the narrator's elder brother, a one-time pimp and homosexual prostitute (p. 96), was also a sadistic criminal, highlighted in the phrase, 'the lurid light of the night of the hunter' (p. 67). In *Yeux*, Duras writes a long and quite remarkable commentary on Laughton's film entitled 'La nuit du chasseur' (pp. 116–26) which deserves our full attention for the way it explicitly connects the idea of aesthetic form with a structured process of identification and transformation, the basis of *écriture courante*.

Duras begins 'La nuit du chasseur' in typical, corrective fashion, declaring that Laughton, by not making the real father (Ben Harper) the same person as the pseudo-preacher, Harry Powell (Robert Mitchum), and thus both the murderer of his own wife, Willa (Shelley Winters), and hunter of his two young children, had essentially 'cheated' on his promise of a full portrayal of family horror. Duras misreads the film here because Harper was not murdered by Powell as she claims but rather executed by the authorities (it was during his period in prison that Powell, imprisoned for stealing a car, found out about the money Harper had entrusted to his children). She proceeds to rewrite *The Night of the Hunter* by focusing on the final scene of 'transformation' where Powell and the two children (John and Pearl) are seduced into singing together a Negro Spiritual initiated by Rachel (Lillian Gish), the old woman who had given the children refuge. The 'Moses' tune is what Powell had been humming while, like Herod, he chased the children downstream in an attempt to steal the money hidden in the girl's doll. Again, Duras is economical with the truth: only the boy, not both children as she claims, actually ran towards Powell the next morning when he was held down by the State Trooper. What is clearly most important for Duras about this 'film within a film' is its decisive double movement of passage, which accomplishes something that could actually have happened in record time if only Laughton had dared to make the father also the criminal, i.e. the children's detachment from their mother (p. 117). In Duras's reading, John and Pearl 'cross over' in song towards the preacher at the very moment that he returns to the realm of grace, or 'the vats of the infinite, childhood'. Here are the selected highlights of this 'miracle':

> The old woman improvises by singing 'Moses' . . . There's the miracle. As the song develops the criminal is transformed. A kind of grace in turn—this grace being a commonplace of the old woman and children—overtakes him, welling up inside him and wending its way through his wickedness, his death . . . The criminal and the old woman together sing of the return of life, of the father's last celebration, and the children bathe in this song till morning . . . It's at the end of this night that the children recover their father in this criminal, that they recover their love . . . Night of the criminal's reunion with his victims, night of the father who at the same time as he created life created death . . . At the end of the night too, this evil rises up out of the father . . . This transfer which the children see of their killer to those who are going to kill their killer—the children see their father arrested—is decisive. This father is going to die because of them. He is going to die for having wanted so very much to kill them. They are the cause of his death. The revelation is overwhelming. Like knowledge itself . . . The children cry out and give themselves up body and soul to the father, their killer. With all the violence inside them, they run away from the old woman and give themselves to the father . . . (*Yeux*, pp. 121–25).[53]

This impressively elaborate exercise in imaginary reconstruction emphasises two main points. Firstly, that the children's 'transformation' of the 'blinding real', once activated by the intertextual 'rampart' of 'Moses', generates its power precisely from the fact that they orient themselves towards a 'false' father. Secondly, that during the period of his 'conversion' to grace, Powell serves to ensure the children's escape from the potentially stifling authority of their maternal saviour and her misleadingly naïve conception of good and evil. This nocturnal turning-point of inversion and substitution is, I would argue, the prototype of all Duras's intertextual adventures with 'deficient' Great Men in *écriture courante*, where the apparently spontaneous and irrational moment is effectively crossed over, even double-crossed, and the pain of the already-written is always overcome where, too, an incomplete, imaginary text is introduced homeopathically into the Duras text to protect against intratextual madness and finds itself transformed in the process. As Madeleine puts it in *Savannah*: 'pain proposes itself as a solution to pain, like a second love' (p. 70). Unlike, for example, in some nineteenth-century novels by women writers like George Eliot where an inadequate father requires that the daughter act as a patriarchal prop, Duras's version of the sentimental romance requires only that a Great Man enter into her textual home, dissolve the female-maternal bond, and, his role fulfilled, depart.[54] His identity in this daughter-plot is necessarily fictive; he must just be there, even if spiritually or structurally flawed, but long enough for imaginary identification to take place and for the Minuit text to come into being. Such a mercenary process of paternal foundation reaches its most self-conscious level in *Savannah*, which refers across genre to an imaginary film (*Savannah Bay*) starring Henry Fonda (*fonda*, third person singular simple past of the verb *fonder*, to found)![55]

It is the at once imaginary and institutional nature of Duras's intertextual Great Men that obliges us to read the 'folly' of the children's love in 'La nuit du chasseur' in the context of Kristeva's theory of primary narcissism. There, the infant's archaic identification and immediate enrapture with a loving Third, i.e. the pre-Oedipal 'Imaginary Father' indicated by the 'gap' of the mother's desire for another, permits the creation of a space of figurative play beyond separation and absence. The mother herself is rejected as abject insofar as the gestures of maternal care are encountered as insignificative marks. Identification, or transference, is shown by Kristeva to constitute the very structure of the sign which opens up the performative aspect of language and metaphoricity and is thus linked to poetic and amatory discourse. In its later, reactivated form as '*le sujet supposé savoir*' during the analytic encounter, the 'Third Party', or 'Great Other', with whom the subject identifies and will paradoxically 'kill', is transformed into an object of love by means of a process of metaphorical drifting, idealisation and affect.[56] As we have seen,

Duras's adventures in intertextual transference possess the same giddy mixture of love and death, of poetic passage and symbolic violation, all at the expense of a maternally figured real (*elle*). In the rhetorical terms proposed by de Man, by transforming its intertextual other 'catachrestically' into a textual whole by means of unnaming, misnaming or renaming, the Duras Minuit text bears the mark of 'defacement', of having given 'intertextual' face, or figure (*prosopo-poeia*), to the indeterminable marks of material inscription.[57] A text like *Homme assis* is successful only to the extent that it reveals in the most graphic terms what happens when the Father is absent, and when, in marked contrast to another sexually explicit story, Bataille's *Ma mère* (1966), where the male protagonist succumbs to the charms of his 'abominable mother', writing cannot even sustain *epiphora*, the metaphorical motility previous to any objectification of figurative meaning.[58]

Duras's tales of intertextual love and identification can be seen, therefore, to revise Kristeva's own theory of intertextuality as a process of transposition played out within the intertext of the unconscious, for they propose a metaphorical notion of transference which resolutely avoids the implications of the missing, irretrievable object of fantasy.[59] Indeed, intertextual transposition becomes in Duras a narrative fantasy of seduction (incestuous and otherwise) which can control, tame and positively reinvest diegetic pain, affect, and *jouissance*. Surprisingly, Kristeva has not linked her loving Father of imaginary identification to her own theory of intertextuality, a move which would allow her to read Duras's formal, replicating intertextual screens of heightened readability as a resolution of blocked repetition. The intricately embedded folds of *écriture cour-ante* offer, at the very least, the subtle pleasures of tracking at first hand the metaphorical process. Moreover, it could be argued that Duras's intertextual erotics of ironic, rhetorical error realises precisely what Kristeva, referring to the work of Crébillon and Marivaux, declares to be the defining moment of the postmodern, i.e. 'the harrowing amusement of parody, the artifice of appearances [*l'artifice du semblant*]'.[60] Using Kristeva's own terms, Duras's Third, an intertextual Great Man chiastically refined, is nothing short of 'jubilatory'.

One matter has not yet been addressed. Why, to take the case of *Amant*, is only one creative artist, Renoir the focus of intertextual revision and not Laughton, nor even Barthes, who also plays there an antithetical role? For indeed, *Amant*'s images of maternal despair (p. 41) and undifferentiation (e.g. the natives' photographs which erase individual traits and create an 'hallucinatory resemblance' [p. 118]) all bear the non-cathartic, 'pathetic' imprint of the photographic image of *Chambre*, specifically that one 'just' image of the missing 'Winter Garden' photograph of Barthes's mother as a young girl. Barthes and Laughton ultimately remain decorative elments in *Amant*, like Montaigne's 'unreadable' *Essais* in *Eté* which, according to Duras, never escaped the 'singularity' of their author's relationship with La Boëtie (p. 68). What, then, makes some artists like Renoir so 'giving' of sublimation but others, like Proust and James, failed candidates for Durasian paternity? If Laughton, who was himself gay, is used by Duras merely to figure the 'bad' homosexual brother, are we then to assume that, like the female 'body' of Dickinson's poetry, the gay-related text must always function in essentialist terms as the body of a maternally fixated, gay man? Or is it just a pure coincidence that Duras's '*pères manqués*', if not always homosexual, are, at the very least, sexually ambiguous, fragile, sometimes even suicidal, like Nicolas de Staël in *Emily* or the unidentified American writer ('Papa' Hemingway?) referred to en passant in the same novel as someone who took life (p. 65)? In short, how are we to read Duras's abjected intertextual others? This is the issue we shall now explore in depth as we leave the twilight world of Minuit and head into the textual and paratextual regions of Duras's 'Outside'.

CHAPTER 5

All Her Sons: Duras, Anti-literature, and the Outside

Parlons des choses gaies. 'Gai', les pédés nous ont pris ce mot. Ils prennent tout. Et puis c'est un très beau mot, gai, oui, quel beau mot.

(M. Duras)

It is clear that the portion of Duras's literary work post-1980 not published by Minuit 'passes' in very different ways from *écriture courante*. At the risk of gross over-simplification, it is unhindered by narrative constraints, resists the heterosexual configurations of textual difference, and does not engage with intertextual 'Great Men'. A brief overview of Duras's major non-Minuit texts of this period can illustrate the point.

Yeux, a heady, unpredictable mix of styles and themes—epistolary, dialogic, theoretical, journalistic, poetic, political—and composed of short texts in assorted typographical fonts, photographs and unidentified stills, has no narrative strategy as such, except for the odd doubling of consecutive chapters (e.g. 'La lettre'/'La lettre') and a sequence of progressively more intimate, close-up images of Seyrig in *India Song* (pp. 163–86).[1] *Douleur*, apart from the erotic montage of its torture scene in 'Albert des Capitales' (see p. 51 above) and its play in the preface to each chapter on the book's uncertain status (i.e. are the 'sacred' texts real, true, invented or rewritten?), is devoid of any concerted intertextual play. Indeed, the naming in the title text of Robert Antelme's personal account of Dachau, *L'espèce humaine* (1947), corresponds exactly to 'Robert L.''s gradual self-cancellation in one double, textual movement: the narrator helps to resuscitate his lifeless body after his return to Paris from Dachau having already planned to divorce him and move over to 'D.'. *Vie mat.*, unbound by any structure or *'formation livresque'*, is a self-styled 'anti-book' of *'écriture flottante'*, neither fiction nor journalism (p. 7) and 'without beginning, middle or end' (p. 11). Although it describes the odd scene of erotic desire (e.g. 'Le train de Bordeaux', 'Le dernier client de la nuit'), it does not 'perform' textually itself and serves merely to enumerate the key themes of the Duras Minuit text (domination/ submission, curability/incurability, reality/invention, etc.). *Pluie* cites texts which are all false (*Vie de Georges Pompidou* is invented, Edouard Herriot's *La forêt Normande* should read: *Sous la forêt normande*), and its obvious pretext, Ecclesiastes, is allowed to take concrete form as 'the burnt book', a symptom of the father Emilio's personal embodiment of the paternal instance. *Pluie* thus remains on the same discursive level as its family of Italian immigrants (*eux*) and indulges in the gentle metonymies of tautology and verbal humour (franglais, slang, phonetic transcription, etc.). Finally, in *Chine*, a novel which declares itself in the preface to be explicitly on the side of '*eux*', a transformative poetics of desire is suggested only in its last three pages divorced from the main body of text. There Duras lists examples of cutaway shots ('plans dits de coupe')—essentially cine-matic conceits—for possible use in the future.

A major reason, of course, for the individual nature of the above texts is that they each have particular functions. *Chine*'s ironic use of footnotes referring to a possible film adaptation, for instance, indicates that Duras has other, more pressing, extratextual concerns on her mind: the repossession of *Amant* both from Jérôme Lindon at Minuit (with whom she fell out over the book after alleged mistreat-ment) and from the film-maker Jean-Jacques Annaud, who was directing at the time a film version of *Amant*. The text, in fact, is based on the screenplay that Duras wrote for Annaud before withdrawing from his project. Its title—*L'amant de la Chine du Nord*—already presents a drama of ownership, i.e. whose lover? Whose China? Who owns Duras?[2] *Vie mat.*, too, has purely functional aims: '[t]his book allowed us [Duras and Beaujour] to pass the time' (p. 7). As for *Pluie*, it seems designed primarily to repay a debt of gratitude to its dedicatee, Hervé Sors, a doctor-friend who helped to retrieve Duras from her long coma of 1988–89 during which she claims to have 'unconsciously' written the novel. It should be read, therefore, more as the after-effect of a 'real' cure.

Despite, however, their many differences in subject matter and purpose, Duras's non-Minuit texts constitute a heterogeneous textual space where sexual passion, including that of incest, can at last be fully realised, notably in *Pluie* where the tune of the mother ('La Néva') usurps the interdicting Name of the Father (*Ne-va-pas*!) which has been unveiled in the form of Emilio. Even more significantly, this mini-corpus of texts can also identify homosexuality and discuss it at length. Such a feature was formally established by Duras in 1981 with her first volume of collected journalism, *Outside*, for the Albin Michel series 'Illustrations', a series which, under the editorship of Jean-Luc Hennig, included work by gay writers such as Hervé Guibert and Guy Hocquenghem. While *Outside* does not itself engage directly with gay themes, except for one very brief moment when Duras raises with a Carmelite nun the possibility of desire between women,[3] it clearly advertises its link with homosexuality since it was Yann Andréa—or 'Y.A., homosexuel'—who assembled and edited all the material (p. 13). It could even be argued that the one enduring trace of Andréa's homosexuality in the collection is what he describes in his 'Note sur le classement des articles' (pp. 15–16) as the book's very inability to impose a (sublimating) order of classification, an impossibility that remains intact even when *Outside* is republished in 1984 as the first volume of Duras's own series for POL, also called 'Outside'. Certainly *Outside* continues the connection between homosexuality and the 'open', unedited image that we have established thus far in Duras's work: the articles were her 'first cinema', 'when the outside would submerge me, when there were things which made me mad, *dehors* [outside]' (*Outside*, pp. 11–12).[4]

What is so remarkable about all of Duras's 'Outside' work is how gay themes and subtexts are invoked, often in subtle and oblique ways, only then to become immediate sites of contestation and even denial. We have already seen how *Yeux* contains both a double dismissal of militant feminism and homosexuality in the chapter 'Femmes et homosexualité', as well as a full-scale attack on Aragon— a communist and homosexual—in 'Il n'y a pas d'écrivains communistes'. During the composition of that text, however, Duras was actually assisted by the editor then of *Cahiers du Cinéma*, Serge Daney, a self-styled, gay *'passeur'* (or 'border-crosser'). Even the title, *Les yeux verts*, represents a negotiation with gay influence, identifying as it does the character 'Yeux-Verts' from Genet's *Haute Surveillance* (1949).[5] Let us also quickly replay Duras's other non-Minuit texts in this specifically gay light.

Douleur, the second volume of Duras's 'Outside' series for POL and where she proposes the idea of an 'anti-literature' that 'puts to shame any pretension to literature' (p. 10), records Duras's first serious attempt to bring together two men face to face without recourse to a female intermediary. Unfortunately, the chapter in question, 'L'ortie brisée', ends on a note of potentially violent non-communication. Another chapter, 'Monsieur X dit ici Pierre Rabier', where Duras infers that a Gestapo agent's lonely existence was founded on a homosexual identification with a dead Frenchman—the result of an unresolved, criminal episode from earlier in his life (p. 110)—is prefaced by a short note explaining that it was Andréa, along with Hervé Le Masson, who insisted on its publication (p. 86).

In *Vie mat.* Andréa, or 'Y.A., homosexuel', proves himself strong enough to bring *écriture flottante* to a point of narrative closure. In the final chapter, 'La population nocturne', he dissolves the mysterious, Aschenbach-like vision that had been accosting the narrator by simply opening and closing the door (p. 159). The narrator never lets us forget, however, that despite this display of calm level-headedness, 'Yann' will always be 'not a *real* man' (p. 152) (original emphasis). In 'Les hommes', where Duras appears to be writing at her most absolute on the tragic solitude of gay men, she is effectively inverting Marcel Jouhandeau's maxims on the uniqueness of gay desire propounded in such texts as *Bréviaire* (1981).[6]

Pluie throughout refers to its original version as a children's book by Duras entitled, *Ah! Ernesto* (1971), where Bernard Bonhomme's lurid, primary-coloured photomontages propelled the story of Ernesto's school-boy recalcitrance into an often dazzling, homoerotic context. In one instance, cigars designed as bombs protruded out of mouths around which circled penile dragonflies. *Pluie*'s account of Ernesto's consummated love for his sister can thus be read as Duras's wish to advance heterosexually beyond the 'juvenilia' of *Ah! Ernesto*, especially if we bear in mind the homosexual ramifications of the name Ernesto which also identifies the sixteen-year-old hero of Umberto Saba's unfinished gay novel, *Ernesto* (1975) (translated and published in French in 1978 by Editions du Seuil).[7]

Finally, during one unforeseen moment in *Chine*, Thanh, the Siamese orphan and family servant, kisses the young girl (*elle*) on the lips and reveals that her brother Paulo (the 'different child') is also an object of his love. The girl replies that she already knew this (p. 206) and Thanh's admission is immediately transformed into a very different, but far more acceptable, statement of male intimacy: Thanh and *elle*'s lover, the Chinaman, agree to come together to mourn their shared love for her once she has departed and abandoned them (p. 207).

We could continue in the same vein and track down further instances of Duras's double-edged engagement with gay subjects and themes in her non-Minuit work. I want, however, to focus in this chapter on a form of Duras's textual 'outside' where the issues of contemporary gay authorship and influence are much more explicitly addressed. I am referring to the articles, interviews, even mock-interviews, which did not find their way into the published collections of Duras's journalism, and which reveal a positively sollicitous desire on her part for contact with contemporary gay writers, even to the point of actively promoting them. How 'positive', exactly, is this desire? Moreover, how long can Duras remain on the 'outside' without resorting to the heterosexual comforts of *écriture courante*? My aim in posing these questions is not simply to establish a pro- or anti-gay basis to Durasian textuality but rather to develop the notion of intertextual erotics which we explored in Chapter 4. By examining the rhetorical ways in which Duras negotiates both gay textuality and gay sexuality we will be better placed to determine the reasons for the figuration within her Minuit corpus of sexually precarious, even deathly, intertextual male 'others', or *'pères manqués'* (Proust, Barthes, Laughton, etc.). Let us begin with Duras's stunning 1987 interview with Denis Belloc in *Libération* on the publication of his first novel, *Néons*.

THE VOYAGE OUT

'L'exacte exactitude de Denis Belloc',[8] an interview edited by Duras herself, is by turns comic and perverse, and dotted with barbed criticisms, provocations and nonsequiturs. The standard roles of gay man and liberated woman often appear reversed (Belloc: 'I don't love men . . .', Duras: 'I love them') and bizarre sequences of circular nonsense are recorded. Take the following exchange: Duras: 'The book is there, startling, magnificent, as the truth always is. And that's the main thing.' Belloc: 'There are some unfortunate people who have not done the urinals'. Duras: 'There are also those people who do the urinals and who have not done your book. There are also those rich people who have done neither the urinals nor your book.'[9] Such jesting is only an appetiser for the final bravura paragraph, a major rhetorical display of hyperbole and inversion signed majestically by a self-troping, transformative chiasmus. Duras states:

Realism has for a long time seemed an out-of-date militantism, a demagogi-
cal truism, perhaps a little the slang of the left. In your book, it becomes a
rigorously personal and inimitable position, it belongs to you, it is of you.
And you are not responsible for it—coming as it does out of your body—
any more than you were before the book. All one can do is to consign certain
things . . . This book that one cannot leave once started, and which seems to
be about your story, is, in fact, about everybody, but counted out one by
one; about all those of the major minorities and all those of the minor
majorities, but counted out one by one [*mais un par un dénombrés, sur tous
ceux des minorités majeures et sur tous ceux des majorités mineures, mais
un par un dénombrés*].[10]

What is Duras doing here with Belloc? By reducing his autobiographical fiction to a realism for which he is not even 'responsible', and by
purposely ignoring the renaissance of his alter ego in *Néons* and that
character's determination to escape on his own terms the nightmare
world of prostitution, she is, in effect, desublimating the full story of
his passage to artistic creativity. Indeed, at the very moment that
Duras appears to be identifying with Belloc's bodily writing and its
often graphic portrayal of the late 1960s Parisian bas-monde,
complete with 'eddies of fucking' and 'shit, piles of dirt in which to
forget oneself' (p. 118), etc., she is essentially troping over it, erasing
rhetorically its creases of genuine complexity and ambiguity through
recourse to a neat binary equation (minority/majority). In the process,
Néons is rendered a dull, literary stereotype, as 'commonplace' as its
publisher, Lieu Commun. Hence, a simple publicist's trick of compression has been sharpened into an efficient weapon of repression. A
little later, in her review in *Libération* of Belloc's second book,
Suzanne, also published by Lieu Commun and dedicated to Duras,[11]
she will go one step further. 'Denis Belloc, la nuit sociale' not only
reinvents the interview form as an imaginary tango between the first
and second person (*vous*), so destroying any idea of verisimilitude,
but it also reformulates the decisive chiasmus of 'L'exacte exactitude'
as elevated intertextual play between titles: 'L'exacte exactitude / . . .
Denis Belloc' / 'Denis Belloc / la nuit sociale'. Finally, in a self-
fascinated meditation on her own handiwork, Duras closes her
review-article of this 'staggering' novel with an appropriate citation
from the mother, Suzanne: ' "I am a mender: I know how to clean
everything, all will be like nickel" '.[12]

Duras's treatment of Belloc highlights in spectacular fashion the
negative force of the chiastic strategies of intertextual sublimation
that we have seen operating in her Minuit work where 'Great Men'
are always inverted and remade. Yet it also poses a new question:

Belloc is positioned by Duras in 'L'exacte exactitude' against an anonymous, male '*eux*', defined as 'the latrines of literature, the fattest misogynists'. What precisely is the purpose of this figuration of an abject Other, and how important is it for the success of Duras's engagement with her 'outside', male others? In search of a possible answer, let us turn to Duras's earlier experience with new writers, her 1986 interview with Gérard Meudal in *Libération* entitled 'Les outsiders de Marguerite Duras', where she publicises her 'Outside' series for POL and its two new additions of 'unlimited writing', Catherine de Richaud's *Monsieur le chevalier* and Jean-Pierre Ceton's *Rapt d'amour*.[13]

In 'Les outsiders' Duras compares her two young authors, both previously turned down by other publishers, to other 'prose poets' such as Louis-René des Forêts and Michel Leiris, her choice of comparison demonstrating, as in the case of Belloc, that she is not concerned primarily with having her current work duplicated.[14] *Monsieur le chevalier* is a harsh tale of colonial life set in 1950s Morocco, reminiscent, if of anything, of Duras's earlier depiction of Indochina in *Barrage*, while Ceton's *Rapt d'amour* comprises nine, highly visual, short scenes of abortive communication and inconsequential desire. The most crucial aspect of 'Les outsiders' is the way in which Duras opposes Ceton and de Richaud to an unspecified male '*eux*' branded an unscrupulous form of social evil. Duras warns: ' "They" cannot destroy them [the two books] whatever they may do. "They" are the imponderable of evil, it is not necessary to give details. Those who are of it will recognise immediately their belonging to that microsociety which wallows in bitterness, the shrinking of the soul, the recuperation by the sum of culture, the regular exercising of evil jealousy.'[15] This is not a new idea in Duras. She had already made it clear in her preface to Henri Choukroun's 1985 polemic, *Pour une nouvelle économie de la création*, that she sees herself as part of a long and distinguished tradition of artists like Jean-Jacques Rousseau victimised by the world of publishing.[16] We have also noted en passant how her work has been imitated and misappropriated by Rambaud, Noguez, Annaud and Lindon, a list to which we can add for good measure the names of Peter Handke[17] and Gérard Lefort.[18] But the expression, 'those who are of it', has a specifically homosexual ring to it made popular by Proust in his phrase, 'ceux qui n'en sont pas' ('those who aren't . . . you know what'). While this is not the space to discuss Duras's possible fear of a gay, male conspiracy, we should remind ourselves that she often fell foul of gay or gay-related criticism. After Sollers's analysis in 1970 of *Détruire* as a failed film suspended between homosexual seduction and the analytic space,[19] she suffered Maurice Blanchot's apparent refusal to engage directly with the key issue of homosexuality during his long analysis of *Maladie* in *La communauté inavouable* (1983),[20] as well as Michel Tournier's article suggesting that the real, untold story of *Amant* is the mother's encounter with the Chinese lover (and, by implication, Duras's own 'bastard birth').[21] Moreover, Duras often found herself the target of fierce personal and political attack at the hands of gay writers. Witness Guy Hocquenghem's vitriolic castigation of her politics as symptomatic of a soft left Establishment that has sold out on its promises,[22] Angelo Rinaldi's contemptuous dismissal of 'Sublime, forcément sublime Christine V.',[23] and Renaud Camus's persistent linking of Duras and Sollers for what he sees as their shared homophobia.[24]

Duras's relaunching in 'Les outsiders' of her 'Outside' series for POL, a relatively new publishing house notable for Renaud Camus's radical gay work (e.g. *Buena Vista Park* [1980]), *Notes achriennes* [1982], *Chroniques achriennes* [1984]), reveals itself, therefore, to be not only a defiantly heterosexual, literary statement, but also a deliberate effort on her part to appropriate a position of power within the despised, gay male world of the media. Indeed, her ability to bind Ceton and de Richaud together as a 'different' ideal should be taken more as proof of her own authorial difference and identity than as an endorsement of the special uniqueness of her two young writers. This point will become more evident if we recall Duras's original, traumatic encounter with Ceton on the occasion of his first novel, *Rauque la ville* (Minuit, 1981). In her two-page preface to the novel later included in *Outside* (pp. 263–64) and already a premonition of her rhetorical approach towards Belloc, Duras confessed to being ravished by Ceton's free-style, 'incomparable' writing and his seemingly unstoppable, matter-of-fact account of urban, bisexual *errance*. Alone in her room, speechless and 'paralysed', she praised the unique and seductively 'innocent' novel in such hyperbolic terms that it began to resemble one of its characters, the loner figure, Leyo, whose death haunts the narrative ('it [the novel] is alone in the midst of the world'). At the same time, however, in a text-book illustration of the Longinus sublime, Duras identified 'body and soul' with the power of *Rauque la ville*, imitating Ceton's breathless style in order to install herself as the novel's creator ('a pain as penetrating as if I had written it [the novel] myself' [*Outside*, p. 263]). Her rhetorical hold was further extended by an insistent use of repetition ('to love, to grow, to laugh, laugh, to love', etc.), affectations of stylistic clumsiness ('lieux . . . où ne faire rien' ['places . . . to do nothing']), and finally, as she imagined the novel's critical reception, by an astonishing and necessarily imperfect event of chiastic inversion: 'Il [*Rauque la ville*] sera donc à la fois haï et adoré, adoré et brûlé' [*Outside*, p. 264] ('It will be both hated and adored, adored and burned').

Yet despite its muscular power and virtuosity, Duras's preface did not succeed in fully containing Ceton's singular 'immensity' and thus restoring her own equilibrium. This may account for why she wrote a short piece immediately afterwards entitled 'Pour Jean-Pierre Ceton, les yeux verts' (*Yeux*, pp. 85–86), where the 'other state' of *Rauque la ville* is personified as 'our sister, our twin', 'so young . . . so beautiful, with her white skin, her green eyes' (p. 86). The level of idealisation achieved here can be measured by the black and white still on page 84 of a resplendent Seyrig from Duras's first film, *La musica*. Shot in close-up and wearing a wide, open-necked blouse, Seyrig stares out of frame to the right and faces head-on the text of 'Pour Jean-Pierre Ceton', her eyes providing a focus for the 'white skin' of *Rauque la ville*'s formless, whirlwind activity which is thereby reshaped into an exclusive, male-female relationship.

Hence, Duras's formal pairing of Ceton and de Richaud in 'Les outsiders', where it is de Richaud with her *Monsieur* le *Chevalier* who assumes the active role, represents merely the culmination of a long and typically involved process of Durasian inversion and intertextual fantasy, one which confirms the extraordinary limits to which she will go in order to effect literary sublimation. For while appearing, as with Belloc, to identify with, and even promote, Ceton's unique, 'outside' writing, Duras is actually protecting herself against the feelings of loss it occasions in her by 'crossing' over it rhetorically. Such a calibrated transformation of an explosive other lacking fixed gender or genre into an intertextual (POL) other—and by October 1980 Ceton was already interviewing Duras for France-Culture[25]—is facilitated, no doubt, by the fact that, although swaying to the noise of the 'ocean city', *Rauque la ville* depicted a bisexual desire that could be remoulded without too much difficulty into the tighter structures of heterosexual fantasy. What matters, as always in Duras, is that there should be some form of fantasy, or a fantasy of form, familial and intertextual, which amounts to the same thing. In fact, bonding of the kind that exists between Ceton and Seyrig/de Richaud is a common sight in Duras's later non-Minuit work. In *Vie mat.*, for example, Michelet's *La Sorcière* (1862) and Woolf's *A Room of One's Own* (1929) are proposed as Duras's only true library (pp. 53–54), while in a 1985 article on reading for *L'Autre Journal*, Racine and Madame de Lafayette are hastily married in a ritual of heterosexual give-and-take ('He withdraws, she receives . . .').[26] Again, it is the female writer who assumes the upper hand, de Lafayette performing Durasian passage twice over: '[s]he chooses to be on top of the flow [*le passage*] of information as it leaves the Court, and also on top of its flow when it returns'. This event takes place, as in 'L'exacte exactitude' and 'Les outsiders', against the backdrop of a chaotic, and undifferentiated, gay '*eux*': the hapless '*entremetteurs*', or 'go-betweens', loitering not so mysteriously inside the Tuileries gardens.

We see now how far Duras has travelled since the days of the early 1970s when she claimed to belong with Genet and des Forêts to a trio of marginal 'outsiders' lacking a theory of the novel.[27] For with Belloc and Ceton she is now the 'insider' turning her own outsiders *in*. With her ever-keen eye for what can be sublimated (and so desublimated), she is constructing an Outside of gay and gay-related textual influence that can always be put 'straight' rhetorically by being cast against an even greater, abject body of '*eux*', at once unreadable and untropable because totally unerotic (the wicked 'microsociety', the 'latrines of literature', etc.). Seen in terms of the Duras corpus as a whole, this circumscribed Outside of young male writers—let us call them 'Outsider-sons'—functions as a spectacular decoy to deflect over-prying eyes from the intertextual passions of her Minuit work. Yet it also adds a necessary touch of perversity to *écriture courante*, similar to that described in 'Le dernier client' in *Vie mat.*, (pp. 17–19) where the narrator's account of her mother's funeral is sandwiched between descriptions of the violent sex she performs with an unnamed stranger. Duras's permanently desired gay Other is thus merely the facilitating 'nickel' in a series of 'inside' acts of textual purification so consistent and regular that even the physical appearance of *Outside* changes from its original, wild, Albin Michel cover—gleaming turquoise striped in blood-red lettering—to the bleached, black, grey and white formula favoured by POL.

Belloc and Ceton replace Duras's previous court of gay writers and interpreters that numbered Yves Navarre, Renaud Camus (now in open revolt),[28] and Isi Beller, whose sexual analysis of the orgasmic 'black zone' in *Vancouver* she approved of, albeit with reservations (see pp. 48–50 above). They should not, however, be confused with Duras's other list of angels and martyrs that includes Daney (who died of an AIDS-related illness in 1992),[29] the actress, Pascale Ogier (who died tragically in 1984 at the age of 24),[30] the film-maker Jacques Tati,[31] the footballer Michel Platini,[32] and the lawyer and writer, Thierry Lévy.[33] This is because they are now endowed with a name, '*l'homme tremblant*', a term Duras coined during her 1980 interview in *Cahiers du Cinéma* with the film-maker Elia Kazan to describe Montgomery Clift in Kazan's 1960 film, *Wild River*. If, in the words of Kazan, Clift was a 'tragic man', a gay actor destroyed by a homophobic industry, in *Wild River* he can at least, according to Duras, participate in a scene with Lee Remick where, like Belloc with Duras and Ceton with Seyrig, he 'passes', however falteringly, for a heterosexual lover. He may indeed represent a 'new state of man', a sexual complicity 'always new because always hazardous, never definite, wandering . . . the closest to desire' (*Yeux*, p. 203), but, as is made clear by the illustration for 'L'homme tremblant', where Clift kneels down to be cradled by Remick, the reason for his 'major seduction' lies more in his eminently malleable gentleness. Clift, Belloc, Ceton: all Duras's *hommes tremblants* are handed a special contract which could not be more simple, and it is one which Duras unveiled in her preface to *L'Histoire de France* (1991), a book of 'untranslatable, irreversible' images of oblique detail by the 'savage' American photographer, Ralph Gibson. She proposes to Gibson, but it could just as easily be Belloc or Ceton: '[y]ou should make me a book and I would write about the unknown in the world and you'.[34]

Not all Duras's gay male others are so tremulous, of course. In her extraordinary 1988 interview in *Globe* with Pierre Bergé, 'Duras est SEXY!', Duras confronted an out-gay man who could not be more influential, being not only one of the richest men in France (he was, at the time, *Globe*'s principal backer and managing director of the House of Yves Saint Laurent) but also a close confidant of Mitterrand. Bergé offered Duras a rich selection of gay French writers including Genet, Aragon and Violette Leduc. She was not impressed by any— Genet is singled out in particular on account of the pure 'bluff' of his sexual exhibitionism—and instead repeated her long-held admiration for de Lafayette and Racine. Their work, she explained, is erotic due to its very pudeur. By the end of the interview she proposed her own literary model, Louise Labé, whose poetry was 'doubled' by the presence of another woman (Clémence de Bourges) chosen by Labé as her first reader. Duras's reading knowingly ignores the many sexual ambiguities surrounding the Labé legend and asks us simply to admire the poet's success in satisfying a normal, human need to feel 'more self-assured, calmer and reasonable'.

Duras's reversal of the opening premise of 'Duras est SEXY!'—i.e. powerful business-man with literary pretensions meets 'difficult' female writer to discuss sex and gay culture (the interview is advertised on *Globe*'s front-cover as: 'Duras the hard-core version. "Mitterrand, Genet and an historic wank" ')—was sealed by the third and final photograph by Alain Duplantier accompanying the text. Here, after previously presenting herself alone in monochrome close-up as forbiddingly Hard, Duras now offered herself in colour as ideally Soft, the precocious daughter of Bergé whose paternal, corporate hand rests awkwardly on top of her left shoulder. While she dominates the foreground and stares impassively at the camera, he is consigned to the shadowed area behind her, as impotent as the man she discusses during the interview who gravitated towards her body at an official reception for the sole purpose of masturbating. Paradoxically, then, Bergé found himself enrolled in Duras's family of 'trembling' sons. A year later, she even recuperated Bergé's gay identity, writing the preface to a book on his former lover, Yves Saint Laurent, in which she lauds the designer for 'possessing' the female form so that women might be 'reborn'![35] (This is all the more ironic when one considers that in an earlier article on contemporary sexual mores Duras held a perceived gay male 'slant' in fashion as partly responsible for the current dearth of (of all things) Chanel clones and the corresponding increase of 'less beautiful', androgynous women, 'dressed too wide, their bodies lost'.[36])

The figural logic of Duras's strategy of pseudo-identification and reappropriation dictates that the only complete rhetorical victory will occur when her Outside Other is as 'other' as it can be while still being amenable to the demands of literary sublimation. As we have seen, however, the problem for Duras is that the host text is often of an undecidable nature and demands a major display of interpretive cathexis and rhetorical might on her part, especially when, as occurs in *Emily*, her gay male interlocutor (*vous*) can suddenly proliferate for no apparent reason into 'vous tous' (p. 47). Duras's increasing unease about infinite, gay undifferentiation is well captured by Andréa in his description in *M.D.* of the visions she experienced during her detoxification treatment in 1982. These were 'bizarre beings, perhaps transsexuals . . . very small, fifty centimetres high . . . [with] a very long nose . . . who are kind and atrociously frightening' (p. 113). In fact, male transsexuality, or the desire to become The Woman, is really how Duras begins to conceive of male homosexuality during the 1980s; it is always feminine, transvestite, and, in the manner of the 'go-betweens' of 'La lecture dans le train', flagrant and intrusive. Duras argues this in *Vie mat.* by loading her terms in the form of a threat: 'the masked, invading, proclaiming, delicious transvestite, ineffable darling of every milieu' (pp. 38–39). Obsessed by the idea of sexual reconciliation, Duras's gay men can be linked to Lacan's equally misguided transsexuals who believe that by ridding them-selves of the organ, they can also be rid of the signifer which sexuates them.[37] In the case of the former, their similarly impossible identifi-cation with a *jouissance* precluded by the Symbolic means that they exist only in the abstract, their one purpose in life being a 'passion for homosexuality', their 'lover . . . native land . . . creation' (*Vie mat.*, p. 41). While the drive for a perfect duality is not limited, of course, solely to homosexuality or transsexuality, in Durasian heterosexu-ality it actually achieves the opposite effect of greatness precisely because it can never be realised: '[i]n heterosexuality there is no solution. Man and woman are irreconcilable, and it's this impossible attempt, renewed with each new love, that makes for its greatness' (*Vie mat.*, p. 40).[38]

We can perhaps best appreciate the full significance of Duras's rhetorical framing of sexual and textual difference and the degree to which it is concretely formalised and controlled if we recall that Duras once celebrated androgyny unproblematically, even in the writing of Pascal.[39] In addition, gay and ambivalently gendered intertexts were once positively inscribed in the folds of her work as a privileged source of dedifferentiated desire. In *Vice-consul*, for example, Proust, identi-fied by name, actively contributed to the insistent, swirling madness of the narrative centred around the vice-consul and Anne-Marie Stretter who 'would read in her robes, rosy reader rosy with rosy cheeks, Proust' (p. 211). A little later, in *Détruire*, Alissa suddenly and mysteriously alluded to 'the theory of Rosenfeld' (p. 123). This reference is apparently worthless, yet, in the bisexual context of the three 'destroyers' and their 'open', 'indifferent' desire, it also conjures up the psychoanalyst Arthur Rosenfeld who opposed Freud by suggesting that homosexuality be seen as a defence mechanism *against* paranoid anxiety (a view that inadvertently sparked off a 'homosexuality-is-paranoia' equation).[40] A little later, in *Nathalie Granger*, Duras linked the domestic violence of the untamable Nathalie with the news item heard intermittently on the radio of two 'killer-children' who, for no apparent reason, killed several people in the Yvelines during the summer of 1971. The fact that the boys were closely connected with a gay circle that had given them the nickname 'the killers' is never mentioned, yet the homosexual specificity of this *fait divers* is not entirely suppressed, returning at regular intervals in the form of the radio's reference to 'Whitman', transcribed in the published screenplay as 'Withman'.

Ever since her interview in 1980 with *Le Gai Pied*, however, Duras personalised her approach to gay textuality by taking Barthes as the official face of gay male influence due to his apparently flagrant disregard for women's writing.[41] Duras's hostility towards Barthes contrasts sharply with that of feminist critics such as Jane Gallop and Naomi Schor who are rightly distrustful of a 'neutral', 'indifferent' text.[42] On one level, she was clearly registering in the interview a response to Barthes's veiled attack on her in *Roland Barthes par Roland Barthes* (1975), where he accused 'M.D.' of lacking on one occasion a proper critical overview, or 'third degree'.[43] Yet the major thrust of her attack, beyond the obviously untenable and risibly homophobic idea that a male writer who has never 'touched' a woman's body is a contradiction in terms (*Vie mat.*, p. 41), was centred on the apparent timidity and weakness of Barthes's writing. In Duras's view, despite his advice in *S/Z* to 'manhandle' the tutor-text,[44] Barthes was only capable of 'a certain static, regular writing', which avoids opening up to the 'blasphemous', the 'forbidden' or the 'unknown' (*Vie mat.*, p. 41). In this respect, she finds herself curiously in agreement with the gay critic, Gregory Bredbeck, who argues that Barthes's textual pleasure imposes ony 'abrasions' on the fine surface of a 'female' text and is thus marked by a 'will to limited play'. Their reasons, naturally, are diametrically opposed, since Bredbeck faults Barthes's work precisely because it appears to validate the tropes of deferral at work in phallocentric mimesis and thus constantly presupposes the doxa of heterosexuality.[45]

I do not propose to enter here into a major debate on the differences between Barthes's 'irenic', parodic fingering of intertextual detail and Duras's own performative ironies of intertextual seduction.[46] I wish simply to suggest that Barthes's lack of interest in staging definitive, potent moments of textual passage throws into acute relief Duras's crossing over in the name of 'love' to such 'inverted' images as Belloc and Ceton, both no more than extreme versions of the standard, male comrade-in-arms ('our opposite . . . our antidote . . . our hell'[47]) of antagonistic, heterosexual desire. (It is surely no coincidence that Belloc's pose in the photograph illustrating 'L'exacte exactitude' echoes that of Barthes at his desk in *Roland Barthes* ([p. 41]). By effectively reversing Barthes's intertextual strategies, Duras is also negating all those gay and queer theories of writing which have used his work as a starting point for the notion of a gay rhetoric. I am thinking here in particular of Renaud Camus who shares Barthes's admiration for Proust's erotic 'discourse of reversal' and its cultivation of the pleasure of surprise, most notably during the final unveiling of the gay characters in the last volume of *A la recherche*. Camus has even proposed that inversion be considered, like the anagram and the palindrome, a specifically gay figure of rhetoric.[48] A little differently, Lee Edelman, working within the American poetic tradition, makes a powerful case for linking the fact of Hart Crane's homosexuality to his preference for the chiasmus, catachresis and anacoluthon rather than metaphor and synecdoche.[49] Duras's restless, chiastic tropings on the static 'mirror-image' of gay desire deny all such theoretical possibilities, performing instead what James Creech, in his analysis of the chiasmus as a 'master-trope' in some recent critical theory, has accurately termed the 'rhetorical seizure of troubling homosexual content'.[50] For however 'open' and non-binding Duras's intertextual chiasmus may appear, it still functions characteristically as the most inward-pointing of all the rhetorical figures, providing her work with a water-tight seal of textual and sexual identity that outlaws even further her chosen *tiers exclu*. This she all but admits to in *Monde* where, after again denouncing the narcissistic inertia of gay relations, she ends up arguing the case for fixed membership in the heterosexual club. In homosexual practice, she writes, there is an interchangeability of pleasure: 'one never *belongs* in homosexuality [*on n'*appartient *jamais dans l'homosexualité*] as one belongs in heterosexuality. It is this hell of not being able to escape the desire for one person that I myself call the splendour of heterosexuality' (*Monde*, p. 13).[51] In this endless game of finding the right erotic and emotional distance, of being neither too close (narcissism) nor too far (promiscuity), the only real winner is Duras.

RE-TURN PASSAGE

If we have now fully captured the strategic force of Duras's rhetorical counter-formation against a homosexual, textual 'image', we have still not yet determined why she should have constructed this Outside space of 'anti-literature' so intently and so comprehensively, beyond the obvious fact that it clearly provides a measure of textual pleasure and power. Why, after all, is it always the case that differently identified gay authors and their texts are reduced to their sexual specifics and defined in essentialist terms as the same, lacking, gay male body? Could there be a specifically gay origin, or origins, to this seemingly inexorable process? To examine these questions we are obliged to return to the period in the 1970s when Duras first began to talk of texts explicitly in terms of real bodies. In one of her interviews with Xavière Gauthier in *Parleuses* she revealed that she had just given a young male writer carte blanche to incorporate into his first novel long, unedited extracts from *Vice-consul* without any indication of their provenance. She accounted for her decision thus: 'The book [*Vice-consul*] has become like a person. It is now in the domain of this young man's imaginary . . . It must circulate' (p. 196). The young man in question is Renaud Camus, his novel, *Passage* (Flammarion, 1975). Let us examine the full implications of Duras's 'free' gift in order to see what it can reveal of the subsequent nature and development of Duras's intertextual erotics.

Passage is a multi-lingual work that quotes often verbatim up to forty authors ranging from Mallarmé to Allen Ginsberg, all listed at the back in alphabetical order and described as constituting over a quarter of the novel's contents. Two sections of miscellaneous illustrations culled from art, photography, cartoons and film-stills are also presented. In a blurring of the usual distinctions between textual irony and parody, all the cited fragments, and in particular those of *Vice-consul*, are repeated, reversed or ruptured. With text and image in such convulsion, clean moments of chiastic inversion of the kind we have just witnessed with Belloc and Ceton cannot take place. Each paragraph runs 'indifferently' into the next, the pre-texts being assembled, according to the back-cover, 'in view of a passage through a text-machine'. The effect is one of a self-reflexive *mise en texte* that is both process and its result, punctuated by bizarre moments of grammar (e.g.: 'Puis je se lève . . .' [p. 12], as opposed to: 'Puis je me lève'). In one case, Duras's novel is brought into close contact with Sand's *Indiana* (1832) on the level of the signifier in such a way that both works are flattened. For instance, the vice-consul's musical score, *Indiana's Song*, is transformed into 'the song of Indiana' before becoming simply the title of Sand's novel, *Indiana*. In addition, Duras's female protagonist, Anne-Marie Stretter, renamed Ann-Mary Straighter, is mocked and her 'straightness' exposed. The caption for plate number 9, a pornographic image of a male nude, returns us to a paragraph from page 125 which reads: '[t]he text does not cease designating the laws of its own functioning, all the better to contradict them immediately they are formulated. Ann-Mary Straighter is not swayed by this duplicity.'[52] Meanwhile, the sequestered 'Whites' of *Vice-consul* are forced into contact with the indigenous population which eventually wipes them out in a massacre.

The topsy-turvy chaos of Camus's *Passage* is, among its many achievements, a tour de force desublimation of Duras's *Vice-consul*, which, despite being an avowedly avant-garde experiment in textual transgression, had clearly not gone far enough in terms of sexuality and gender. The eponymous, outlawed character, 'Jean-Marc de H.', is finally outed as the emblem of a homosexuality that was always latent in the novel yet misdirected into erratic acts of sadism (firing 'on to Calcutta', for instance). The character now brings renown to the toilets of the French embassy (p. 107)! As for the resident writer of *Vice-consul*, Peter Morgan, he is confused here with a certain Peter Walsh, rescued, we suppose, from his wasted adulthood in Woolf's *Mrs. Dalloway* (1925) and diverted outside into a garden where acts of fellatio and anal intercourse are regularly being performed by three young transvestites. The narrator explains: 'In order for the tape [*la bande*: tape, group, erection] to continue it would be necessary . . . to introduce a new coin into the machine sucking his sex' (p. 109). In this primal scene of writing, the destabilised narrator penetrates texts as surely as he is 'plugged into' from behind like the deterritorialised, transindividual 'desiring machines' of Deleuze and Guattari's 'anti-Oedipal' desire.[53] For this reason, *Passage* enacts on a textual level the same radical risk of male self-dismissal that Bersani views as unique to gay sexuality,[54] one where extreme, narcissistic self-absorption may be viewed as only 'the last desperate effort to resolve a grave doubt

. . . the doubt about which self to adore'.[55] It is as though Duras had suddenly found herself absorbed into a generalised, anonymous site of male loss over which she has ultimately no control. Like the anonymous *elle* who is obliged to perform a rite of passage (p. 161), she has unwittingly become an agent of 'gay passage', forced into intertextual/intersexual liaisons with George Sand 'dressed up as a man, with soft cigars in her mouth' (p. 162). Polyphonic textuality here is polymorphous desire, a sustained *perturbation* of intertextual self-shattering and fusion. As the epigraph of *Passage* commands: 'Giocate, giocate pure . . .'.

Duras's later commitment to defining clear spaces of literature and 'anti-literature' in the interests of sexual/textual desire can be read on one level, therefore, as part of a deliberate strategy to avoid the implications and repercussions of Camus's 'abysmal', libidinal economy. For having been 'inserted' into the transvestite desire of the homosexual Other of *Passage*—a text which contributes to a long, modern tradition of homoerotic (mis)appropriations and subversions of heterosexual romantic love (Wilde, Gide, Woolf, Gertrude Stein, Barthes, etc.)—[56] Duras was, in her Minuit work, systematically reclaiming her warped textual identity by means of an ironically controlled, heterosexual erotics of literary montage which, as we have seen throughout this study, always emphasises the gap between (heterosexual) text and (homosexual) image. *Emily*, to take only the most obvious case, appears to write over Camus's text by reworking key elements from Sand's *Indiana* which also posits foreignness, betrayal and doubling (even the possibility of a suicide pact) as possible ways to survive the rigours of love. Indiana and Sir Ralph are the doomed English couple of *Emily* who act as a screen on which *je* and *vous* project their imaginary powers, correcting in the process the errors and excesses of Emily L.'s (i.e. Indiana's) frenetic passion. In fact, all Duras's stagings of textual difference can be viewed as a form of rhetorical troping on the kinds of sexual oscillation and fluid indeterminacy found in other texts such as *La petite Fadette* (1848) and the multi-(male)voiced *Lettres d'un Voyageur* (1834–36), manifestations of what one critic has called Sand's 'bisextuality'.[57] After all, Duras's intertextual Third is not a new, third, unclassifiable sex but rather a powerful, because temporarily unstable, eroticised text which ensures the boundaries of sexual difference. *Emily*'s neutralising of the very real lesbian threat posed by Miss Fellowes in Huston's *The Night of the Iguana*—she and her female coach-load of tourists are simply transformed into a passing band of Korean men—is only the most visible aspect of this intertextual process of heteroerotic recuperation.

In short, *Passage*'s muddy waters of undifferentiation are reprojected by Duras as an external immobilised *trans*, whether that be—to take only the most lurid example from Duras's Minuit margins—*Eté*'s suspended image of the dying Proust, or the indefinable, abject, gay '*eux*' stalking her Outside. This perfectly formatted flux of otherness parodies Barthes's always dutiful referencing of sources and it allows *écriture courante*—Duras's Inside—to assume all the greater mobility. Two ideas that Duras had once viewed as totally irreconcilable—Bataille's anonymous *indifférence* and Genettian *différence*[58] —have thus been effectively collapsed into a single movement. This transfantasmatic, intertextual, gay Other functions a little like Alexandre's all-encompassing discourse in Tournier's *Les météores* (1975), i.e. as a 'homotext' in which all difference is accounted for and yet which must be finally annulled in order for the non-negotiable otherness of some form of heterotextuality finally to emerge.[59] Whereas this paves the way in Tournier for a playful theory of imitation and the fake, in Duras it constitutes part of an intense and unending struggle for (hetero)sexual identity. Even the strange pairing of Racine—a Camus 'text-machine' and Barthesian cause célèbre— with de Lafayette—a writer Barthes freely admits to never having read[60]—may be read as an attempt by Duras to reinvest and 'crystallise' romantically the diffuse sexuality of *Passage*.

For all these reasons, Duras's discursive strategies of reappropriation and sublimation do little more than subscribe to a rhetorical tradition of difference which installs the gay man as a point of impossibility within the system, i.e. as its 'other face'. A glance at the recent work of Edelman on the rhetorical inscription of the homosexual within Western discourse, which he terms 'homographesis', can help to place Duras's work in proper context.[61] Taking as an exemplary case Otto Preminger's 1944 film, *Laura*, a murder mystery illustrating Hollywood's obsessive preoccupation with faces, Edelman argues that a constitutively defensive masculinity projects 'the intolerable face of the faceless, specularly fixated, and mother-identified male, on to a specific category of person against whom it then can define and defend itself' (p. 237). A paradox is thus created: 'The gay male body . . . must be *marked and indeterminate* at once; consequently, it is imagined to be marked *as* indeterminate with the result that indeterminacy effectively ceases to *be* indeterminate and becomes, instead, the gay male body's determining mark' (p. 237). As we have seen, Duras's Outsiders allow her specifically to 'project' the inevitable indeterminacy and undifferentiation of the (inter)textual process by positing an intertextual 'face' to embody and so reject it, even if that face is the very facelessness of promiscuous gay sexuality itself. The use of Seyrig's eyes in *Yeux* to focus a response to Ceton's textual 'trembling' reveals both the need and value of this trope, and it is one to which Duras naturally turns when she wishes to depict the state of the French right (Jean-Marie le Pen, leader of the Front National, has, like all gay men, 'death in his eyes' [*Monde*, pp. 32–33]). The gleaming white physical appearance of Duras's POL texts functions in similar fashion as a pure 'cover' for the blue, black and white fantasies of her Minuit project.

The logical conclusion to all Duras's experiments in outsiderhood, intertextual reclamation and sublimation is *Yann*, published by POL in 1992, for here she goes one step further by troping on her own rhetorical practice. At first glance, *Yann* appears to be an archetypal Outside text, even acting as a gay meeting ground. Ceton is referred to by name and in connection with the editor of *Outside* whom the narrator addresses thus: 'Yann Andréa, I met someone that summer whom you know, Jean-Pierre Ceton. We spoke of you. I could not have guessed that you knew each other' (pp. 9–10).[62] The text also repeats key elements from *Vie mat.*, including the narrator's dismissal of Barthes's suspect brilliance, her account of Yann's letter-writing in advance of his arrival at Trouville, and, on a formal level, *Vie mat.*'s style of discrete textual segments. Even when *Yann* replays episodes from Duras's previous Minuit work, for instance, the story of the monitor and the young boy in *Eté* and the dialogue between *je* and *vous* on the plight of their love affair in *Emily*, it does so with a recognisable, 'outside' difference. The monitor of *Eté* now has a name (Jeanne Goldberg), and the discordant sexual desire of *Emily* is effectively consummated, as the narrator relates with wonderfully narcissistic aplomb ('you told me that I had an unbelievably young body' [p. 31]).

Yet *Yann* is unlike any other POL text that bears Duras's name because it is working from the outside in.[63] As in a typical Duras Minuit text, there are plenty of named, decoy intertexts, although these are now mainly Duras's own (e.g. *Yeux bleus*). The only other author mentioned is George Orwell, signposted early on, and in most unsubtle fashion, as 'G.O., the English writer' (p. 45). As for a fully performative, intertextual other, the narrator is enjoined by *vous* to elaborate on a text which can be identified by the name of its protagonist. 'Théodora' is a short, three-page extract from an unpublished novel by Duras called *Théodora* and which constituted the last chapter of *Outside* (pp. 293–95), where it was prefaced with a brief statement by Duras to the effect that the novel was 'unfinishable'. 'Théodora' is certainly an unusual piece of Duras prose: a male narrator, 'T.', encounters a certain Jacques in a hotel as he goes to meet his lover, Theodora. The reader senses a temporary confusion in sex and gender reminiscent of Théophile Gautier's 1835 novel, *Mademoiselle de Maupin*, where, at one point (Chapter 16), Théodore/Madeleine realises the bisexual potential of her androgyny by visiting in quick succession the rooms of d'Albert and Rosette. What 'Théodora' ultimately offers is the discrepancy between a set of male doubles and an affair between a man and a woman destroying itself in casual indifference and over-familiarity (p. 295). The text peters out with a description of nudity and discordant speech intensified by threatening sounds emanating from outside (p. 295).

Like a typical Duras Minuit text, *Yann* resolves the heterosexual crisis of 'Théodora''s 'outside' tendencies through recourse to an impressively foreign other: the war-time story of an English woman, Théodora Kats, as provided by the Germanist (Duras's term), Georges-Arthur Goldschmidt.[64] In fact, what makes *Yann* so compelling despite its effect of déjà vu is the patent gleefulness of its intertextual heteroerotics. Here is how the narrator describes the desire she shares with Yann for Théodora (Greek for 'God's gift'): 'We were nourished by the child-like body of Théodora Kats, that frail body, its bright eyes' (p. 30). Naturally, *je* is in complete control of her literary creation ('I have done my best to recreate the phenomenon of the station . . . it has happened again' [p. 48][65]), and as soon as Théodora is fully dressed and made up, she is peremptorily dispatched, 'dead as alive, dead' (p. 48). Indeed, as *Yann*'s 'immaculate white' double blank, ThéOdOra is hollowed out in a game of self-conscious excess and falseness that outstrips even Rambaud's earlier pastiche of Duras, *Virginie Q. de Marguerite Duraille*. The final play on 'trop' ('TROP. Trop peu' [pp. 137–38]), repeating as it does the cover's upper/lower case dialectic, is matched by the queasy campiness of Théodora's blanched, cancer-ridden body waiting eternally for the train to Auschwitz under the protective gaze of a station-master. Most astonishing of all is the scene of naming promised by the title. After a typical Durasian moment of imaginary compression—'I brought them both back [Jeanne, the boy] just as I do you, out of the sea and the wind, and I enclosed them in this dark room lost above time. That which I call The Room of the Jews'[66]—*vous* is eventually reborn by association with Théodora as a Jewish husband: 'Yann Andréa Steiner'. This remarkable sleight of hand represents the summation of all Duras's tropings on sexuality as heterosexual form, for with it she has formally rewritten her homosexually-encoded Outside as the very Inside of personal, heterosexual, Minuit fantasy.

We see, then, that the later history of Duras's publishing itself constitutes a narrative achievement. Her outside, intertextual margins, comprising works published by POL and Gallimard and embodied by writers such as Belloc and Ceton, are finally sublimated as the very centre of her textual practice. This highly aggressive rhetorical approach to contemporary gay writing and influence reveals that textual and sexual alterity in Duras's literary work must always conform to a predetermined and essentialist image of undifferentiation, and that a self-styled, ethical 'heteroerotics' is really no more than an aesthetic practice of appropriation and recuperation.

Yet what happens when Duras is no longer dealing simply with 'trembling' texts, or even intertexts fantasised as real, but rather with living, in particular, female others? Can she fashion a political 'passage' with the same command that she has exerted over the image, intertext and gay man? Furthermore, can she afford to be so cavalier when it comes to the more everyday reality of current affairs and contemporary French politics? In short, is there a Duras political sublime? These questions we shall explore in Chapter 6 where we examine the rhetorical workings of Duras's media work and her public persona, beginning with perhaps her most famous, if not infamous, intervention, 'Marguerite Duras: sublime, forcément sublime Christine V.'.

CHAPTER 6

Sublime, forcément sublime Marguerite D.?
Sex, Lies, and Politics in the Real

Qu'est-ce que c'est cette route parallèle, cette trahison fondamentale de tous et de soi?

(M. Duras)

On 16 October 1984, the body of a four-year old boy, Grégory Villemin, was found washed up along the banks of the river Vologne in the Vosges region of north-west France. He had been murdered. On the 273rd day of what became known as 'L'affaire Grégory', and with the boy's mother, Christine, still incarcerated on charges of infanticide, *Libération* published 'Marguerite Duras: sublime, forcément sublime Christine V.'. This three-page article by Duras was prefaced by a short note from the editor who had commissioned it, Serge July, in which, as if to preempt hostile criticism, he defended her right to stage publicly Man's *'part maudite'* as part of the natural 'transgression of writing'.[1] As it turned out, the article was almost unanimously attacked by feminists including Simone Signoret and Benoîte Groult who viewed it as a scandalous contravention of the acceptable limits of literature in the name of sisterhood,[2] citing in particular Duras's statement: 'What would have made Christine V. a criminal is a secret common to all women'. In a letter addressed to Duras and subsequently published in *Libération*, Nelcya Delanoë inveighed against the 'fantasmatic arbitrariness' of a writer expressing herself publicly in order to make an 'innocent criminal' out of a woman who had not yet been put on trial.[3] And a year later, in *Esprit*, Paul Thibaud, mindful of the general history of French intellectuals defending the damned (Zola in the Dreyfus affair of 1898, for example), ascribed to a Camusian romanticism dating from the Liberation Duras's tendency to oppose every law with the rights automatically 'granted' by suffering.[4]

115

The most substantial critical response to 'Sublime', a joint article by David Amar and Pierre Yana published in the *Revue des sciences humaines*, is, however, much more favourable towards Duras, and it makes some powerful claims.[5] Linking 'Sublime' with Barthes's famous article in *Mythologies* on the 'Dominici affair' of 1952,[6] Amar argues that it serves to reveal the real stakes of a public affair and could even signal a future community of reconciliation. Yana offers a more sober reading of 'Sublime' which falls in line with recent approaches to the Duras corpus: by blurring the distinction between fact and fiction (Christine V. is a Duras heroine in the Lol V. Stein mould), Duras's article becomes a text of tragedy yet supplies no statement of guilt necessary for catharsis. Rather, Christine V., whose body was apparently violated by her husband, opens up an irreversible wound in Duras's fragmented and melancholic textual body which cannot be healed. According to Yana, Duras's article accompanies Christine V.'s 'crime' in its exploration of the materiality of *'le pire'*. But can the aims of Duras and Christine V. be so easily collapsed together to form a 'double', female discourse'? And what exactly is the status of the 'real' and the 'sublime' in 'Sublime'? To answer these questions and thus determine the precise nature of Duras's textual relations with real others, we are obliged to enter fully into the article's syntax and rhetorical structures.

Perhaps the most striking feature of 'Sublime' is its remarkably mobile range of subject and object positions, including *on*, *eux*, *ils*, *vous*, *elle*, *elles* and *nous*. *On*, for example, refers variously to the media, the judiciary and 'the murderers', while *nous* first signifies the *Libération* team working with Duras before developing into a strictly female identification between the narrator and Christine V. articulated thus: 'Innocent Christine V., who perhaps killed without knowing as I write without knowing'. As the article progresses, however, and its hypotheticals and oxymorons acquire an insistent, rhetorical force ('Who knows?' 'Why?'), the idea that Christine must have killed her son becomes an overwhelming certainty. The logic goes like this: because Christine V. experienced such a bad pregnancy, and because she had already endured such a brutalising marriage, she had no other choice but to kill Grégory. The suffering of her life was cancelled out by the very pain she felt in executing the deed. How could she be guilty except in the eyes of a male judiciary which upholds 'the law of the couple made by man'?

If Duras, as self-styled *voyante*, appears here to be defending her heroine's female nature against an indiscriminate but always discriminatory *on* (the recurring 'on dit') so as to establish a new 'intelligence' of the crime 'beyond the bounds of reason', she is nonetheless invoking Villemin as Christine V. all the better to silence her. Even Villemin's own account of her actions is exposed by the narrator for its 'errors' and moments of carelessness (the fact, for example, that Villemin first went to look for Grégory in the place he was least likely to be, at the home of his nurse over a kilometre away). In fact, the process of identification reveals itself to be a trick of distancing and substitution, for once Christine V. has violated 'Sublime' as an unknowable absence or void, she is then voided of her own crime, and in spectacularly convoluted fashion. The narrator declares: 'From the moment that, in the particular situation she was in of having to commit this crime, no-one could have avoided it, guilty she was not' (p. 6).[7] Amar remarks at this point that such a parody of judicial discourse divests Christine V. of individuality and gender, therefore rendering her experience of pain universal.[8] Yet what we are witnessing in this inverted sentence is more a public instance of Duras's use of form both to crystallise the essentials of her argument and to reverse them, all the time drawing the reader (or viewer) into an ironic awareness of his/her own stake in the process. The sentence is typically chiastic in nature, hinging on the 'criminal but not guilty' conceit which underlies the entire article and which requires us, if it is to work at all, to read a pronoun ('le') as a noun ('le crime'), i.e. 'personne n'aurait pu l'éviter, coupable elle n'a pas été' ('no-one could have avoided / it [the crime], / guilty / she was not'). We are, of course, compelled to make this syntactical move and let the sentence cross over itself, the result being that the crime is now directly juxtaposed with the idea of guilt, and Christine V., guilty by association, is linked precisely with 'no-one' ('personne . . . elle n'a pas été').

This double emphasis on *elle*'s negativity means that Christine can now be totally 'deserted'. The narrator states: 'There is no-one in this crime, it's a desert like the bare hill' (the accompanying photographs by Pierre-Olivier Deschamps of the Villemin home and a country lane record a complete lack of human presence, living or dead). It also paves the way for the narrator's effortless take-over of her victim's voice. For the imagined thoughts of an 'ordinary' person are brutally rendered in direct speech, a pale echo of *je*'s own mediated and rhetorical language and one which reduces Villemin's story to the level of a courtroom soap-opera. The narrator imagines the scene: 'If she shouted I think it would be like this: "*Let everybody around me die, my new child, my husband, me, but guilty as the Law would have it I will never be*" ' (original emphasis).[9] The text's inexorable contraction of *nous* to *je* is emphasised a little later in a telling typographical error of grammatical agreement between noun and verb: 'd'autres gens n'aurait-il pas été "*supprimés*" . . .?' (original emphasis) ('would not other person have been "*suppressed*" . . .?'), before being ironically reversed by the escalating number of deaths now involved (we are told that Villemin's traumatised daughter may actually constitute a fourth 'murder' after those of her son and brother—'that other crime'—and the arrest of her husband).

It is not so much, then, that the narrator has repeated the alleged crime of infanticide by means of a doubling discourse, rather that she has inverted it by committing a textual version of matricide. In a twisted double movement, Christine V. has been 'rescued' from the silence of a case that was sub iudice, only to be compelled to speak as a representative of the criminal subclass of child-killers. The aesthetic gains of this textual manoeuvre satisfy the narrator's textual desire more successfully than Christine V.'s own, apparently short-lived feelings of fulfilment after seeing her husband arrested. For if Christine V. could desire again a man whose 'abominable pain' she has just created, one equal to the misery he had caused her ('it [*elle*] [*la douleur*] has rendered all misfortune equal'), the narrator, for her part, can sustain a higher level of erotics through her dialogue with the implied reader, *vous*, a pronoun which also denotes the judges (as opposed to 'la justice' [*'elle'*]). Only one true crime can be committed and it is rhetorical. Having been scissored into by the lure of a female real, 'Sublime' finally enjoys the pleasure of sewing itself up by doubling and reversing Christine's 'V.' into an anonymous X.

As such, Duras's Medea-like 'deification' of Villemin displays none of the ethical concerns raised by Barthes at the unhealthy, mythological collusion between French literature and the French justice system. Indeed, Duras appears to be doing almost exactly what Barthes attacked the judge, police and prosecution in the Dominici trial for doing, i.e. taking into the courtroom a Realist 'literature of repletion' based on a universal (bourgeois) language and articulated in the form of classical rhetoric (antithesis, metaphor, etc.) (Duras will later talk in *Au-delà des pages* of the 'sumptuous' beauty of 'Sublime'). Even more disturbing about 'Sublime' is the self-conscious degree to which Duras acknowledges her absolute need for the structuring framework of a real crime ('The affair can be imagined in its principal form', 'For the sake of form . . .', etc.). We are forced to conclude that Duras's ostensible concern to restore 'the horizon of the crime and, let us say the word, its spirit' in the interests of intelligence (*elle*), is ultimately nothing of the kind. 'Sublime' renders the body of Christine V. doubly alone and doubly (im)material, a point underscored by the narrator's final remarks:

> She [Christine V.] is still alone in her solitude, where the women from the depths of the earth and darkness, still are, in order that they remain just as they were before, relegated to the materiality of matter. Christine V. is sublime. Necessarily sublime [*Christine V. est sublime. Forcément sublime*]. (p. 6)[10]

If we retain the full power of the French '*forcément*' as 'per-force', we can see that a personal theory of literary sublimation is being proposed by Duras. The final three words—'Sublime forcément sublime'—could also be read as: '[le] sublime [c'est la] force [qui] ment [donc] sublime', i.e. '[the] sublime [is the] force [which] lies [therefore] sublime'. This simple equation is the author's unveiling of her own knowingly coercive and duplicitous rhetorical strategy, prepared for in advance by the reflexive use of the verb, '*démentir*' (to deny, contradict) in the phrase: 'Her [Christine's] fear when she [the daughter] contradicted herself [*s'est démentie*]'. Perhaps one of the reasons why the phrase 'sublime, forcément sublime' quickly became so notorious is that phonetically it is a chiastic formation of seven syllables hinging crucially on the conjunction of juxtaposition, 'et': 'sublime / force / et / ment / sublime'. The phrase could even be taken to mean: '[sa] sublime / force / est / mon / sublime', i.e. 'her sublime force is my sublime'.

There are two individual sublimes, then, operating in 'Sublime', one innocent and therefore weak (Villemin), the other strong because self-consciously criminal (Duras). Together they make for the real interest of the article which is revealed as a drama of female self-differentiation. Behind the carefully worded rhetoric of equivalence ('Christine V. who *perhaps* killed like I write' [emphasis added]), *je* always insists that she 'knows' how to write, as opposed to *elle* who, due to her social class, is unable to transgress, even as a reader. We are informed, for instance, that even during the worst of times, thrillers are of limited use for the likes of Christine V. ('one must not transgress ancient taboos'!). 'Sublime'''s intertextual erotics contrives to escape the kind of proximity and 'contamination' caused by a fascination with '*la mère*' (or '*elle*', or '*elles*', or 'les autres femmes', etc.) and found in some accounts of the feminine, horizontal sublime where the desire for pre-Oedipal bonding is not repressed.[11] In fact, with Christine V. absent from the very outset of 'Sublime' and hence already merely a 'reality-effect' ('I will never see Christine V.'), the narrator happily relies on the words of a male judge to portray a woman consumed by what is termed in the article the most 'ravishing' of all death drives: inertia.

Could the chiastic identification that *je* establishes with *elle* in order to abject Villemin represent, perhaps, another instance of the Imaginary Father of primary narcissism, a process which Neil Hertz in his study of the Romantic Sublime has mapped on to an asymmetrical chiastic structure found in the poetry of Wordsworth (what Hertz calls 'a T on its side')?[12] Certainly the scapegoating of Christine V. surpasses the aims of the impersonal sublime as defined by Amar, which are to parody to excess official discourse, present the unrepresentable, and render the real untouchable because 'accursed and sacred'. If anything, the narrator's usurping of the role of God— '[o]nly her can I see at the centre of my world, the concern of time and God alone'—connects 'Sublime' to the vertical, Romantic sublime of masculine self-aggrandisement and domination over the Other. For the masochistic state of checking in one's vital powers in the face of a disarrayed sequence (i.e. a real crime) has been resolved in a one-to-one confrontation which retrieves them rhetorically. In the terms that she uses elsewhere to describe the 'genius' of Yves Saint Laurent's tailoring of the female form, Duras forces Villemin to 'pass through' a 'sacrificial' form of exchange,[13] just like the man from the waterboard who, in a short text from *Vie mat.* entitled 'Le coupeur d'eau' (pp. 101–05), cut off the water supply one suffocatingly hot day and so precipitated the suicide of a mother and her children. The fact that another is 'reborn' aesthetically in the process is purely incidental, for this is alterity in the service of self-possession and self-identity. What counts is simply the other's potential for abjection, and, as 'Sublime' illustrates, this functions most successfully when it is veiled in the metonymical mode of feminine realism and identification. Duras is effectively isolating and honouring in the 'tragic' figure of Villemin a particular femaleness and sisterhood which she makes external to herself. Her projection of discrete, feminine personae on to a subordinate becomes, on one level, simply a means of poetic self-empowerment, and it has led one critic of 'Sublime' to argue that

Duras's negative narcissism and textual deliverance is founded on a masculine tradition of sacrifice and negativity that also includes Bataille and Blanchot.[14] It is certainly true that whereas she once considered any idealisation of women as evidence of male misogyny (e.g. Bataille's 'false' and 'blasphemous' transgression'[15]), she deems it a viable reappropriation of masculine power if women now do the same, especially if they are reversing the 'natural order' ('It doesn't hurt women to be idealised', she casually remarks in *Vie mat.* [p. 62]).

If we step back a little and look at Duras's work as a whole, we can see clearly that there is a marked change in its figuration of female influence. In 1969, for example, Duras helped quite literally to stitch back together the manuscript of Barbara Molinard's *Viens* in order to lift it out of the 'realm of the unsayable'.[16] We recall also from our discussion of *Baxter* in Chapter 2 that she lent artistic support to women writers and film-makers during the early days of feminism. Her later, 'outer' corpus, however, is littered with the tired images of women who have been 'crossed out' once accessed as the real, part of what Annie Le Brun (referring to *EVC*) has winningly described as Duras's '1980s kit of clean desire'.[17] In *Yeux*, for instance, Barbara Loden 'floats' by in her unhappy role as Wanda under the gaze of a police officer (p. 195), while slumped on a sofa on p. 227 lies a stony-faced Laure Duthilleul, Juliette in Aline Issermann's distressing film about enforced marriage, *Le Destin de Juliette* (1983).[18] The novelist and poet Leslie Kaplan, interviewed by Duras in *Le Nouvel Observateur* on the publication of her fourth book for POL, *Le Pont de Brooklyn* (1987), finds herself reduced pictorially to the size of a small incised photograph within a larger view of the Brooklyn Bridge stretching away towards an inaccessible Manhattan sublime.[19]

Yet Duras's abject female real is not always strictly 'female', of course as we see if we return briefly to the 1986 interview, 'Les outsiders de Marguerite Duras' where, we recall, she suddenly lashed out against an unspecified, gay-encoded, male '*eux*', the potential predators of her two young novelists, Ceton and de Richaud. What is significant here is that *eux* is linked metonymically to 'microsociety', which in French is gendered not masculine but feminine ('la microsociété'). It thus might be the case that the transvestite and mother-identified, gay *eux* represents only one manifestation—albeit the most extreme—of *ELLE* and its epiphenomena of female-female relations (Christine V., *elles*, the '*femmes-écrivains*' who know nothing about (hetero)sexual passion, etc.). Duras's perfectly formalised *hommes tremblants* would thereby already constitute her troping on a more fundamentally dangerous, feminine force which can, at its worst, assume the deadly, political proportions of the French right, i.e. '*la droite la* mort' (emphasis added).[20] Similarly, her hypervisible, 'outside' homotexts (literary and otherwise) would function more as simulated doubles of an otherwise unreadable, because invisible, 'female' real, to be compared, for instance, with Thomas Pynchon's paranoid structures in novels such as *Gravity's Rainbow* (1973).[21]

The question of an 'essential', female, paranoid force subtending Duras's work is not, however, one I wish to pursue here, although a touch of paranoia can indeed be detected in the way Duras conceived of her beloved reading public when it edged too close and became '*VOUS*' ('YOU . . . whom I love and for whom I write . . . you who are sometimes as terrifying as criminals' [*Vie mat.*, pp. 121–24]). Instead, having now crossed over from 'Sublime' to the 'microsociety' in general, let us continue our specifically rhetorical investigation of Duras's work in the media by examining how she negotiates its most pervasive form, television.

BEYOND THE WHITE PAGES: WITHIN AND WITHOUT

Duras's studio encounter in 1984 with Bernard Pivot on *Apostrophes* to celebrate the publication of *Amant* was extraordinary for many reasons, not least for the way in which she rewrote the time of live television as a literary tense and used the occasion to realign herself with Blanchot and Bataille, dismissing in the process the 'transitive', because always strategic, (non-)writing of Sartre, once her political 'Father'.[22] What is most original and exciting about Duras's dealings with television, however, is not how she performs in the House of the Father but rather how she forces the Father to operate in her own. One example is her 1987 television interview, 'Deux ou trois choses qu'ils se sont dites' where, as the 'voice' of Literature, Duras invited Jean-Luc Godard, the 'image' of Cinema, into the inner recesses of her private apartment in Paris.[23] Capitalising on his frank admission that he would never have succeeded as a writer, Duras gradually wore Godard down during fierce interrogation, to the point where he functioned as no more than a screen on which to project further ideas about her newly published novel, *Emily* (which he had not read). Godard, of course, had once employed Duras as a barely-audible voice-over in his 1979 film, *Sauve qui peut (la vie)*, where, as though introducing its central, Sadean scene of perversion, she explained the abjection involved in writing ('it is to be behind something . . . suspicious, I would say almost immoral'). As she reveals in her account of the shooting of this film in *Yeux* (pp. 47–48), Duras never took this to be a satisfactory cameo role, and in 'Deux ou trois choses', arguably the realisation of their longstanding project to make a film together,[24] she cut Godard off and out as though she were scolding a child ('If you snore', she warns, 'I'll cut!') ('Si tu baîlles, je coupe!')). In so doing, she confirmed the precise nature of her role in *Camion* as a master-editor of textual erotics.

It is the four-part series *Au-delà des pages*, filmed again in Duras's Paris apartment during the first three months of 1988, which merits most attention, for there Duras goes more public than ever before. Sporting her stage-dress of polo-neck and cardigan—the 'M.D. uniform'—and bedecked in rings and bracelets, Duras projects herself in *Au-delà des pages* as 'other' and as a natural friend to disorder ('Elle écrit, M.D.. Elle dit n'importe quoi. Elle dit n'importe comment', she repeats). In a collage of passages and sequences identified on the screen by the different months in which they were filmed, she discusses at length not only herself and her work but also more general topics such as the 'scandal' of writing, the status of the French left, the Second World War and man's capacity to commit acts of violence and torture. In fact, *Au-delà des pages* is a prime example of Duras's remarkable ability to work various seams of cultural passage simultaneously. As with Bergé in 'Duras est SEXY!', she presents herself as both Soft and Hard, crossing between the public and private positions of passive desired object and active *voyeuese*, victim and aggressor. An instance of the latter is when she faces the camera head-on and relates in graphic detail, and with unconcealed pleasure, a dream she recently had of the brutal murder of le Pen by three North-African men (this from a writer who consistently disavowed the dream-work![25]). Duras here is both Outsider, the self-proclaimed foreigner within the French language, *and* the Insider of the literary Establishment, delivering lessons to Perrot on how to recite and interpret her work, notably *Maladie*. While she may claim a personal right to the 'femme fatale' scandal of being unfaithful to men, she nevertheless reserves her highest praise for the Father (here the intertextual father of *Savannah*, Henry Fonda, blessed with 'that gait, that elegance'). In addition, although deadly serious and adult on political issues, she is at times playfully skittish and fanciful, appearing to play up the role of what Jean-Louis Barrault once rather slyly called a 'grown-up-child' ('un-enfant-qui-a-grandi').[26]

If such a seductive display of polymorphous potency has any equivalent in Duras's work, it is surely the young girl's hyper-determined crossing of the Mekong in *Amant*, during which she wears a combination of her mother's silk dress, one of her brother's belts, gold lamé shoes and a fedora hat. Yet by crossing from monitor to monitor and from image to image in *Au-delà des pages*, Duras also ends up occupying every part of the chiastic map. She is at once self and other, the point of reversal, and all points in between. We hear her talking over her freeze-framed image, we feel her coaxing us towards her as she 'gives face' like the Maillol statues in *Césarée* or the streets of Paris in *Mains*, extracts of which punctuate the programme. At other moments we are invited to rest our gaze on Duras surrounded in the editing suite by the images and background noise of Perrot and anonymous others—another indiscriminate *eux*—while she surveys the same footage yet again, and with increased fascination, before then being restored to full-frontal close-up where she revises her previous statements. Duras's face, her image, her writing: all is being rhetorically controlled through the montage of delicate self-revision. It is as though Duras had reappropriated for herself the trope of irony usually associated with fetishism, the Freudian male perversion par excellence,[27] and made it endlessly displaceable, somewhere between the caress of her glasses and the cut between frames. If Duras is deconstructing here her passionate, symbiotic relationship with her own cult audience, just as she once did the phenomenon of Maria Callas, or 'that other woman who was encased within her',[28] she is also, more fundamentally, 'cutting herself up' self-reflexively for purely autoerotic pleasure.

As in Duras's cinema, then, the formal rhythms of desynchronised sound and image in *Au-delà des pages*, where a break into black often highlights the separation between different footage, are superimposed over the ostensible message of alterity. There is no pretence of a dialogue of love, and certainly not with Perrot whose presence is all but eclipsed. For this is a monologue of narcissism writ large, and larger, 'from me to me', as Duras puts it elsewhere,[29] and one which anchors the viewer firmly in the role now of ravisher, now of ravished, according to whether she is playing the seductive fausse-naïve nonchalantly discussing late-night television, or the cold, oral mother recounting fantasies of violence and revenge. At times the forbidding nature of the latter, a constant of Duras's media image during the 1980s although much softened after her coma in 1988–89 when she underwent the literal 'cutting' of a tracheotomy, ranks in power with the photograph taken by her son for the 1987 interview in *Le Nouvel Observateur*, 'Comme une messe de mariage', where Duras, hand on hip, a faint smile on her stern face, defies the camera to get any closer as she preaches the 'butchery' of writing. The audience is invited first to look at the fetishised woman who looks back, then to surrender with pleasure to the penetrating 'cut', the moment when the subject is severed from the phallic M/Other and accedes to difference and the fantasy of self-possession.[30] All the while, we pay silent homage to the vertical power of Duras's fantasy of controlled self-violation. It is precisely for this reason that Duras's image in *Au-delà des pages* never reaches the dangerous proportions of an androgynous ideal which, when taken to extremes by other cross-dressing female writers, can sometimes risk provoking sexual and cultural anxiety (Emily Dickinson, for example, who often dressed up exclusively in white as a mark of submission to a mystical marriage, was trapped for life in the House of the Father[31]). As Duras explains in *Vie mat.*, the 'M.D. uniform' already constitutes a 'definitive' creative achievement, a perfect marriage of form and content', since it diverts public attention away from the natural 'error' of her small body and waist (*Vie mat.*, pp. 75–76).

The intensive glamour of Duras's media presence should not, however, distract us from the gravity of certain aspects of *Au-delà des pages*, in particular its inclusion of extracts from *Mains*. These place her work directly in the context of racism and racial difference, raising questions about Duras's political and cultural practice which will occupy us for the rest of the chapter. At one point in the programme, just before Duras recited her dream about le Pen and just after she had accused *Libération* of exploiting 'le scandale Duras' because it published 'ignominious' letters addressed to her concerning 'Sublime', a short scene from *Mains* is repeated twice in a row with the music on the sound-track redubbed to heighten the effect. This is the highlight of that film's slow, dawn tour through the streets of Paris, when Duras suddenly found herself face to face with her post-colonial Other. Following one quick edit, the camera veered left towards a corner of the street and picked up within its frame a team of about eight black refuse-collectors on the pavement sweeping up the past evening's debris. The male figures, all indistinguishable, were caught converging on to the corner as if deliberately seeking unison with the camera, although they seem unaware of its presence. After several long seconds of contemplation the camera starts to move forward again, a white Peugeot van gliding past in front as if delivering the camera back to the open road.

This brief encounter with France's under-class touches at the core of Duras's public relations with the Other for how are we to interpret the episode: as a spontaneous gesture of sympathy by Duras towards France's immigrants? As a failed rapprochement between two mutually estranged sections of society, the worker and the intellectual? For Duras, the issue is simple: *Mains* is intended as a gift to those who populate the big cities of the West in the early hours of the morning and call out to be loved and recognised as human beings ('La caverne noire'). In *Yeux*, where she emphasises the range of foreigners on view in *Mains*—blacks, Portuguese, Puerto Ricans, 'mulattoes'—Duras explains: '[s]ince Indochina, since my youth, I had never seen such a colonial population gathered in one single spot. It's to them that love is addressed' (*Yeux*, p. 154). Certainly in the context of *Au-delà des pages* where it assumes quasi-documentary status, the constant—if not always continuous—movement in *Mains* appears to exemplify Duras's proclaimed aspiration towards the Other. According to the film's spoken prologue, the title, *Les mains négatives*, refers to ancient traces of hand-prints found in sea-caves along the Atlantic coast of Southern Europe, underlining the fact that Duras is concerned here with France's submerged, 'negative' Other.[32] Just as the spoken text recovers from oblivion the silent cry of a man who placed his hands anonymously on granite to address a woman, or indeed anyone, who might hear his simple plea—'I shout that I wish to love you I love you / I will love whosoever hears that I am shouting [that I love you]'—so, too, Duras's solitary camera projects workers from the Third World into a new visibility. Even the lateral-tracking shots which temporarily suspend the predominant forward-tracking mode of the film appear to correspond to the imperfect tense used by the text to express the continuity of love (as in: 'I am the one who shouted that he loved you, you').

Yet how does Duras presume both to identify lovingly with the captured object of her gaze—'the colonial given of humanity', as she puts it—and at the same time speak in its place (the only sounds heard in the film other than Duras's voice are the screeching and at times piercing chords of Amy Flamer's violin)? The key would seem to be the film's very mobility; *Mains* represents a pure circulation rather than a traditional 'journey' with a fixed destination, a circulation which terminates almost by chance before it reaches the top of the Champs-Elysées. The constant motion between the viewing camera— a slave to whatever passes through its frame—and the viewed object would seem to guarantee a free-flow of difference and passage to the Other. In fact, mobility of movement has been a determining issue for the few critics who have explored Duras's postcolonial thematics. Panivong Norindr, for example, has argued that if Duras does not sustain a coherent critical position in texts such as *Amant* and *Chine*, nevertheless the *errance* of urban passage depicted in her work is a transgressive strategy aimed at undermining the discursive power of colonialist discourse.[33] Christine Holmlund goes even further and considers that although no reflection on racism and colonialism is offered in *Mains* on the level of the image, the actual disjunction between sounds and images is so complete that it throws into question all representation of difference as fixed.[34] Duras herself presents *Mains* as a film not about the state of immigration but rather the process of 'emigration', and the confrontation which ensues between self and outside. In a brief article in 1985 entitled, 'Une certaine idée de la France' (*Monde*, pp. 44–45), she claimed that 'foreigners' like those in the film have always remained foreigners in France and have had the chance to experience change both from within and from without. She added that the attempt in France over the last forty years at 'assimilation' was false and misguided, although she offered no alternative solutions, declaring only her pride in the fact that France's open borders made her a world model for democracy!

The approach by Duras almost to wish away the history of racism and return to some kind of 'prehistory', like the cave-paintings of 'negative hands', connects her to a certain French literary tradition of attitudes towards racial difference that includes the writer Victor Segalen, whose work she claimed during the 1980s to have read with great excitement (see *Vie mat.*, p. 119). In his exoticist strategies of mediation and transference pitched between the poles of the Real (Tahiti, China) and the Imaginary, Segalen prefigures Duras's poetics of displacement and its attempt to reconcile the need both for identification and difference. His advice to the 'new traveller' in his *Essai sur l'exotisme* (1904–18) could just as well apply to the roving yet non-committal eye of *Mains*: 'state not just crudely your vision, but, through an instantaneous and constant *transfer*, the echo of your presence'.[35] What underlies Segalen's so-called 'aesthetics of the diverse' is a perception of the irreducible foreignness of cultures and languages and the sense that no real fusion or exchange of differences is ever possible. For Baudrillard, Segalen is even to be admired for going beyond the contemporary 'melodrama' of difference and for insisting on the Other's excessive, radical otherness, which, like the 'incomparability' of sexual difference and the 'irreducibility' of the Object, can sometimes erupt in sublime, reversible fashion.[36]

What is striking, however, about the chance and troubling encounter in *Mains* is that Duras cannot leave it alone in its radical otherness; she immediately replays it but in reverse. Once the camera has regained equilibrium by returning to its neutral position—a measured forward tracking movement in the middle of the boulevard—the shot is cut and, at the mention of 'c'est la terre / vide' ('it's the land / empty'), the viewer is carried off swiftly to another corner on the left. This time, however, in place of the refuse-collectors, there is a large white object standing on the pavement and occupying the centre of the frame. The white object is an isolated and boarded-up commercial stall on which are printed in black lettering words which only come into proper focus as we pass it by. The camera continues down the side of the boulevard to the words: 'These hands will remain on the wall of granite facing the roar of the ocean / Unbearable / No-one will hear any more / No-one will see'.

This is a typical Duras manoeuvre, for three reasons. Firstly, because of its effect of pleonasm: working as so often the border between English and French, Duras presents us with a standing object called 'STAND F.N.D.I.R.' (for a second it even looks like STAND F. NOIR!). Secondly, because it sets up a scene of focused reading: the general ambivalence of the preceding shot is replaced by a series of specific and even banal oppositions and differences between the two shots which we are obliged to register: the difference, for example, between black and white, people and object, immobility and movement, plural and singular. Thirdly, and most importantly of all, because the two shots are motivated into a definite structure, the second shot reversing the configuration of black and white in the first, thus forming a chiasmus: shot 1: black workers, white car; shot 2: white object, black writing. This formal play on the theme of colour is continued in the next shot. Following another cut, a white Peugeot appears on the right (perhaps even the same one as before), and then soon after a black car penetrates the frame, gently stealing in front of the white car. At the same time Duras pronounces the words: 'those hands there, black' ('ces mains là, noires'). It is as though Duras had deliberately called up the black car into the frame, *là*, with the power of her own voice, in the same way that she ritualistically recalled the blue lorry into the frame of *Camion*. Whereas in the first shot of the encounter the camera was the passive observer of an indiscriminate and invading area of blackness, now Duras is the active controller of a black object in an almost abstract and decorative play of colours. From now on the film will offer only scattered shots of refuse-workers who appear as so many marks of urban shade.

The three shots, then, constitute a discrete narrative scene and illustrate that if Duras has a natural affinity for sublime moments— moments of total otherness, loss and confusion—she also treats them as challenges to be negotiated and resolved. (The entire film, in fact, is set up as Duras's answer to the mystery of why hand-paintings were originally made.) A space open to the Other is created only to be superseded by a space which predates and exposes it, where rubbish still stands and where paradoxically the frame is at its most open (i.e. devoid of people and action). A potential meeting point between self and other in a new corner of the world, a point of radical otherness and no return, has become a purely formal matter, an ironic play of signs, structured around a point of chiastic reversal (the cut). This represents a tribute to Duras's own hands, the authorial and not so 'negative' hands of cinematic montage.

We can now rerun the scene quite matter-of-factly as a play of contrasting angles and positions. As *lui* reaches out in the text to speak to *elle* who is blessed with identity ('[y]ou who have a name, you who are endowed with identity, I love you'), the camera, *'elle'* (*la caméra*), operating in the hands of a white, female, metropolitan writer (*je*), singles out an undifferentiated *eux*, cruising it briefly as a preferred *vous* but always at a distance apart. Warmed up transferentially by the camera, the objectified male Other is subsequently cooled down and, because unable to return the camera's look, rendered invisible. Desire in *Mains* is thus inscribed as totally female, whether that of the text's reader (Duras) and its addressee (*elle*), or that of the camera (*elle*) and the authorial hand of montage (Duras). The fetishistic qualities of this totally self-referring movement are brought out in spectacular fashion in *Au-delà des pages*, where the almost obsessive repetition of the encounter is linked directly to the personal situation of Duras's own 'scandal'. It is the kind of fetishism which, because founded on the pointing of Duras's camera at the black object, performs the demonstrative gesture of colonial discourse as defined by Homi Bhabha. According to Bhabha, '[t]he visibility of the racial/colonial other is at once a *point* of identity ("Look a Negro"!) and at the same time a *problem* for the attempted closure within discourse'. He adds: 'in that form of substitution and fixation that is fetishism there is always the trace of loss and absence . . . the recognition and disavowal of "difference" is always disturbed by the question of its re-presentation or construction'. Hence, the need to continue repeating the same gesture.[37]

Bhabha accounts for the ambivalence of the colonial object—at once an object of desire and derision—by proposing the concept of 'stereotype-as-suture'. As we saw during our discussion in Chapter 2 of *Camion*'s use of the shot/reverse shot structure, suture—a psychoanalytic term signifying the founding cut, or the subject's transition from the Imaginary to the Symbolic—can also describe the constant fluctuation between the imaginary plenitude of a cinematic image and the loss of that plenitude through the agency of the cut, the cut marking an integration of the image into syntactic structure. In *Mains*, although there is no shot/reverse shot as such, suture is also sealed in the form of cinematic montage: in shot one, we experience first the sudden plenitude of Duras's post-colonial object—'Look! Black men!'—then, with the cut into shot two, its total eclipse. This movement of presence and absence is repeated on a different level in the third shot with the two cars ('those hands there, black!'). Taken together, the three shots form a tight syntactic structure in which the black men are reduced to a mere signifier—'black'—and their general alien status reinforced. Hence, the possibility for radical difference has been elided, evacuated of any substance like the 'empty land' mentioned in the text. If the film seemed initially to be heading towards the point of no return, it turns upon itself self-reflexively and withdraws chiastically into its own, totally private space.

The way Duras first creates, then colonises, an open space in *Mains* clearly recalls some of the rhetorical techniques of negative identification, hypothetical generalisation and inversion employed by the early colonists in order to stereotype the Other and thus make it the containable opposite of their own ideal.[38] In this respect, the film can be linked to another scene of urban passage in Duras's work, the moment in *Emily* when the narrator catches sight in the distance of a group of fifteen or so 'Oriental-looking' men dressed uniformly in white. She identifies them first as '*eux*'—'[t]he same person indefinitely multiplied' (p. 11)—then as 'Korean', thus choosing to ignore completely the crisis of ideological and political difference posed by North and South Korea (she willingly acknowledges the charge of 'pathetic racist' made by her male interlocutor, *vous* [p. 14]). Perhaps the best way, however, of grasping the full implications of Duras's unstoppable, structuring and colonising impulse is to show it in action in a context which is not directly (post-)colonial at all. In a small chapter from *Yeux* entitled 'Vous, l'autre, celui de notre séparation' (literally, 'You, the other, he of our separation'), we are presented with another scene of cross-identification, another ambiguous moment of alliance between the first-person narrator and a chosen *vous* (a former friend or lover). As in *Mains*, subject and object positions seem to be on the move and expanding (you / the other / he / our), and again the need for dialogue with the Other is considered essential: the narrator will call out into the void to *vous* even though he has caused her harm and will probably not receive her message. Here are the chapter's key moments:

> You don't matter to me any more . . . I have given up on you . . . But you see, I am calling you anyway . . . The distance separating us is precisely that of death. It is one and the same distance for you and me. In the same way that you want to keep it pure between us, I cover it by my shouting and my calling. Like you, I know that this distance is insurmountable, impossible to cover. The difference between you and me is that for me this impossibility is a minor drawback. So you see, we are similar, we both of us keep to our respective niches, to our scorched, incalculably narcissistic territories, but I shout *towards* the deserts, preferably in the direction of the deserts. (*Yeux*, pp. 41–43) (original emphasis)[39]

In this scene of impossible exchange, equivalences and similarities are established but only to emphasise difference or negative opposition. This leads to an acceptance of the absolute and unbridgeable distance between self and other. Yet if *je* and *vous* are portrayed as equally entrenched and narcissistic, the first-person narrator has the additional ability to act and shout vigorously '*towards* the deserts' and so make empty space her own (a matter of personal preference). *Vous*, meanwhile, remains in the same position as he was at the beginning of the chapter, i.e. apart. Hence, in a chiastic reformulation of the title, the word 'separation' refers not to a shared situation ('our separation') but to a fixed and abstract state of human relations: '*vous*' / '*moi*' // '*moi*' // 'the deserts'. The first and fourth parts of this structure—'*vous*' and 'the deserts'—could just as easily be '*vous*' and '*eux*', or even '*eux*' and 'the deserts', for to some degree these terms are all interchangeable and indistinguishable. Piling up multi-layers of difference and chance to sift through and clean, the Durasian first-person always differentiates herself from a projected second-person to which she remains ultimately indifferent (i.e. a third person). In Duras's hands, alterity can become a purely reversible concept.

This gives the lie to Duras's assertion in 1985 that it is the 'mark of genius' to experience one's interior and exterior as 'communicating spaces'.[40] For if she claims to love only the Other, she quite happily, like Segalen, redirects the Real into a fascination with what, for both of them, is probably the only, truly exotic self, i.e. the writing self. In the case of Segalen, his most constant 'transfer' is from the Chinese Empire to the 'Empire of oneself' and it will lead him in *Voyage au pays du réel* (1915) to state that the simplest thing to do is to despise and detest the Chinese 'in their skin'. In the case of Duras who aims to move forward towards the absolute, the *post*-colonial Other is just that: positioned *behind* in order to be crossed out. Otherwise, the Durasian first-person would itself become the object of a potentially engulfing Other.

TO KNOW OR NOT TO KNOW

What could the final outcome be of Duras's presentation of herself as other, where the 'real' other is abstracted and made ultimately redundant, if not her appropriation even of violence against the Other as her own? So it is with Duras's remarkable, manifesto-style article 'Moi' published in *L'Autre Journal* in 1986, where she discusses President Reagan's raid on Libya.[41] Duras defends her earlier 'physical' and moral approval of the raid. It was, she argues, perfectly natural for America to mount a raid on Tripoli because a surgical operation (one, no doubt, as effective as that already performed on Britain by the 'very efficient' Mrs Thatcher[42]) was urgently required on a defective, 'cinematic' region of the political body. A 'faulty circulation' was 'normalised'; disease was cured. Should Duras feel ashamed of such a position which is so radically opposed to that of her co-editors? No, she answers herself, and she doesn't. In fact, politics and Kadhafi soon become a side-issue in 'Moi', for, as Duras admits, even when she is commenting on international violence she is only ever describing her own innate and absolute potential for brutality. 'I don't know what non-violence is', she declares, '[w]hat moves me is myself. What makes me want to cry is me, my violence.' Lacking the quick-silver allure of its intertextual cushions, Duras's work is exposed here at its most naked or, as Duras puts it herself here, 'indecent'. What counts above all else is the free circulation of her own aggression and violence.

Something similar happens in the chapter 'L'image écrite' in *Yeux*, where Duras makes it now the turn of the Jews to figure as the projected violence of her brilliantly self-reflexive writing practice. She states: 'I think that the question of the Jews, that incredibly strong anxiety for me, which I see in full light and before which I remain in a state of exhausting clear-sightedness, comes back to writing. To write is to go looking outside oneself for what is already in oneself.'[43] While Duras may emphasise elsewhere the Jewish foundations of the 'European' ability to be, like Charlie Chaplin,[44] simultaneously oneself and other, in 'L'image écrite' she is using the history of the Jews merely to represent the confirmatory other of writing which is, in the end, always self-sufficient. It is to the Jews that Duras again naturally turns when she tries to account for her previous attraction to militant activism. The only advantage, she stated in 1983, 'in having left oneself, in having gone outside, "*dehors*", as I did for 10 years as a militant, is that the reasons I will have had for dying were exterior to me. Like the fate reserved to Jews, the pain of seeing people tortured . . . these are reasons exterior to my life.'[45] Far from absolving her of all responsibility, however, political activity only further entangled Duras in a series of social obligations to an undefined Other ('this life which stretches out of doors, which develops tentacles' [ibid.]).

In fact, only after the successful completion of *Camion* was Duras finally able to live her sadomasochistic fantasies *as* the political, inviting us to ride them with her because they tap so easily into our own deepest fantasies of aggression and control. The fact that Duras is merely extending pleasures automatically granted by the evil 'microsociety' (publishing a book, for example, is already, in her eyes, an act of prostitution, the chance to 'become common, sleep in the street'[46]), exposes her to the charge that she is merely colluding with it. Yet Duras proposes such pleasures as the natural extension of 'belonging to the left' (*Au-delà des pages*): man is nature's 'evil-doing', a 'wicked emanation from God';[47] society is inherently false and scandalous. Hence, the only true politics requires a 'terroristic' approach (*Au-delà des pages*). Duras's public airing of violent fantasies is further legitimised precisely by being framed rhetorically in a post-'68 discourse of passivity and 'indifference'. At a time when, for Duras as for Baudrillard, the left's only legacy is a knowledge of 'divine' despair or 'fabulous disenchantment', and when political loss is always 'self-loss', or 'the loss of one's anger',[48] there is nothing left to do, it seems, but join the currently swelling ranks of neo-conservative revisionists in France and suffer, solipsistically ('To suffer [is] not to be able to avoid suffering'[49]). When all 'errors', past and future, are completely acknowledged, one can finally begin again to play, fetishistically: 'The left also means to play. It is a very great pleasure. It means listening out for others, even enemies, and not being able to do anything else. It is *to know and not know* at the same time' (emphasis added).[50] The kind of breathtaking licences taken in 'Sublime' offer the *only* valid transgression worth pursuing, the *only* way left to transume the political blockage of the French left which, already by 1985, was in disarray and, according to Baudrillard, in full 'parodic effect'.[51]

There is no better illustration of the effects of Duras's gradual depoliticisation than her own rewriting of her political history. In 1985, twenty-five years after its publication, Duras proposed in *L'Autre Journal* that the 'Déclaration sur le droit à l'insoumission dans la guerre d'Algérie' (or 'Manifeste des 121'), a document conceived by Blanchot and Dionys Mascolo as a collective response by writers and intellectuals to the French government's foreign policy during the Algerian War and to which she was a signatory, should now be read as an 'absolute' text. This is because, if the document invoked man's fundamental right of political refusal at a specific historical moment (i.e. the refusal to fight for France in the war), it also, more importantly, addressed the question of his 'sovereignty', in particular his capacity for 'criminal' violence:

> It ['La Déclaration des 121'] does not have a police-type function. Where it is innovatory is elsewhere, in that it places the man 'called up' in front of his essential responsibility: his sovereignty. It asks the man 'called up' to know himself, but in this case from what he knows of himself, of his will, of his refusal and of the criminal violence which resides in him and which he discovers to be the lot of all humanity . . . Only a fundamentally reciprocal relation between all men, between everyone, with each always alone in his thoughts, is the single point of reference for the 'Déclaration des 121'.[52]

Such self-mystifying reflections as these, mathematically expressed as so often in Duras and reliant on extravagant universal truths, provide, in fact, for the very continuity of the Duras corpus, even when it seems to be heading in totally opposite directions. If, in her first published work, *L'Empire français. Avec trois cartes* (1940), written under her maiden name of Donnadieu in collaboration with Philippe Roques and long since missing from the official bibliography, Duras sought very differently to defend France's colonial ambitions, she also had recourse to the same kind of totalising idealism.[53] She indulged there in pure Republican universalism, presenting France's outer territories as happy providers for the metropole in return for the values of a global, French identity, or what the book termed 'the treasures' of French kindness and intelligence. The preface set the tone: '[t]hese pages aim to substitute for a fragmentary vision the vision of an organic entity'. When asked in 1991 about this forgotten chapter of her career, the fruit of two years spent at the Ministère des Colonies from 1937 to 1939, Duras replied uncompromisingly that she had never even considered the question of anticolonialism since, being a 'Creole' and speaking Indochinese as a child, the colonies were *her* country. Again, as in *Mains*, an aggressive act of self-identification precludes all questions of political and historical responsibility.[54]

But what exactly are the immediate social and political consequences of Duras's personal culture of redemption, where the political can be intercut by the personal *as* the personal, and where real difference is always a stimulus for yet more (self-)sublimation? Let us look, finally, at Duras's treatment of the 'Greenpeace affair', a crisis which began in 1985 when French Secret Service agents blew up *The Rainbow Warrior*, the boat being used by Greenpeace to protest against nuclear-bomb testing in the Pacific. A photographer was inadvertently killed during the attack, resulting in a cover-up at the highest levels of the Socialist government. Despite the complex twists and turns of the story which slowly trickled out through the media, the main issue for Duras writing in *L'Autre Journal* was simple: the government may have acted in a contradictory manner that lacked any sang-froid and even evaded the truth for reasons of personal shame, but Mitterrand himself (whom she invokes at one point as *vous*) was innocent of all the charges of duplicity levelled at him by the press.[55] Drawing on personal, 'inside' knowledge, Duras argues that Mitterrand's only fault—but one easily put right—was just an inability to speak out publicly with the same ease that he displays in private. In fact, it was the press itself that was guilty of dishonesty because it chose to link the capsizing of *The Rainbow Warrior* to one man's death, thus aggravating a tense situation to the level of 'pathos'. Moreover, Greenpeace was the most suspect of all the parties involved due to its naïve pacifism, the 'major lie of our time' since it plays into the hands of the Soviets. Duras concludes rather preposterously that the entire Greenpeace movement deserved to be blown up along with the boat because it betrayed the ideas of the Mitterrand left: 'I believe that Greenpeace has only an absurd explanation. To be on the left means to know what I am saying here. If Greenpeace does not know that it might as well no longer bother with this earth.'[56]

What should we conclude from this statement and the other profoundly ambivalent social and political ratiocinations that we have studied in this chapter, beginning with 'Sublime'? Is Duras reinventing *Libération*, *L'Autre Journal*, *Globe* and *Le Matin* (for whose survival she actively campaigned in 1987) as literary models of political engagement which can simply transcend practical and ethical constraints? Is it the case, indeed, that, as she explained to Mitterrand in 1986 during their series of self-congratulatory interviews in *L'Autre Journal* later adapted for the Paris stage, 'only art can withstand all changes' and that it alone is always justified in whatever form?[57] I think that the answer lies more in the way that Duras exploits the media and allows herself to be exploited by it, since she was, in effect, performing there the role of a national healer. This is not so much because she is a witness to much of France's most painful recent history (Ames[58]) which she then dressed up in 'the luxurious masochism of bourgeois love' (Bersani and Dutoit),[59] or because, as one of France's most 'nationalist of stylists' (Probst Solomon),[60] she permitted readers to indulge in a 'racist nostalgia' while fantasising that questions of racism and oppression could be explained by the mystical (Smock).[61] It is rather because, in an age of deep uncertainty, the aesthetic and rhetorical gaps or 'partitions of difference' (Segalen) which Duras cultivated within the political and cultural real always took a traditional form (sublime heroes, abject villains, etc.), thus giving her public statements an air of the reassuringly familiar and worldly-wise. For example, in an instance of the media functioning as a confessional, Duras was called upon by *Globe* in 1993 to receive the personal story of Bernard Tapie, a fallen star of the popular left, then under criminal investigation for financial mismanagement of his football club, Olympique de Marseilles.[62] Elsewhere, she provided a stern sense of therapeutic closure, as when she offered witty, bite-sized captions for the twelve 'images of emotion' collected from around the world by *France-Soir* during 1990,[63] or when she proposed in *Globe* that the only way to solve the drug-trade was to suppress by any means necessary the 'abominable world' of dealers and sellers.[64] Similarly, her television special with Godard, a Christmas gift to the nation, ensured that festive fun in France would not sink to the level of the purely frivolous. With her long campaign against enforced incarceration, Duras could even fulfil the country's enduring need for a safe, utopian, republican conscience.[65] It is precisely in recognition of her ability to perform these and other types of social and cultural role so consummately that in 1984 one critic declared Duras 'the last perfect idol'.[66] Six years later, in *Le Nouvel Observateur*, Jean-François Josselin spoke for all those straddling the centre-left in France when he remarked that if Duras did not exist, she would have to be invented.[67]

This is not to suggest, of course, that Duras's work in the media had the wider interests of the community in mind. Her sacred dramas of ritualised violence and sexual differentiation do little to resolve the present 'sacrificial crisis' as described by René Girard, where the disappearance of sacrificial rites marks the collapse of sexual difference and leads instead to an impure and contagious form of violence.[68] Indeed, Duras's ethical commitment to the Other often disappears in scenarios of future apocalypse and chaos, whether that of another ice-age or the 'new harvests' of the unemployed (*Yeux*, p. 87).[69] Even the apparent spectacle of self-sacrifice—i.e. Duras giving herself up to the 'image' of the Other—can, as Borch-Jacobsen has shown, be experienced as purely 'economic' and offer immediate returns.[70] What characterises most of Duras's interventions in the media, however, and what makes them so compulsively terrifying, is a desire to swallow the real whole in order for the hunger of Durasian passage to be completely satisfied. Such is the force behind her extraordinary public announcement in *Le Monde* in 1981 that those not already predisposed to her individual style of film-making spare themselves the effort of going to see the film *Atlantique*. For those that do, however, she would ideally lock the doors behind them (*Yeux*, pp. 222–23). We see here fully exposed in the guise of public concern Duras's parallel and much underestimated view of passion as the putting to death of the Other, an event as vertiginous in its implications as the boa-constrictor attacking its victim 'musically' and 'impudently' in her early short story, *Le boa* (1954).[71]

Of course, the Other can never be so easily consumed in aesthetic transubstantiation. Christine Villemin is a stubbornly *real* object of sublime fantasy and, like Bhabha's impossible, fetishised object of colonial fantasy, cannot be fixed forever in someone else's personal narrative. All charges against Villemin were officially withdrawn on 3 February 1993 by a court in Dijon, leaving her free to sue Duras and *Libération* for damages (albeit unsuccessfully).[72] Despite, therefore, the temptations of a mighty authorial power, the fragile swing-door between writing self and real other in Duras's media work always remains necessarily, if not sublimely, open.

Let us now return one last time to Duras's literary work proper in the company of Yann Andréa, who, as a gay man involved in writing, cinema, and the media, would appear to represent the most intensely 'other' of all Duras's others. In October 1986 she published the novel, *Yeux bleus*, a Minuit text dedicated to Andréa but which, seven months later, she admitted was not a success. During a long and impassioned post-mortem in *Vie mat.* entitled 'Le livre' (pp. 86–91), Duras explained that the novel told only of an impossible story between one heterosexual woman and one homosexual man whereas what was originally intended was not even a positive version of the same story, but rather an account of love which is always made possible through writing (p. 89). Although at a loss to explain the reasons for this unusual outcome, Duras linked it to her experience with Andréa during the writing of the novel. Chapter 7 will unravel the mystery of *Yeux bleus* and its continuing saga in *Pute* and *Vie mat.* as a basis for examining Duras's creative partnership with Andréa and what it reveals further both of the Duras Sublime, and of the erotic and aesthetic possibilities of collaborative form.

M.D./'Y.A., homosexuel': Literary Collaboration and the Sexual Cure

I rose—because He sank . . . My soul / grew straight . . . I lifted him
(E. Dickinson)

Agonising in *Vie mat.* over how to account for the mysterious failure of *Yeux bleus*, Duras refused to identify the novel as anything other than 'the book', treating it with the same paranoid fear displayed by its male protagonist towards the female body, i.e. as a 'hostile, wounding object, a weapon levelled against her' (*Yeux bleus*, p. 90). She declared it to be simply false and weak prose, 'an essay à la Barthes'. If homosexuality creates 'a shadow on a word', the text itself 'lied' in the space of a word (p. 89). However, Duras did relate the writing of *Yeux bleus* to her relationship at the time with Yann Andréa, stating as follows:

> We [Duras and Andréa] scoffed at all the compromises, all the usual arrangements between people. We confronted the impossibility of this love, we did not retreat, we did not run away . . . we would laugh at it [this love], we couldn't recognise it, and we lived it as it came, truly impossible, and without intervening, without doing anything to suffer less, without running away, without destroying it, without leaving. And that was not enough. (*Vie mat.*, p. 91)[1]

The problematic links between the real and the imaginary are tantalisingly raised here but left unresolved. How could living the impossible have resulted in a text telling only of love's impossibility? To explore this mystery and determine in the process the specific nature of the creative relationship shared by Duras and Andréa (or 'Y.A., homosexuel'), we need first to analyse why *Yeux bleus* constituted such an aberration in her aesthetic Minuit practice of error, and why it necessitated such a vehement denial.

The opening pages of the novel reveal immediately that it lacks the fundamentals of *écriture courante*. There is no first-person narrator to bind the material and the reader into a consummate whole, and the decisive, 'scandalous' event of visual rapture at the Hôtel des Roches—the passing sight of a sailor with blue eyes and black hair—is viewed both from the window-frame gaze of the unnamed male protagonist (*lui*) and by a silent, third-person narrator in whom we are expected, unusually for Duras, to place our automatic trust. If this event sets in motion the central relationship between *lui* and *elle*, it nevertheless refuses to become the transferable stuff of textual memory and fantasy. Similarly, the irregular presence in *Yeux bleus* of incised blocks of text containing stage directions for a future adaptation produces only a series of self-enclosed entities divorced from the main body of narrative. The novel's first line, 'A summer evening, says the actor, would be at the heart of the story' (p. 9), leads us to expect an integration of the narrative and its hypothetical adaptation, especially if we link it to the ambiguity of 'ici' ('here') recorded in the first block of stage directions (p. 21). However, this textual synthesis never happens because *Yeux bleus* is unable to perform symbolic acts of (self-)penetration and equivalence. In the absence of any dynamic metaphor or chiastic event of the kind we have seen elsewhere in Duras's Minuit work, it sinks instead into a prosaic literalness and pronominal confusion which, for many critics, stretches the limits of self-pastiche.[2]

Yeux bleus reads, in fact, like a text haunted and undermined by always just missed ideals. The requisite Durasian moment of naming had already taken place before the text began in one transformative instance of female authorship performed between *elle* and the sailor ('It was she who had taken him; she had had herself penetrated by him, while he lay below her, dead with the grief at having to leave her. And it was then that he had called her by his own name, the name of the Orient, which she had distorted' [p. 94][3]). In the real time of the novel, change through sadomasochistic gratification is an intangible and impossible prospect. Sexual 'passages', or writerly instances of recognition between complete strangers (p. 102), are taking place out of the textual frame along the beach, and *elle* has to visit another anonymous man to enjoy the perfect programming of sexual violence, or 'profound culture' (p. 123). By far the most serious lack of an ideal is provided by the figure of the actor-cum-director portrayed in the stage directions. He presents himself as powerful enough to cut erotically and self-reflexively into the final silence of his troupe with his own dialogic space of doubt ('peut-être') (p. 151), and his mise en scène even manages to turn the maternal roar of the sea to metaphorical and symbolic effect ('the river . . . the audience, the outside, reading, the sea' [p. 150]). He is also able to envisage a final night that would bring the lovers' story to a close, something inconceivable in the opposing main narrative. For this reason, the final four blocks of adaptation which encase *Yeux bleus*, and where one actress describes language as an '*empêchement*', or the 'inhibition one feels about not being able to express this inhibition [i.e. the recognition of what one does not yet know] due to the meagreness and inadequacy of words when faced with the enormity of pain' (p. 151), must be read more as a comment on the non-theatrical void of the narrative itself than as a contradiction of the actor-director's word.[4]

Yet if the actor stands in direct counterpoint to the profound negativity of *Yeux bleus*, he does not resolve it. He is merely another symptom of its crisis, occupying the place of all those intertextual Great Others that *Yeux bleus* could perhaps have embraced but did not. The opening episode, for instance, redolent both of Aschenbach's first sighting of Tadzio in Thomas Mann's *Der Tod in Venedig* (1911) and of Saint-Loup's passage through the hotel lobby that one hot day in Balbec in *A la recherche*, is never returned to its pretexts in the interests of intertextual betrayal.[5] In fact, rather strangely, the novel appears to wash up verbal and thematic debris from other contemporary French fiction such as Monique Lange's *Les cabines de bain* (1984) and Maurice Roche's *Maladie Mélodie* (1980).[6] In addition, like *lui*'s face smeared with rouge, it displays only literal, overt references, to 'La Callas' for example (p. 69), and her interpretation of *Norma*—all too casual, however, to generate precise fantasies of murderous, intertextual desire. Indeed, in its depiction of 'cinematically' sad protagonists ('he shouts, he cries, like desperate people in bleak films' [p. 13]), *Yeux bleus* appears to have fallen foul of the gloomy tendencies of 1980s French gay cinema represented best by Patrice Chéreau's *L'homme blessé* (1983), a highly pessimistic film about the seamy side to male gay life in Paris.[7]

In short, *Yeux bleus* is whatever Durasian sexuality and textuality are not. Neither Inside nor Outside, it performs what is essentially a 'desublimation' of *Maladie*, an elliptical text already described by Duras as 'that which would remain with you once you had read a book of that title—which does not exist—a very old book that would narrate the story in long form'.[8] *Yeux bleus* is that 'ancient book', risen, it seems, *après-coup* to supply information lacking in the earlier text (e.g. the sexual cause of *elle*'s bruised hands [p. 79]). It vomits up phrases and ideas from the earlier text as though arrested in a fantasy of incorporation, and *Maladie*'s occasional impudence (*elle*'s caustic dismissal of *vous*'s idea that the sea is black, for example) rebounds paraphrastically into the final stages of *Yeux bleus* as no more than a vain after-thought in reported speech (p. 149). Similarly, the novel's chunks of estranged adaptation contrast with the short, supplementary text included at the end of *Maladie*, 'La maladie pourrait être représentée au théâtre . . .', in which still further creative possibilities of ironic inversion are proposed (e.g. the suggestion that the male narrator speak in a high–pitched, female voice).

We can now understand better, perhaps, why Duras treated *Yeux bleus* as an alien body, for it has effectively succumbed to the *empêchement* of its male protagonist, the 'beast' (p. 41), a 'false lover' because unable to love (p. 86). In this extreme case of text as psyche, the novel, locked in the hold of *Maladie*, enacts *lui*'s unresolved mourning for the loss of an inaccessible sailor-double, an *homme fatal* in a white yacht. Failing to impose a definitive form on its material which it thus maintains as an untouchable, archaic mother,[9] *Yeux bleus* constitutes an instance of Kristeva's melancholic caught in unresolved mourning for his 'auto-sensual pre-object', the hidden force of which is figured powerfully by *elle*'s sex, that 'abhorred' and 'monumental thing'. Even the one successful moment of contact in the novel is immediately disavowed as an 'entire secret, a happiness that must be sacrificed' (p. 130), like the 'criminal and mad secret' lying under the surface of our 'diplomatic behaviours' (Kristeva).[10] And just as the male protagonist is inexorably drawn towards the hotel's pre-Oedipal, glass space containing women and children (p. 88), so, too, *Yeux bleus* wraps itself in a narcissistic envelope of abstract patterns and reflections, a fact underlined by the denotative and fetishistic force of the recurring titular phrase, 'les yeux bleus cheveux noirs'.

Of course, it could be argued very differently that the novel is more radical than any Duras Minuit text which presents itself as a performance of the possible by demonstrating universal truths of sexual difference. For it also represents Duras's first real confrontation with the female body without the mediation of a male gaze or Father-text. Indeed, much of the excitement in reading *Yeux bleus* derives precisely from our anticipation of how long Duras can remain in such close proximity to her female creation.[11] Certainly, in its

unremitting self-absorption in the impossible and its perverse wilful-
ness not to conform to the conventions of Duras's self-ironising
textuality, the novel inspires our genuine empathy for two equally
absent characters stranded contiguously on the edge of the void, and
who struggle to love each other without recourse to orgasm, or the
'comfort' of wild and murderous desire.[12] This is what Duras herself
eventually concedes when, in an interview four years later, she
acknowledges that just as there exists in *Yeux bleus* more 'orgasm'
than in *Maladie*, so, too, there is now more love 'for' someone, as
opposed to simply love 'of' homosexuality.[13]

How Duras finally regains her critical equanimity and re-estab-
lishes firm, authorial control over the aberrant, 'homosexual body' of
Yeux bleus is what interests us most here. Her rewriting of a deficient
Minuit text will not only reveal the full scope of her rhetorical
commitment to 'heterotextual' reclamation but also elucidate her
literary relationship with 'Y.A., homosexuel'. Already in the first,
limited edition of *Yeux bleus* designed for journalists and critics,
Duras took the rather unusual step of writing her own afterword. This
was an impassioned plea to the reader for special tolerance in the face
of an exceptional text, one which tells of a 'feeling' so far unnamed in
novels and which has neither vocabulary nor rituals. Contrary to
appearances, this is not just a crude example of commercial self-
promotion on Duras's part, for what she is attempting to do here is
regenerate, à la lettre, a literary accessory which has begun to fall out
of use.[14] The afterword, or *prière d'insérer* (literally, a 'request for
insertion'), is an eleventh-hour attempt by Duras to 'insert' into the
project of *Yeux bleus* its so far missing dose of sadomasochistic desire.
The reader (*vous*) is summoned directly to 'detest':

> Read the book. In every instance, even one of fundamental loathing
> [*détestation de principe*], read it. We have nothing left to lose, neither you of
> me, nor me of you. Read it all . . . Continue to read, and suddenly you will
> have traversed the story itself, its laughter, its agony, its wildernesses. Yours
> truly.[15]

Yet despite its chiastic, transferential force ('neither you / of me / nor
me / of you'), Duras's afterword arrived too late to achieve its goal.
Within weeks it was withdrawn from the pages of *Yeux bleus*
(although it still lingers on in the Italian version, and in an abridged
form on the cover of the English). It was, after all, only a 'request', not
a fully willed textual event.

And so, on 14 November 1986, to coincide with Marianne

Alphant's review of *Yeux bleus* in *Libération*, 'Le faux amant', Duras published an article on the genesis of the novel entitled, 'La pute de la côte normande', republished a month later by Minuit as a twenty-page text of the same name and sold with *Yeux bleus* as 'two by Duras'. Although treated by most critics as a straight-forward personal account of the writing of *Yeux bleus*, *Pute* requires careful critical attention.

THE BEAST

From its in medias res beginning accentuated by an ellipsis (this is *Yeux bleus* continued), *Pute* is nothing if not a tease, skirting around the phenomenon of *Yeux bleus* which, like *Vie mat.*, it stubbornly refuses to identify by name. A giddy sense of triangular structures is quickly created (three dots, 'three voices', etc.), yet no idea that *Yeux bleus*, which also made Duras the 'toy of a formal formality' (p. 8), might itself be a failed version of *Maladie*, is ever forthcoming. Despite the fact that *Maladie* is described as impossible to adapt for the stage due to its 'so evident ambiguity' and its 'closed and unitary form'. Similarly, a vaguely defined, 'ten to twelve scenic passages' ('couloirs scéniques') (p. 7) are mentioned en passant but no attempt is made to link them with the blocks of theatrical directions lying washed-up in the margins of *Yeux bleus*. Instead, with coy obfuscation, *Pute* hints in its central section at a possible source of meaning: 'that Quilleboeuf episode'. Another text, *L'homme menti*, is alluded to, then dropped. Finally, the summer of 1986 arrives, writing begins (p. 10), and Yann immediately appears on the scene as a figure of disorder, prone to lengthy periods of shouting and yelling. He it was, we learn, who stopped the natural progress of what was destined to be a standard Duras Minuit text of imaginary self-projection featuring an eighteen-year-old, first-person, female narrator. As regards the narrator of *Pute*, she herself became the victim of Yann who is revealed as a confused, promiscuous and destructive homosexual man drowning in a flood of speech not his own.

After the abortive 'detesting' of Duras's textual body in the afterword, we have now arrived at a case of concrete aggression directed against Duras's own physical body. The framing for this manoeuvre is made secure because we are back in the familiar world of *Atlantique* and *Maladie* with their confused and self-ignorant young men, variants of *l'homme tremblant*. Like them, Yann is lost in the minutiae of the real, unable to separate the 'detail' of what he desires from the 'totality' (p. 11) of what he has always wanted and lacked. Originally an innocent homosexual tapper (or '*tapette*') of the typewriter keys typing up Duras's manuscript under her dictation, he has now become a beast, thrusting his way physically into the narrator's private space. Yet could it be that the narrator herself has deliberately provoked this situation due to her particular choice of subject matter? Has she, that is, actually programmed Yann's 'unpredictable' nature by invoking a former model of disgust towards her body (the novel was meant to include a man who hated the narrator's body), thus defying him to do better (or worse)? Certainly, Yann goes out cruising with other men, returning only to harangue the narrator, a precise schedule of pain and gratification begins to take shape: '[a]fterwards, we'd sometimes laugh . . . I lived with that all summer. I was to hope for it, too' (pp. 17–18). As this strange passion continues to develop, the narrator's autobiographical project is inverted into its 'other', i.e. pure fiction, a fact somehow linked to the exotic foreignness of Yann's 'mad' desire for 'big barmen' from Argentina or Cuba (p. 19). The narrator is still always in charge, however, for although she presents her situation as one of involuntary loss and pain, she effectively controls it as a personal fantasy of sadomasochistic desire. Yann, for instance, will always carry with him an old blue bag that she had sewn for him to run her errands (p. 11). Moreover, because all possible threats of male doubling in *Pute* have been removed from the outset (Siam, we are reminded, is no more), the narrator can easily single Yann out and reify him as 'the taxi's friend' prior to making the necessary move of separation: 'I completely separated him from his words, as if he had caught them unwittingly, and they had made him ill' (p. 16).[16] In the process, he is made writable, and thus readable, as *ça*: 'Eventually, it [*ça*] could begin to be read. We had arrived in a place where life was not totally absent' (p. 19).[17]

During a scene of nomination of the type denied in *Yeux bleus*, Yann's insults are eventually reclaimed by the narrator as the personal seal of a fictional identity—'la pute de la côte normande'—which she had sought perhaps all along in *Pute* by 'whorishly' identifying him by his real name. That this scene might constitute part of the narrator's on-going treatment for the real or imagined trauma of being physically rejected when she was eighteen is a matter for conjecture. What we can say, however, is that *Yeux bleus* has now been redefined by Duras as a personal, even heroic attempt to confront the unhealthy body and mind of Yann ('I knew more and more things about Yann', she states [on page 18]). Not only that, but by first rendering him mute and then remoulding his sadistic impulses into fantasies of proper heterosexual difference, she is eventually able to domesticate him. He has been transported from his cruising-ground of Caen to Quille-boeuf, that mysterious, blunted point of reference which reads literally as a violent game of skittles (*quilles*) hurled over beast-like matter (*boeuf*). The narrator writes: 'All directions [or senses: *sens*] would converge in him [Yann] at the end of the day . . . There were the tides, too, and then Quilleboeuf, which one knew to be far away, as everpresent as Yann' (pp. 19–20).[18]

Yet if *Pute* sublimates wild, indiscriminate and promiscuous (Y)an(n)ality in the precise, readable contours of a heterosexual narrative of sadomasochistic sexuality, thus producing a recognition of Yann's latent, *heterosexual* desire, it does so through recourse to the rhetoric and ideology of the 'homosexual closet', in particular the use of disclosure and revelation as a truth of sexual identity. In this respect it echoes the narrator's efforts in *A la recherche* to reveal retroactively the double identity of Charlus by placing the signs of his sexual identity in the 'correct' order.[19] The narrator of *Pute* also appears to fit into the common literary pattern of heterosexual women who know male sexuality better than men, especially when the latter are undergoing what Eve Kosofsky Sedgwick has called the 'crisis of homosexual panic' in male homosocialisation,[20] or what Duras herself depicts as the violent metamorphosis, or 'passage', from heterosexuality into homosexuality, where a man represses the hypothesis that he is gay and, unlike his wife, 'recognises' nothing (*Vie mat.*, p. 46). However, by avoiding the literary topos of the omnipotent, yet unknowing, mother of cognitive ignorance who cannot, and must not, know her inscrutable son, the narrator of *Pute* never falls victim to her own interpretive skills. And unlike Catherine Bartram in Duras's stage adaptation of James's *The Beast in the Jungle*, who tried to manipulate her lover, John Marcher, by steering him towards (homo)sexual self-awareness, she will live to tell her story, that of her own sadomasochistic desire.[21] What this means, in short, is that her transferential needs win out over those of Yann.

The narrator's counter-aggression against Yann is played out characteristically in the form of a textual event. She first reconfirms

Yann's taste for scandal which seemed to place her life in so much danger but which was always handicapped because expressed in contradictory terms: '[i]t went beyond the *reasonable limits of reason, or the unreasonable limits of the same reason. It was like a target: kill that*' (p. 18, emphasis added).[22] She then concludes the text with a deliberately self-convoluting but chiastically-arranged argument on the semantic difference between *se passer* (to happen) and *arriver* (to take place), designed to provoke the reader as surely as her earlier withholding of the secret of Quilleboeuf. She writes:

> Here [*Yeux bleus* or *Pute?*], readers are going to say, 'What has taken hold of her? *Nothing happened*, since *nothing takes place*'. Whereas in fact *what took* place is *what happened*. And when nothing else takes place, then the story is truly out of the reach of writing and reading. (*Pute*, p. 20, emphasis added)[23]

This self-ironising play on the facts of knowledge and non-knowledge offers concrete proof of *Pute*'s erotic potency. In addition, the final sentence of self-mystifying, solipsistic logic appears to reinvent the paradox of Wittgenstein's precept about the unsayable limits of language as discussed by Blanchot at the end of his account of *Maladie* in *La communauté inavouable* (pp. 92–93), i.e. that in order to express the thought: 'That about which one cannot speak must be kept silent', Wittgenstein had to use language. It is as if Duras were not simply redefining all criteria for the reception of *Yeux bleus*— 'passing it' off as an error of *male* homosexuality, a 'homo-thing'— but also attempting to draw a complete distance from the whole saga, one that includes the novel's fatal precursor, *Maladie*, and its 'formal weight' of misleading criticism. The *Maladie/Yeux bleus* cycle would thus appear to have run its course.

The vapid hyper-logic of *Pute*'s final paragraph, in particular its parallelling of violence (*prendre*) and textual coming (*arriver*), illustrates, however, the limitations of Duras's self-reflexive, literary technique. In a direct reversal of the Baudelairean fear that art might emasculate the artist, nothing could take place in *Yeux bleus* because *everything* had already happened in the real. In effect, the novel was already 'desexualised' by the erotic events related in *Pute* and thus unable to perform for itself a sublime, sadomasochistic poetics. This is surely what Duras is referring to when she remarks in one interview that what she 'writes' in *Maladie* she 'lives' in *Yeux bleus*.[24] An 'error' in the production of *Yeux bleus* has been formally, and only too logically, played out in the novel's 'false', homosexual prose, where a male actor-cum-director usurps the word of Duras. Yet despite its stunning recuperation of *Yeux bleus*, *Pute* represents only a Pyrrhic victory. The two texts quickly lost their joint identity on the French bookshelf and were sold separately. Hence, the ironic play between them is completely lost, there being no clear textual referent to anchor the meaning of words like 'ici' and 'le livre'. For this reason, *Pute* achieves little more than the inserted afterword, both pieces ending up a curious irrelevance to *Yeux bleus*. The result is that Duras now has three disarticulated moments of sublimation on her hands: (1) an abject text (*Yeux bleus*); (2) loose transferential affect (the after-word); (3) rhetorical play (*Pute*). If only these three events had occurred at the same time, they could have formed one perfect Duras text! Instead, they have all fallen victim to the 'formal fatality' of *Maladie*. What is there left now to do?

The answer, as we would expect from Duras, can only be a 'counter-fatality' of form, or a 'second voyage' back into normality. A whole study could be devoted to illustrating how the deathly homosexual *thing* of *Yeux bleus* is finally reversed into a heterosexual triumph. It would trace, for example, the intertextual network of rhetorical inversions which are staged in *Vie mat.* as soon as Duras's admission of failure has been made, notably in the statement—directly refuting *Pute*—that 'what took place every day was *not* necessarily what happened every day' (p. 91, emphasis added). Textual 'errors' and reversals are also committed in the chapter immediately following 'Le livre', 'Quilleboeuf', where Quilleboeuf is truncated into 'Quillebeuf' and a confusion of dates assails the reader ('I told you that Quillebeuf had triggered the desire to write. In fact, it's the reverse' [p. 92]). These are then developed in the following chapter, 'L'homme menti', which returns us to the borders of desublimation, or *'empêchement'*, before then playing itself out mock-tragically through recourse to a dead metaphor, 'to die of love'. The strictly heterosexual figure of the 'man who is a lie', and who ironically attains his final 'deliverance' during the moment of sexual climax, tropes theatrically on the deathliness (or 'lie to life') that is Durasian homosexuality. Happily poised somewhere between truth and fiction, he can do everything that the 'false' lover of *Yeux bleus* cannot, i.e. write a 'man's book', read difference *'à travers'*, overcome an otherwise fatal infarctus, and, most importantly of all, make love exclusively to women through his expert application of 'a brutality at once controlled and savage, frightening and polite' (p. 94). *Empêche-*

ment as a psychological disease is transformed into a purely physiolo-
gical, and thus curable, minor ailment, the inevitable victory of
healthy heterosexual desire being sealed by the narrator's active
penetration of masculine space. On the eighth day she 'resisted' and
'mounted the scaffold' (p. 98), entering the café to meet her man.

'L'homme menti' performs, in short, a double triumph of the
Possible. Firstly, it effectively writes up the text described in *Pute* as
unfinished. Secondly, by demonstrating the ascension of heterosexual
desire and commenting on it axiomatically with a universal manifesto
of love based on the 'permanency' of female desire (p. 96), it
completes the maturational cycle of genital heterosexuality. Hence, a
protracted series of Duras texts has now been straightened out and
reshaped heterosexually, rendering impossible any description of gay
'passage', or even of one man's rebirth into life through the 'incidental' discovery of his latent homosexual desire. This is despite the fact
that, by Duras's own admission, there exists no greater instance of the
powers of transformation (*Vie mat.*, p. 46). To relate such an epic
story would run counter to Duras's formal thematics of textual 'love',
a sadomasochistic mode of heterosexualised violence which can go
only one way, from manic Eros to sublime Eros. Duras's later writing,
where textual 'accidents' must be read as so many sublimations of the
unforeseen, violent 'accident' of male homosexuality, constitutes
what we may term a 'homotextual closet'. For although a gay man
provides the very foundation of *Yeux bleus* and *Pute*, he is never
allowed to cruise openly the grounds of Duras's (inter)textual space
nor indeed is he able to experience the rapture of his first coming out.
If that were the case, how would a Duras text possibly 'come'?

M.D.

We have now firmly established that formal deformation is Duras's
only effective guarantee against two *empêchements*, one sublime (the
influence of a perfect text: *Maladie*), the other abject (beastly
inversion: Yann). This fact raises several key questions. Firstly,
because they so closely skirt each other, might not the sublime and the
abject in Duras's writing be considered the same thing? Secondly,
what kind of partnership is it that allows Duras to displace responsibility for an aberrant text on to Yann while at the same time claiming
Andréa's *M.D.* as one of her own, sublimely 'intangible' books (*Vie*

mat., p. 88)? What, in other words, are the limits of possession and appropriation of the gay Other in Duras's cross-textual relations, and how do they inflect the lines of gender and textual difference we have traced so far in her work? We need to turn now to Andréa and his own text, *M.D.*

The narrator of *M.D.* relates with the scrupulous care of a faithful archivist the last three weeks that Duras spent writing *Maladie*. He reveals the extremes and paradoxes of a situation in which M.D. (Duras, although this is never spelt out) is about to complete a book on the 'malady of death' while herself in grave personal danger due to treatment for detoxification. Stylistically, *M.D.* reads like a pastiche of the normal Duras Minuit text in its overt, sometimes verbatim citation of the recent corpus, notably *Night*, and in its snatches of choicest Duras (e.g.: 'You are my absolute preference, from now on inevitable' [p. 45]; 'You say: To write is to know how to resist writing' [p. 133][25]). This impression is further confirmed by the text's principal features, including its joint thematics of pain, loss and the possibility of love by 'definitive separation' (p. 121), its constant recourse to an originary scene of rapture at Trouville in 1980, and, finally, its reliance on a foreign intertextual other, Jack London's autobiographical novel, *Martin Eden* (1909). *M.D.* even performs a standard Durasian negation of its chosen intertext: whereas Martin's life and literary career ended with his own drowning, M.D., after almost literally sinking in alcohol since 30 August 1980, eventually returns home to Paris to sign the final proofs of yet another masterpiece (p. 133). Unlike in Duras's own Minuit texts, however, the over-explicit nature of this intertextual event produces an effect of plodding awkwardness and even prosaic decoration, exacerbated by the complete absence of irony. Such earnestly delivered sentences as 'You look around you, you see' (p. 110) have none of the figurative playfulness of the repeated 'Vous voyez?' in *Camion*. Indeed, the erotic Durasian touch of intertextual 'holding' is only a literal, half-hearted gesture here, as when the narrator describes how he merely 'wished' the doctor (J.D.) to remain close to both himself and M.D. (p. 15).

Why, then, does Andréa mime Duras's style so imperfectly? Let us continue for a moment with our description of the text. If M.D. is on the point of death for much of *M.D.*, the narrator, in a dramatic reversal of the situation recorded in *Pute*, continues to write and transcribe even under fierce verbal assault. Here is a brief sample:

'You say: "I don't understand how one can live as you do, in such a cowardly manner. You might as well be dead"'. I don't reply, I barely manage to avoid crying' (p. 67).[26] But what is the exact nature of Andréa's apparently selfless and objective writing? Certainly he has authorial power over M.D., coolly observing her *delirium tremens* just as Duras once did the overwhelming intensity of *l'homme tremblant*. He even remarks at one point: 'You tremble. I am the only one to notice it, this trembling' (p. 19). Could it be, in fact, that Andréa's text is 'trembling' intertextually with *Maladie*, published only months before, for both texts, engaged as they are in an intertextual dialogue with '*vous*', seem to be working with and against each other? Take the following examples:

> *Maladie*: You continue to speak, alone in the world, as you like it. (p. 49)
> *M.D.*: I am the only one in the world. (p. 36)
> *Maladie*: . . . your sex cocked up in the dark . . . calls out where to go, where to get rid of the tears that fill it up. (p. 7)
> *M.D.*: I don't cry, I do not want to cry. The tears remain in my eyes. (p. 23)[27]

This degree of intertextual echoing has led one critic to suggest that *M.D.* might even have been 'edited' by Duras herself.[28] If so, it would perform a literary 'crime' of the kind executed by *The Autobiography of Alice B. Toklas*, a book unattributed when it first appeared in 1933 and which only on the last page revealed itself to be a history of Gertrude Stein's life in Paris authored by Stein.

If, however, in its cross-textual relations with *Maladie*, *M.D.* is not simply a personal exercise in narcissism—Marguerite, like her namesake in Dumas's *La Dame aux Camélias*, offering to 'immortality' (p. 121) the 'millennial contents' of her genius (p. 60)—we might well wonder which of the narrators of these two texts is the real aggressor and which the victim. *M.D.* is shown to have refashioned her surrender to illness into a 'sublime submission to the erasured page' (p. 91). Yet what of Andréa's own passive submission to her spoken word: *M.D.*: 'Write!' (p. 135); the narrator: 'I write' (p. 37)? The narrator's transcriptive act of love, made, he claims, 'to make the separation less great, to save you [M.D.] from mortality' (p. 137), is presented as an identification even to the point of osmosis, one that requires his own self-cancellation as a fully active author à la Duras.[29] Might this be the sign of a destructive wish on his part, like that first sublime yet fateful day when he met M.D. at Trouville and immediately started to collude with her in alcoholic excess? Or is he, in fact, not so much identifying with the character of *lui* in *Night* and his doomed desire for an ailing, unavailable *elle*, as killing off M.D. even more thoroughly so as actually to desire her? After all, Duras subsequently revealed that Andréa began to desire her body when it was reduced during the course of treatment to the helpless state of a mute vegetable (*Vie mat.*, p. 80). Furthermore, what are we to make of such sentences in *M.D.* as the following: 'Around midnight, I leave the room. I am leaving you there, a stranger, abandoned, I am leaving you' (p. 23), and: 'Always, this barely visible trembling of life, the unstoppable wound, the damage done to your numbed body, this splendour returned from afar, this marvellous mess [*ce ratage merveilleux*], you' (p. 131)?[30]

We can surely agree without too much difficulty that *M.D.* is Andréa's counter-reaction to an extreme, involuntarily induced state of impotence, of waiting and confusion, when he feels that M.D. wants to die and therefore abandon him ('I want to die if I know you're dead . . . That's what you want, for me to die, and for the world to disappear' [p. 34][31]). All the remembered and fantasised scenes of love in *M.D.* contain, in fact, a barely concealed anger at M.D.'s seemingly limitless powers of imaginary projection and invention (e.g.: 'That over which you have no influence, you deny. You say: That doesn't exist' [p. 35]). Yet is it not also possible that Andréa's patient, self-effacing and submissive text constitutes no less an imaginary fantasy of aggression against *vous* than *Maladie*, where the narrator aids and abets *elle* in her attack on a homosexual man (*vous*)? If this is the case, then Andréa's authorial desire would be as sadomasochistic in nature as that of M.D., whose wish to die, we are told, goes hand in hand with a desire to head 'straight for the kill' (p. 76) ('droit là où ça tue'). Clearly, *M.D.* and *Maladie*, two texts directed at specific referents (Duras and Andréa respectively), form between them a violent ritual of aggression and eroticised revenge more complex than the simple games of contradiction played out on the sound-track of the film *Dialogo di Roma* (Andréa: 'You'd think it rained'/Duras: 'No, it wasn't raining', etc.), and certainly more profound than Duras's earlier film collaborations with men such as Depardieu and Jacquot.[32] As such, this private, intertextual affair— what the narrator of *M.D.* means perhaps when he refers to a 'continual to-ing and fro-ing [*va-et-vient incessant*] between life and death' (p. 45)—functions as a second, higher stage of the verbal erotics of 'love' that he experienced with M.D. during their first days together, when she commanded him to bandy insults she herself had invented (p. 36).[33] Not only does it write over the hollowness of alcohol, which, as Duras has remarked elsewhere, 'transfigures' the 'phantasms' of solitude at grave, nearly fatal risk to one's health,[34] but it also compensates for the 'passage' of non-consummated desire, that 'tenacious lack' and 'privation' (p. 27), experienced after M.D.'s return to Paris from the hospital.

Out of two opposing negatives, then—a young non-heterosexual man and an ageing heterosexual woman whose age and sex make her, according to Lois Banner, 'doubly the Other' in Western society[35]— Duras and Andréa pull off a double triumph of the Possible. Theirs is a self-styled, illegal romance between 'liars', with Duras misquoting her significant other through rhetorical manoeuvres of literary fantasy. One could go even further and say that Duras and Andréa are troping vertically on the so-called 'horizontal', sexual collaboration between Nazi soldiers and French women during the Second World War, a subject Duras explored in her own cinematic collaboration with Resnais, *Hiroshima*.[36] Moreover, in an inversion of the courtly love equation, Duras's reconfiguring of the non-coincidental nature of her desire for a gay man supplements the lack of a heterosexual, sexual relation, i.e. she pretends that it is he, and not her, who presents the real obstacle. In her hands, collaboration has become a 'safer-sex' practice, a dandified discourse, or 'gaieté-lyrique' (*M.D.*, p. 59), between two self-styled 'princes' lying on, and over, each other's texts. As the interlocutor of *Emily* states: 'What we prefer to do is write books on each other [*l'un sur l'autre*]. And we laughed' (p. 61).

The reality, of course, of these magical textual operations is less a splitting of the Author in a radical, Bakhtinian *heteroglossia* of shared authorship than an orchastration of literary sex-toys moulded by Duras over Andréa. For like the Stein-Toklas 'marriage', the Duras-Andréa partnership illustrates just how easily literary collaboration can degenerate into the confusing rhetoric of collusion or, in Duras's own vocabulary, 'connivence' (Stein: 'There is collaboration that in collusion that there has been collusion'[37]). This should not detract, however, from the scale of Duras's achievement, for by sublimating Andréa in an intertextual relationship where she is, and has, the phallus, she reinvents a literary tradition of legendary French lovers that includes the epistolary exchange between Héloïse and Abélard (where the latter was thought to have been the sole author), the chaste *tendre amitié* between Madeleine de Scudéry and Paul Pellison (eighteen years her junior), even Marguerite Yourcenar's last, tempestuous affair with her young, gay male lover, Jerry Wilson.[38] Already the name Andréa, gendered feminine when used as a first name in German and charged with Proustian resonances, constitutes a concerted literary act by Duras—her troping on Andréa's original surname, Lemée.[39] What, in fact, could be more autoerotic than for M.D. to sublimate the sub-Duras of *M.D.*?

Such intertextual play may not perhaps produce anything 'new', as it can, for example, in heterosexual male collaboration where, according to Wayne Koestenbaum, expressed and repressed homoerotic feelings give rise to a textual intercourse that is at once a female body the men can share and the child of their partnership.[40] Yet, as an *'entreprise de séduction'*, the Duras-Andréa partnership possesses the same, efficient, erotic power as the sexually explicit novel, *Histoire d'O.* (1954), key to Dominique Aury's successful strategy to keep alive a secret love affair with Jean Paulhan.[41] This is because it performs for Duras two specific functions. Firstly, it allows her to overcome once and for all the rival, gay influence of Barthes from whom Andréa had tried (in vain) to obtain a position in Paris shortly after the publication of *Fragments*.[42] Secondly, it outrivals the most famous model of political and literary collaboration in post-War France, that between Sartre and de Beauvoir, which ended with Sartre's death in 1980, the year Duras and Andréa began. If the pain of Andréa's *M.D.* matches at times de Beauvoir's own sad record of her mother's last days in *Une mort très douce* (1964) (also set in the American Hospital at Neuilly), and if his apparent obeisance reproduces some of the negative effects of what has been described as de Beauvoir's 'erotico-theoretical transference relation' with Sartre,[43] the unresolved intertextual ambiguities and ironies of *M.D.* are still a world apart from de Beauvoir's often monotonous and lugubrious testimony of Sartre's incontinent last years in *La cérémonie des adieux* (1981) (a book for which she was even accused of illegally seizing an inheritance[44]). Furthermore, if de Beauvoir, like Duras, used and abused an incestuous and surrogate family of homosexual thirds, she did so 'authentically', that is to say, masochistically, by consigning herself to the traditional role of *entremetteuse* for her young entourage. As Tante Simone she would enlist various *'femme-lettes'* (Olga, Wanda, Bianca) to supplement a literary marriage of dependence which, by her own admission, always made her feel inferior and which left her ultimately a depressed alcoholic.[45] Compare this sorry tale with Duras's 'cross-age', rhetorical relations with Andréa, whereby Duras is able to generate a fixed dose of erotic excitement as a way of surviving the climacteric passage of old-age. Following one gerontological tradition outlined by de Beauvoir herself in *La Vieillesse* (1970), Duras magnifies the sexual power of her diction and thematics—one of the few outlets for older women's still potent libido and narcissism—and, by means of the happy intermediary of Andréa, crosses the ever-widening gap between the imaginary she seeks to realise and the reality working to prevent it.[46]

But why 'Y.A., homosexuel' exactly? For Duras, male homosexuality represents that part of man's natural wildness which has not yet been tamed or 'transgressed'.[47] Its particular 'provocation to violence' derives from a constant 'recalling of the taboo'.[48] For this reason, Andréa's 'delinquent' capacity for self-combusting rage is simply a natural expression of his sexuality, and as such, according to Duras, provides the means for understanding sexuality in general.[49] In fact, Duras's use of Andréa fully exploits homosexuality's Freudian status as the principal energising force behind homosocialisation. In textual terms *M.D.*, like Renaud Camus's *Passage* (see pp. 108–11 above), serves as a general source of reference for the heterotextual erotics of *écriture courante*.[50] It is the prosaic and abject 'behind' not only of the self-troping *Maladie* but also of texts as varied as *Douleur*, with its common store of fantasised images of death, and *Emily*, with its predominant dialogical form (*je/vous*). It can even be regarded as the early prototype of all Duras's 140–50 page experiments in metadiscursive writing, beginning with *Amant*.

Paradoxically, then, Y.A.'s deathly, homosexual body is impressively productive, functioning as a bankable quotient of anality and 'realness' ripe for literary sublimation through the processes of metaphorical equivalence and conversion. In fact, Y.A. is writing itself, even though he does not write (in his own voice, that is). He can reverse the direction of the narrator's project in *Pute* 'without having to do it at all, without any idea whatsoever other than to destroy it' (p. 14). In *Tout*, which see-saws between affirmation and negation and where the 'indecipherable' Yann is both the 'author of everything' (p. 41) and 'a double zero' (p. 51), the narrator declaims: 'Everything has been written by you [*toi*], by this body that you have. / I am going to stop this text here and take up another one by you, written for you, written in your place' (p. 42).[51] The narrator of *Emily* is more precise: 'You [*vous*] don't write because you know everything about what it is, that tragic thing, writing, about doing it or not doing it, about not being able to do it. You know everything. It's because you are a writer that you don't write' (p. 56).[52] Just as the story of the failed, impossible love in that novel is prevented from being completely written due to the residual love *je* feels for *vous*, so, too, homosexuality, or 'failed' heterosexuality, like Lacanian love, can never cease not being written.

In such a way Y.A. is both abject *and* sublime. He constitutes a reliable site of 'passage' which can be immediately sublimated, then desublimated, to be ironically resublimated, and so on. In the filmic terms proposed by *Atlantique*, he is both an absent image and a fully inked-in screen of black writing. In fact, he performs almost mathematically as a chiastic point of reversal—'Y./A.'—for the entire later corpus, the point where its abject and sublime axes intersect most visibly and where the rhetorical structure of the Duras Sublime—literary and filmic—folds over into the psychoanalytical process of sublimation. If Andréa's identity is never stable, it is only because Duras is never quite at the same stage of sublimation. He ranges in status from editor and classifier of *Outside* to pseudo-chronicler in *M.D.*, from minor assistant during the 1983 staging of *Savannah* to silent interviewer and amanuensis in *Tout* and interviews for *Libération*[53], and from sexual partner and Jewish husband in *Yann* to simply 'friend' in *Douleur* (p. 86). He can also function as Duras's privileged agent of sublimation, adapting and abstracting the core fantasy structure of *Eté* for Duras to read aloud on audio-cassette in *La jeune fille et l'enfant* (1981). As we noted briefly in our discussion of *Vie mat.* in Chapter 5, he can even be schooled in the paternal gesture.

Andréa is thus always more than either a simple 'pendant' to Duras (*Tout*, p. 33) or, to take the other extreme, the sole inheritor of her work (*M.D.*, p. 59). He may indeed appear as the superfluous background to Duras's prolific late period—an impression cultivated in publicity shots where, like Toklas with Stein, he is a silent, secondary presence—but this is only because we have not yet properly learned to read the Duras image. Take the case of the photograph which accompanies Duras's interview with Gilles Costaz in *Le Matin* to celebrate the publication of *Yeux bleus*. Andréa, facing left while fingering his glasses in the Duras manner, appears as only a fragile silhouette reflected in the mirror behind Duras who is seated in the foreground and is looking up to the right but at a different angle

(Andréa's own reflection is visible behind Duras but to the left). Situated in a structure of transversals recalling the shot/reverse shot sequence of *Camion*, Andréa is already a simulation and parody of the 'real thing', rendered, like Charlus's 'almost symbolic *derrière*' in *A la recherche*, both hypervisible and invisible.[54] Although the photograph might initially signal a spectacular dramatisation of the negative mirror stage of old age as defined by Lacan (Duras rejecting her mirror image in order to reject old-age itself), it actually reveals how, with Andréa's presence, Duras can project an intensified (self)aggressivity on to an easily recognisable other.[55] The play of reflections here presents less a feared trajectory from wholeness to final physical disintegration than the elation of the first mirror-stage, that originary passage into narcissism and identity.

The crossed relations between Duras and Andréa are even more subtle in a remarkable article produced for the November 1993 issue of French *Vogue* and entitled 'Une journée à Trouville'. This is a ten-page collection of texts and images comprising three main elements: photographs by Dominique Issermann of Duras, Andréa, and odd personal objects (Duras's hand-bag and pen, for example); a letter written by Andréa beginning 'à vous, M.D.'; and small extracts from her work, notably the newly published *Ecrire*. The first photograph presents Duras seated and alone while confronting the viewer's gaze head-on, the second (see Frontispiece) shows Andréa standing against a window and staring down at her (she appears unaware of his presence). The caption—red on black—reads: 'I find that it's like cinema . . . A certain type of cinema. He's really looking at me. And I'm looking sideways.'[56] The effect of discordance created by this sequence seems to be the main subject of Andréa's letter on the facing page (p. 161), which speaks of the need to possess a true, if impossible, image of *vous*. If it were not for the fact that the letter is titled and that Andréa's name appears at the bottom of the page, we might suppose that this piece was actually written by Duras herself. For lacking any gendered features of grammar to anchor it one way or the other, it reads, like *M.D.*, as a typical Duras piece on writing, silence, and the need for human contact. Take the following sentence, for instance: 'You see, I'm writing to you. I'm writing a letter to you as if it were possible, as if the address were possible in this case.' Included in the letter are some of the trade-marks of Duras's style such as the intensive use of the conditional tense, sequences of rhetorical questions and the repetition of familiar words like 'tellement'. In fact, it is only the last, rather naïve line depicting physical proximity—'[t]o be silent and give you a kiss [*Se taire et vous donner un baiser*]'—that allows this letter to be read as *not* a piece by Duras.

The dialectics of identity and difference begun in the title of 'Une journée à Trouville' (is this a typical day in Trouville or the one exception?) is continued in the paradox of the caption supplied for the image of Duras's pen: this is a pen resembling all pens but recognisable from a thousand. It is, however, the concluding double-page spread of Duras and Andréa pictured together in close-up that brings the article to its appropriate climax. Both are now facing the camera, both are wearing similar Russian-style hats, and, lying at the bottom of the page, are these patently false words: 'We're anyone. It's not bad to be like everybody. But where is the sea [*On est n'importe qui. C'est pas mal d'être comme tout le monde. Mais où est la mer*]'. Typically, the last enigmatic phrase, a question lacking a question mark, falls under the eyes of Andréa and places him once again in the sphere of the Thing. Thus, if the photograph appears to unite Duras and Andréa even to the point of a shared identity, the caption sets them definitively apart, demonstrating that Duras's unique voice will always make its difference felt even if it is actually unclear who is speaking, Duras or Andréa, her perfect foil. In this, a consummation of all the previous performances of Durasian passage and error that we have explored in this study, Duras 'passes over' to an agent of gay *passage* (the 'death' of sexual difference), and thus protects herself from prematurely 'passing on' (the death of all difference). Andréa— 'Y.A., homosexuel'—has thus become like one of the visions recounted in *M.D.*, where what actually saves M.D. from indefinite abjection is its most potent, oral and anal manifestation:

> there's one of them, it's the leader . . . he has a dwarf-like body with a hairy piglet's tail. He puts it all the time into his mouth as if he were smoking it. Initially it makes me afraid and want to vomit. And then I realised that he was guarding me against invasion by the other animals. (*M.D.*, p. 113)[57]

Duras has succeeded where psychoanalysis and reason have both failed: homosexuality, a dominion, like death, accessible to no-one except God,[58] has been recuperated as an erotic form of heterosexual object-relations. This represents the climax to all her textual and cinematic experiments in erotic pleasure which produce a sublimatory, rhetorical appropriation of the Other as a defence against the threat of homosexual undifferentiation. It is an uncomfortable fact, however, that our own discussion has, in the manner of Duras, written over the silence of Andréa and so created a mystery. Andréa's capacity for intertextual abuse appears without limit, and, as the voice of the Other shaping the theoretical reception of the Duras corpus with such public statements as: 'She [Duras] is a witness to the arrival of the Other [*la venue de l'Autre*], the text', he appears to have an all-consuming purpose, that of guaranteeing Duras's futurity.[59] Until Andréa speaks out and writes for himself, an act which may well reduce the compulsive terror and excitement of the later Duras corpus, our only recourse is to continue theorising the desire of 'Y.A.' and submit once again to Duras's reinvention of the collaborative form—all form—as sexual cure.

Notes to Chapter 1

pp. 1–24

1 Danielle Bajomée, *Duras ou la douleur*, Paris, Editions Universitaires, 1989.

2 'La douleur du dialogue', in Maurice Blanchot, *Le livre à venir* [1959], Paris, Gallimard, 'Folio', 1986, pp. 207–18.

3 Jacques Lacan, 'Hommage fait à Marguerite Duras, du ravissement de Lol V. Stein', *Marguerite Duras* [1975], ed. François Barat and Joël Farges, Paris, Albatros, 1979, pp. 131–37.

4 Carol J. Murphy, *Alienation and Absence in the Novels of Marguerite Duras*, Lexington, KY, French Forum, 1982.

5 'La maladie de la douleur', in Julia Kristeva, *Soleil Noir. Dépression et mélancolie*, Paris, Gallimard, 1987, pp. 227–65.

6 Bernard Alazet, 'L'embrasement, les cendres', *Revue des sciences humaines*, Vol. 73, No. 204 (October–December 1986), pp. 147–60; p. 152.

7 The present study takes *L'Empire français. Avec trois cartes*, written in collaboration with Philippe Roques and published by Gallimard in 1940 under Duras's maiden name of Donnadieu, as Duras's first book.

8 Patrick Rambaud, *Virginie Q. de Marguerite Duraille*, Paris, Balland, 1988. See also Dominique Noguez's skit, 'Aurélia Steiner (Trouville) de Marguerite Duras', in *Sémiologie du parapluie et autres textes*, Paris, Différence, 1990, pp. 114–20.

9 Guillaume Jacquet of the magazine *Réaction* retitled an extract from *Andesmas* as 'Margot et l'important' and dedicated it to Marguerite 'qui ne sait pas'. Duras did not take legal action. *Le Figaro* published a letter on 22 September 1992 written jointly by Antoine Gallimard, Jérôme Lindon, and Paul Otchakovsky-Laurens, in which they defend their 'rigorous' standards of professionalism.

10 In *Duras. Biographie*, Paris, François Bourin, 1991, for example, Alain Vircondelet uses Duras's work as a source of biographical information in order to prove that she is both a lay mystic in the tradition of Pascal and a champion of the 'exploited'. Uncritical as it is, and while no doubt a personal reaction to his earlier impressionistic study, *Marguerite Duras ou le temps de détruire*, Paris, Seghers, 1972, *Duras: Biographie* is still not as crude as Frédérique Lebelley's undiscriminating hatchet-job, *Duras ou le poids d'une plume*, Paris, Grasset, 1994, or even his own, more recent hagiography, *Pour Duras*, Paris, Calmann-Lévy, 1995.

11 Michel de Certeau, 'Marguerite Duras: On dit', *Ecrire, dit-elle. Imaginaires de M. Duras*, ed. Danielle Bajomée and Ralph Heyndels, Brussels, Université de Bruxelles, 1985, pp. 257–65.

12 See, for example, Christiane Blot-Labarrère's *Marguerite Duras*, Paris, Seuil, 'Les Contemporains' 14, 1992, which uses an astonishing volume of citation to argue that Duras's work offers a liberatory aesthetics of the possible.

13 'Le silence, c'est les femmes. Donc, la littérature c'est les femmes' (*Vie mat.*, p. 104) ('Silence is the domain of women. Thus, literature is the domain of women').

14 According to Duras, only women can 'operate the big, organic, political

transgressions'. See 'Marguerite Duras' (an interview), Suzanne Horer and Jeanne Socquet, *La création étouffée*, Paris, Pierre Horay, 1973, pp. 172–87; p. 177.

15 According to Duras, *Vice-consul* is 'submerged' in madness. See Germaine Brée, 'An interview with Marguerite Duras', *Contemporary Literature*, Vol. 13, No. 4 (1972), pp. 401–22.

16 Duras speaks in *Yeux* of 'l'indifférence', or 'the new grace of a world without God' (p. 40).

17 Duras stated that she spent two months writing *Maladie* in order to reduce it to its thinness, to 'what it was no longer possible to efface'. See Didier Eribon, 'Marguerite Duras: "C'est fou c'que j'peux t'aimer" ' (interview with Marguerite Duras and Yann Andréa), *Libération*, 4 January 1983, pp. 22–23; p. 22.

18 For Duras in 1971, a progressive loss of identity was 'the most enviable experience one could know'. See Bettina L. Knapp, 'Interviews with Marguerite Duras and Gabriel Cousin', *The French Review*, Vol. 44, No. 4 (1971), pp. 653–64; p. 656.

19 '[L]e cinéma que je fais, je le fais au même endroit que mes livres. C'est ce que j'appelle l'endroit de la passion. Là où on est sourd et aveugle. Enfin, j'essaie d'être là le plus qu'il est possible.'

20 'Ces livres sont douloureux à écrire, à lire . . . cette douleur devrait nous mener vers . . . un champ d'expérimentation . . . C'est douloureux, parce que c'est un travail qui porte sur une région non encore creusée peut-être.'

21 According to Duras, a double 'murder' of the author is committed during the production of a book: the first during the actual process of writing by the author him/herself, the second at the moment of the book's publication. See Eribon, ' "C'est fou c'que j'peux t'aimer" ', p. 22.

22 See Jean Narboni and Jacques Rivette, 'La destruction, la parole' (interview with Marguerite Duras), *Cahiers du Cinéma*, No. 217 (November 1969), pp. 45–57.

23 See Pamela Tytell, 'lacan, freud et duras', *Magazine littéraire*, no. 158 (March 1980), pp. 14–15.

24 Leslie Hill has given perhaps the most interesting reading of 'Hommage', revealing that Lacan, while he abuses literature in order to make it conform to his own 'pre-emptive fable of sublimation', is also paying homage to another Marguerite, a would-be novelist, Marguerite Anzieu, whom he analysed (and renamed) in his 1932 doctoral dissertation on paranoid psychosis, and whose maternal grandmother was called Marguerite Donnadieu (coincidentally Duras's original surname). See 'Lacan with Duras', *Journal of the Institute of Romance Studies*, Vol. 1 (1992), pp. 405–24. For a more formalist reading of 'Hommage', see John O'Brien, 'Metaphor between Lacan and Duras: Narrative Knots and the Plot of Seeing', *Forum for Modern Language Studies*, Vol. 27, No. 3 (1993), pp. 232–45.

25 See Jean-Louis Sous, 'Marguerite Duras ou le ravissement du réel', *Littoral*, No. 14 (1984), pp. 59–70.

26 See 'Sur *Le Ravissement de Lol V. Stein*' in Michèle Montrelay, *L'Ombre et le Nom: sur la féminité*, Paris, Minuit, 1977, pp. 9–23.

27 See Patricia Fedkiw, 'Marguerite Duras: Feminine field of hysteria', *Enclitic*, Vol. 6, No. 2 (1982), pp. 76–86.

28 See Mary Lydon, 'Translating Duras: The seated man in the passage', *Contemporary Literature*, Vol. 24, No. 2 (1983), pp. 259–75, and 'The forgetfulness

of memory: Jacques Lacan, Marguerite Duras, and the Text', *Contemporary Literature*, Vol. 29, No. 3 (1988), pp. 351–68.

29 See the special issue of *Didascalies* (Cahiers occasionnels de l'Ensemble Théâtral Mobile, Bruxelles), No. 3 ('Aurélia Steiner') (April 1982), pp. 3–31.

30 See Michèle Druon, 'Mise en scène et catharsis de l'amour dans *Le ravissement de Lol V. Stein*, de Marguerite Duras', *The French Review*, Vol. 58, No. 3 (February 1985), pp. 382–90, where Druon emphasises Lol's ability to perceive the 'theatricality' of love.

31 See Alice A. Jardine, *Gynesis: Configurations of woman and modernity*, Ithaca, London, Cornell University Press, 1985, in particular Chapter 8, 'Towards the Hysterical Body: Jacques Lacan and his Others'.

32 See Marie-Claire Ropars-Wuilleumier, 'The Disembodied Voice: India Song', *Yale French Studies*, No. 60 (1980), pp. 241–68.

33 See Sharon Willis, *Marguerite Duras: Writing on the Body*, Urbana, University of Illinois Press, 1987.

34 See Marcelle Marini, *Territoires du féminin. Avec Marguerite Duras*, Paris, Minuit, 1975.

35 See Susan D. Cohen, *Women and Discourse in the Fiction of Marguerite Duras*, Oxford, Macmillan, 1993.

36 See Trista Selous, *The Other Woman. Feminism and Femininity in the work of Marguerite Duras*, New Haven, London, Yale University Press, 1988, in particular, Chapter 4, 'The Blanks'.

37 In 'Marguerite and the Mountain', *Contemporary French Fiction by Women*, ed. Phil Powrie and Margaret Atack, Manchester, Manchester University Press, 1990, Selous reveals how feminists have appropriated Duras even though her work does not lend itself to a feminist reading.

38 See Susan Rubin Suleiman, 'Nadja, Dora, Lol V. Stein: women, madness and narrative', *Discourse in Psychoanalysis and Literature*, ed. Shlomith Rimmon-Kenan, London, Methuen, 1987, pp. 124–51; p. 146.

39 In her interview with Michel Foucault, 'A propos de Marguerite Duras', *Les Cahiers Renaud-Barrault*, No. 89 (October 1975), pp. 8–22, Cixous argued that one cannot talk of despair in Duras since there is no possibility of, or even wish for, the act of mourning (p. 14). Cixous also uses Kristeva's metaphor of the black sun to describe the engulfing effect of Anne-Marie Stretter's fascination on her male courtiers.

40 This situation is not helped by the fact that Kristeva is sometimes inaccurate in her use of primary sources. She claims, for example, that the arrival of Anne-Marie Stretter early in *Ravissement* is that of Lol's mother, and the article's epigraph, extracted from Duras's brief introduction to the title-text of *Douleur*, misreads Duras's opinion of 'La douleur' as a general statement on pain.

41 See Marianne Hirsch, *The Mother/Daughter Plot. Narrative, Psychoanalysis, Feminism*, Bloomington, IN, Indiana University Press, 1989, pp. 146–54, in particular the chapter, 'Waiting outside the Closed Door: Duras's *The Lover*'.

42 See Kathleen Hulley, 'Contaminated Narratives: The Politics of Form and Subjectivity in Marguerite Duras's *The Lover*', *Discourse*, Vol. 15, No. 2 (Winter 1992–93), pp. 30–50; p. 33, where Hulley employs Elizabeth Ernath's notion of the 'posthistorical subject'.

43 Daniel Sibony, 'Repenser la déprime', *Magazine littéraire*, No. 244 ('Littérature et Mélancolie') (July–August 1987), pp. 54–56.

44 '[T]outes les femmes de mes livres, quel que soit leur âge, découlent de Lol V. Stein. C'est-à-dire, d'un certain oubli d'elles-mêmes. Elles ont toutes les yeux clairs. Elles sont toutes imprudentes, imprévoyantes. Toutes, elles font le malheur de leur vie.'

45 '[Le] désir de la femme pour un homme qui n'est pas pas encore venu à elle, qu'elle ignore encore . . . La frigidité, c'est le non-désir de ce qui n'est pas cet homme.'

46 See Didier Eribon, 'Comme une messe de mariage' (interview with Marguerite Duras), *Le Nouvel Observateur*, 16–22 October 1987, pp. 60–61; p. 61. Duras's motivation for not including Proust in her definition of masculine literature (he is simply 'literature') is something we shall explore in Chapters 4 and 5.

47 See Gilles Costaz, 'Ce qui arrive tous les jours n'arrive qu'une seule fois' (interview with Marguerite Duras), *Le Matin*, 28 September 1984.

48 Pierre Bénichou and Hervé Le Masson, 'Duras tout entière. Entretien avec Marguerite Duras (un écrivain au-dessus de tout Goncourt)', *Le Nouvel Observateur*, 14–20 November 1986, pp. 56–59; p. 58.

49 'Mes livres sont-ils difficiles, c'est ça que vous voulez savoir? Oui, ils sont difficiles. Et faciles. *L'amant*, c'est très difficile. *La maladie de la mort*, c'est difficile, très difficile. *L'homme atlantique*, c'est très difficile, mais c'est si beau que ce n'est pas difficile.'

50 See Susan Husserl-Kapit, 'Marguerite Duras' (interview with Marguerite Duras), *Visions Magazine* (Spring 1993), pp. 8–12.

51 'Quelquefois je sais cela: que du moment que ce n'est pas, toutes choses confondues, aller à la vanité et au vent, écrire ce n'est rien. Que du moment que ce n'est pas, chaque fois, toutes choses confondues en une seule par essence inqualifiable, écrire ce n'est rien que publicité.'

52 See Liliane Papin, *L'Autre Scène: Le Théâtre de Marguerite Duras*, Saratoga, Anma Libri, 1988. In 'Place of Writing, Place of Love', *Remains to be Seen. Essays on Marguerite Duras,* ed. Sanford S. Ames, New York, Peter Lang, 1988, pp. 81–94, Papin even claims that Duras chooses to be 'the voice of the "Mother" and "Love", as opposed to one of authority and encompassing knowledge' (p. 82). In 'La présence du Rien', *Les Cahiers Renaud-Barrault*, No. 106 (1983), pp. 17–36, Cohen describes Duras's 'nomination' (as opposed to 'seizure') of the real ('le vide') in utopian terms as a gesture of love.

53 See Marie-Paule Ha, 'Duras on the Margins', *The Romanic Review*, Vol. 83, No. 3 (1993), pp. 299–320.

54 See Claire Cerasi, *Marguerite Duras: de Lahore à Auschwitz*, Paris, Geneva, Champion-Slatkine, 1993, p. 188.

55 Jacqueline Aubenas, 'Entretien avec Marguerite Duras', *Alternatives théâtrales*, No. 14 (March 1983), pp. 11–15; p. 14.

56 See Emmanuel Levinas, *Totalité et infini: Essai sur l'extériorité* [1961], The Hague, Martinus Nijhoff, 1971, p. 12.

57 See Judith Still, 'Literature', *Feminism and Psychoanalysis: A critical dictionary*, ed. Elizabeth Wright, Oxford, Blackwell, 1992, pp. 231–32.

58 See Janine Ricouart, *Ecriture féminine et violence. Une étude de Marguerite Duras*, Birmingham, AL, Summa, 1991.

59 Bénichou and Le Masson, 'Duras tout entière', p. 58. In *Marguerite Duras à Montréal*, ed. Suzanne Lamy and André Roy, Montreal, Spirale, 1981, Duras describes Marxism as an 'autism' and feminism as 'a rotten proposition' (p. 33).

60 This five-part video-set, produced by Pascal-Emmanuel Gallet and directed by Jean Mascolo and Jérôme Beaujour, includes post-face interviews with Dominique Noguez: 'La classe de la violence' (on *Nathalie Granger*), 48' (with Gérard Depardieu); 'La couleur des mots' (on *India Song*), 63' (with Delphine Seyrig, Carlos d'Alessio and Michael Lonsdale); 'Le cimetière anglais' (on *Son nom de Venise*), 48' (with Delphine Seyrig, Michael Lonsdale and Bruno Nuytten); 'La dame des Yvelines' (on *Camion*), 59' (with Dominique Auvray, Gérard Depardieu and Bruno Nuytten); 'La caverne noire' (on *Césarée, Mains, Melbourne, Vancouver*), 57', followed by 'Work and Words' (a short video afterword by Duras). In the accompanying booklet are transcriptions of the interview, short articles by Duras and Noguez, descriptions of the films, a filmography and an index. I will refer to each interview individually by name.

61 See, for example, Aliette Armel, 'Nouveau Roman et autobiographie', in *Marguerite Duras et l'autobiographie*, Paris, Le Castor Astral, 1990, pp. 25–36, and Raylene O'Callaghan, 'The art of the impossible', *Australian Journal of French Studies*, No. 25 (1988), pp. 71–90.

62 Maurice Cagnon, 'Marguerite Duras: willed imagination as release and obstacle in *Dix heures et demie du soir en été*', *Nottingham French Studies*, Vol. 16, No. 1 (1977), pp. 55–64; p. 61.

63 Montrelay, *L'Ombre et le nom*, p. 21.

64 See Catherine Rodgers, 'Déconstruction de la masculinité dans l'oeuvre durassienne', *Marguerite Duras: Rencontres de Cerisy*, ed. Alain Vircondelet, Paris, Ecriture, 1994, pp. 47–68, for a valuable account of Duras's subversion of the 'model' of strong and weak masculinity in Duras's work. Rodgers also emphasises Duras's negative representation of gay men and contends that the first-person female narrator has now assumed the 'phallic' sadism once embodied by Duras's male narrators.

65 'A des années-lumière de la connaître et qui en reçoit déjà le signal.'

66 See Selous, *The Other Woman*, in particular Chapter 8, 'Order, Chaos and Subversive Details'. In 'A Triumph of the Will', *Free Associations*, No. 9 (August 1987), pp. 97–101, Selous argues that the lack of rhetorical devices, metaphor and irony in *Amant* demonstrates how the vagaries of the unconscious being are bent to Duras's implacable will, the result being that there are no 'surprise collisons' of ill-assorted signifieds to produce uncertainty and an 'unconscious excess of meaning'.

67 Dominique Noguez, 'La gloire des mots', *L'Arc*, No. 98 (1984), pp. 25–39. Another notable attempt to address the question of Duras's use of rhetoric is Liesbeth Korthals Altes, 'L'ironie ou le savoir de l'amour et de la mort. Lecture de quatre oeuvres de Marguerite Duras', *Revue des sciences humaines*, Vol. 73, No. 202 (April–June 1986), pp. 139–52, although it opts in the end for a descriptive reading of situational humour.

68 Hulley, 'Contaminated narratives', p. 31.

69 Jean Laplanche sums up Freudian sublimation as an issue of non-repression: 'there no longer remains in what's sublimated *either* the aim, *or* the object, *or* even the source of the drive, so that it is thought that we are finally finding only "sexual

energy"; but a sexual energy . . . itself desexualised, disqualified, yet in the service of non-sexual activities'. See Laplanche's *Problématiques III: La Sublimation*, Paris, PUF, 1980, p. 122.

70 In *Women and Discourse* Cohen discusses various elements of Duras's style, including grammatical manipulation, indicative language, onomastics and syntactic dislocations (e.g. the switching of pronouns and antecedents), but proposes them more as evidence of a poetics predicated on Duras's critique of the cultural-discursive order (p. 202).

71 In the chapter 'Aggressiveness and Sadomasochism' in *Life and Death in Psychoanalysis*, trans. Jeffrey Mehlman, Baltimore, Johns Hopkins University Press, 1976, Laplanche analyses a passage from Freud's 'Instincts and their Vicissitudes' (1915) to demonstrate that not only is the masochistic fantasy fundamental but it is within the suffering position that pleasure resides. Developing Laplanche's idea that the sadist identifies himself with the suffering object only because of a mental representation of that suffering, Bersani and Ulysse Dutoit conclude that sexuality should be understood in terms of the reflexive pleasures of desire: 'In fantasy, an object of desire is introjected; the pleasant or the unpleasant effect which the individual wishes to have on that object is therefore felt *by* the desiring subject himself. . . *desire produces sexuality*' (Leo Bersani and Ulysse Dutoit, *The Forms of Violence. Narrative in Assyrian Art and Modern Culture*, New York, Schocken, 1983, pp. 32–33).

72 Leo Bersani, *The Freudian Body. Psychoanalysis and Art*, New York, Columbia University Press, 1986, pp. 114–15.

73 See Leo Bersani, *The Culture of Redemption*, Cambridge, MA, Harvard University Press, 1990, in particular, 'Erotic Assumptions: Narcissism and Sublimation in Freud' (pp. 29–46).

74 Cixous and Foucault, 'A propos de Marguerite Duras', p. 18.

75 See Jean-Michel Ribettes, 'La troisième dimension du fantasme', in D. Anzieu et al., *Art et Fantasme*, Seyssel, Champ Vallon, 1984, for a fine discussion of the distinction between the 'erratic' movement of desire and the 'hieratic constancy' of the forms of fantasy (p. 188).

76 Pierre Bergé, 'Duras est SEXY!' (interview with Marguerite Duras), *Globe*, No. 30 (July–August 1988), pp. 78–83; p. 81.

77 In *Monde* Duras proclaims that, as opposed to commercial film-makers, she 'signs' all her work, films and books, adding: 'If something is signed, it's my work' (p. 189).

78 'La douleur, chez les hommes, jusque-là, à travers le temps, l'histoire, elle a toujours trouvé son exutoire, sa solution . . . Nous n'avons jamais eu aucun recours que le mutisme' (*Yeux*, pp. 181–82) ('For men, up until then, through time and through history, pain has always found its outlet, its solution. . . We have never had any other recourse except to remain mute').

79 See *Parleuses*, pp. 13–14. Compilations and periodisations of the Duras corpus vary enormously. They include Brée's assertion of four clusters: 1943–55, 1958–1969, 1969–76, 1977– (the last not linked to *Camion*) (see 'A Singular Adventure: The Writings of Marguerite Duras', *L'Esprit Créateur*, Vol. 30, No. 1 [Spring 1990], pp. 8–14); Murphy's dividing of the corpus (up to *Son nom de Venise*) into three parts: the traditional autobiographical novels from *Impudents* to *Barrage*,

the 'invitation to the voyage' from *Gibraltar* to *Andesmas*, and *Ravissement* onwards (see *Alienation and Absence*); Yvonne Guers-Vilate's emphasis on continuity over discontinuity (see *Continuité/Discontinuité de l'oeuvre durassienne*, Brussels, Université de Bruxelles, 1985), and Micheline Tison-Braun's choice of two thematic frameworks, '*la vie tranquille*' and '*la vie intense*' (see *Marguerite Duras*, Amsterdam, Rodopi, 1984).

80 See Nicole-Lise Bernheim, *Marguerite Duras tourne un film* (*India Song*), Paris, Albatros, 1975, p. 104. It should be pointed out that following the success of *Hiroshima* and prior to making her first film, *La musica* (1966) (with Paul Seban), Duras had gained first-hand experience of mainstream French cinema. She wrote the screen-play for Henri Colpi's 1961 film, *Une aussi longue absence* (published by Gallimard in 1961), and produced scripts for Michel Mitrani (*Sans merveille* [1964]), Georges Franju (*Les rideaux blancs* [1965]) and Jean Chapot (*La voleuse* [1966]). She also wrote the text for Marin Karmitz's *Nuit noire, Calcutta* (1964), an experimental, twenty-five minute short which anticipates certain aspects of her own film-work, including its choice of setting (Trouville and the Seine estuary near Ouistreham) and its technique (e.g. the separation of text and image, alternation of a fixed frame with lateral tracking shots).

81 'Celui qui n'écrit pas et le cinéaste n'ont pas entamé ce que j'appelle "l'ombre interne" que chacun porte en soi et qui ne peut sortir, s'écouler en dehors, que par le langage. L'écrivain, lui, l'a entamée. Il a entamé l'intégrité de l'ombre interne . . . C'est sur cette défaite de l'écrit que—pour moi—se bâtit le cinéma . . . Car ce massacre c'est justement le pont qui vous mène à l'endroit même de toute lecture. Et encore plus loin: à l'endroit même du subissement tout court que suppose toute existence vécue dans la société actuelle . . . vouloir faire du cinéma c'est justement vouloir aller droit vers le lieu de son subissement: le spectateur.'

82 Cited in Robert Chazal, *Gérard Depardieu: L'autodidacte inspiré*, Renens, 5 Continents, 1983, p. 73.

83 For a discussion of these devices in *Camion*, as well as the use of periphrasis, see Jill Forbes, *The Cinema in France after the New Wave*, Bloomington, IN, Indiana University Press, 1992, pp. 98–104. For notable introductions to Duras's cinema, see Madeleine Borgomano, *L'écriture filmique de Marguerite Duras*, Paris, Albatros, 1984, which is grounded on an analysis of 'primal scenes' from *Barrage*, and Susan H. Leger, 'Marguerite Duras's Cinematic Spaces', *Women and Film*, ed. Janet Todd, New York, London, Holmes and Meier, 1988, where Leger argues that by constructing interior spaces Duras founds a new, feminine, cinematic language. One of the few attempts to examine the effects of desynchronised montage in Duras's early film-work is William F. Van Wert's 'The Cinema of Marguerite Duras: Sound and Voice in a Closed Room', *Film Quarterly*, Vol. 33, No. 1 (1974), pp. 79–88.

84 Elisabeth Lyon, for example, presents *India Song* as simply the mise en scène of Lacanian desire in her article, 'The Cinema of Lol V. Stein', *camera obscura*, No. 6 (1980), pp. 7–23. For Constance Penley, *India Song* stages a representation which is fundamentally about loss and distance and thus achieves what theoretically 'women' cannot do, i.e. create a repetition of lack (the predication of all symbolic meaning). See *The Future of an Illusion: Film, Feminism and Psychoanalysis*, Minneapolis, University of Minnesota Press, 1989.

85 See Thomas Weiskel, *The Romantic Sublime: Studies in the Structure and the*

Psychology of Transcendence, Baltimore, Johns Hopkins University Press, 1976. See also *Longinus on the Sublime*, trans. W. Rhys Roberts, Cambridge, Cambridge University Press, 1899.

86 Hulley, 'Contaminated narratives', p. 47.

87 'Moi, j'écris avec Diderot, j'en suis sûre, avec Pascal, avec les grands hommes de ma vie, avec Kierkegaard, avec Rousseau, j'en suis sûre, avec Stendhal, pas avec Balzac, avec les autres, mais totalement à mon insu, c'est ma première nourriture que je lis avidement' (Lamy and Roy, *Duras à Montréal*, p. 23).

88 Duras had stated in *Lieux* that when women are not writing from the space of desire they are effectively plagiarising (p. 102).

89 See Husserl-Kapit, 'Interview with Marguerite Duras', p. 425.

90 See Michael Riffaterre, *The Semiotics of Poetry*, London, Methuen, 1978, where he argues that any ungrammaticality within the poem is a sign of grammaticality elsewhere (pp. 164–65), adding that the half-hidden relationship between the 'textually grammatical' and the 'intertextually ungrammatical' is so disturbing that the reader continually seeks relief by retreating from dubious words to a safe reality (or to a social consensus as to reality).

91 One notable exception is Aliette Armel who even conceives of a 'Yann Andréa cycle', although her reasons for doing so are non-theoretical. See *Marguerite Duras ou l'autobiographie*, Paris, Le Castor Astral, 1990, in particular 'Le cycle Yann Andréa: la vie devenue écriture, l'écriture devenue vie'.

92 See Costaz, 'Ce qui arrive tous les jours', p. 144.

93 Duras's statement in *Vie mat.* that all men are potential homosexuals and lack only the incident or evidence that will reveal this fact to them (p. 38), can be linked with Freud's notion of homosexuality as a vicissitude of masculinity which is itself based on the universal capacity to take as objects members of both sexes. According to the Freud of 'Three Essays on Sexuality' (1905), unconscious homosexual object-choices are found at the heart of heterosexual normality, and homosexual inversion installs a repressed heterosexuality at its heart, proceeding from a very intense, but short-lived (maternal) fixation to a woman which is then converted into an identification (the young man looks narcissistically for another who resembles himself and whom he may love as his mother loved him).

94 See Gilles Costaz, 'La vie est illégale ou elle n'est pas' (interview with Marguerite Duras), *Le Matin*, 14 November 1986, pp. 24–25; p. 25.

95 See Cynthia Chase, ' "Transference" as trope and persuasion', in Rimmon-Kenan, *Discourse in psychoanalysis and literature*, pp. 211–32; pp. 212–13, which exploits the metonymical development of Freud's concept of transference, from a displacement of meaning and intensity (*Verschiebung*) to the displacement of love toward the person of the analyst (*Übertragung*).

96 Bernard Pivot, 'Marguerite Duras' (interview with Marguerite Duras), *Apostrophes*, prod. Jean Cazenave, dir. J.-L. Léridon, Antenne 2, 28 September 1984.

97 Luce Perrot, *Au-delà des pages* (interview with Marguerite Duras in four parts), prod. Guy Lopez, TF1, 26 June–17 July 1988.

98 See Leslie Hill, *Marguerite Duras: Apocalyptic Desires*, London, New York, Routledge, 1993, in particular Chapter 1, 'Images of Authorship'.

99 Ibid., p. 37. An indication of the problems created in reading the corpus in this way is that the importance of Andréa is given short shrift in a footnote on p. 176,

where he is summarily linked with previous Duras collaborators like Dionys Mascolo.

100 See Lamy and Roy, *Duras à Montréal*, pp. 55–57.

101 Duras accounted for this unexpected decision by claiming that it was really her way, as an 'incurable' Marxist, of voting for Mitterrand. See Maurice Najman, 'L'enfer, nous dit Marguerite Duras' (interview with Marguerite Duras), *Globe Hebdo*, 24–30 March 1993, pp. 8–9.

102 For Bersani, masochism, 'far from being merely an individual aberration, is an inherited disposition resulting from an *evolutionary conquest*' (*Freudian Body*, p. 39).

103 See '20 Mai 1968: texte politique sur la naissance du Comité d'Action Etudiants-Ecrivains', *Yeux*, pp. 71–84.

104 Michel Bergain, 'Duras, de gauche complètement', *Globe*, No. 13, 1987.

105 'Moi', *L'Autre Journal (hebdo)*, No. 10, 30 April 1986, p. 9.

106 'Marguerite Duras: Sublime, forcément sublime Christine V.?', *Libération*, 17 July 1985, pp. 4–6.

107 See Mary Ann Caws, *A Metapoetics of the Passage: Architextures in Surrealism and After*, Hanover, London, University of New England Press, 1981, pp. vi–vii.

108 Paul de Man, *Allegories of Reading: Figural Language in Rousseau, Nietzsche, Rilke, and Proust*, New Haven, London, Yale University Press, 1979, p. 53.

109 See John Guillory, *Poetic Authority: Spenser, Milton, and Literary History*, New York, Columbia University Press, 1983, p. 169.

Notes to Chapter 2
pp. 25–46

1 See Raymonde Carasco, 'Vers une érotique fragmentaire. Le nouveau cinéma', *Revue de l'Esthétique (nouvelle série)*, No. 11 (1986), pp. 93–102, where Carasco compares the different innovations of Duras, Godard and Resnais.

2 *Camion*, p. 7. All citations from *Camion* refer to the published text; the numbering of shots is my own.

3 For an account of the Hollywood acoustic regime where the male voice is disembodied, unlocalised and omnipotent, and where the female-encoded synchronised voice functions as part of a maternal fantasy of compensation, see Kaja Silverman's *The Acoustic Mirror. The Female Voice in Psychoanalysis and Cinema*, Bloomington, IN, Indiana University Press, 1988, in particular 'Lost Objects and Mistaken Subjects: a Prologue' (pp. 1–41).

4 See Maurice Merleau-Ponty, *Le visible et l'invisible*, Paris, Gallimard, 1964, pp. 142–53, where Merleau-Ponty argues that perception takes place in the vast, reversible 'intertwining' of the tangible and the visible, the world and the self. In *Ethique de la différence sexuelle*, Paris, Minuit, 1984, Luce Irigaray argues convincingly that this idealistic criss-crossing of the tactile and visible has solipsistic implications and that the vital osmotic exchanges between the maternal world and its substitutes must necessarily be cut in order for the flesh to be sublimated (see in particular 'L'amour de l'autre'). As we will see, this idea is brought out in spectacular fashion in *Camion*.

5 See Ropars-Wuilleumier's 'How history begets meaning. Alain Resnais's *Hiroshima mon amour*', *French Film. Texts and Contexts*, ed. Susan Hayward and Ginette Vincendeau, London, Methuen, 1990, pp. 173–85, where she argues that fragmented montage is the only way to acknowledge the event of Hiroshima and links the victims of Hiroshima with the lovers' bodies. Montage, she claims, discharges on to the erotic encounter the 'disjunctive power emitted by the explosion' (p. 179). However, the editing style does not correspond to the specifically sadomasochistic 'event' of *elle*'s desire as expressed in the key phrase, 'Tu me tues . . . tu me fais du bien'.

6 René Prédal, 'Entretien avec Marguerite Duras', *Jeune Cinéma*, No. 104 (July–August 1977), pp. 16–21; p. 19.

7 Kaja Silverman, 'Masochism and Subjectivity', *Framework*, No. 12 (1981), pp. 2–9; p. 4.

8 See 'The Hitchcockian Cut' in Slavoj Žižek, *Looking Awry. An introduction to Jacques Lacan through Popular Culture*, Cambridge, MA, MIT Press, 1991, where Žižek analyses what is and is not possible in Hitchcockian montage, emphasising in particular the role of the death drive in the climax of *Sabotage*.

9 In 'Suture' in *The Subject of Semiotics*, Oxford, New York, Oxford University Press, 1983, pp. 194–246, Silverman, building on the work of Jean-Pierre Oudart, analyses the absence of cinema's enunciating agency in montage as an absent Field

(the 'Absent One'). The viewer's trauma of castration is created by his discursive dispossession in the face of a transcendental Other.

10 See Joan Copjec, 'The compulsion to repeat; *India Song/Son nom de Venise dans Calcutta désert*', *October*, No. 17 (1981), pp. 37–52.

11 Jacques Grant and Jacques Frenais, 'Un acte contre tout pouvoir' (interview with Marguerite Duras), *Cinéma 77* (July 1977), pp. 48–58; p. 57 (reprinted in Barat and Farges, *Duras*, pp. 119–30; p. 129). All subsequent references to this interview will refer to its reprinted version.

12 See 'A Child is Being Beaten: A Contribution to the Study of the Origin of Sexual Perversions' (1919), in the *Standard Edition of the Complete Psychological Works of Sigmund Freud*, trans. and ed. James Strachey, in collaboration with Anna Freud, assisted by Alix Strachey and Alan Tyson, London, The Hogarth Press and the Institute of Psycho-Analysis, 1953–73, Vol. 17, pp. 179–204.

13 In his literary study of masochism in the work of Leopold von Sacher-Masoch, *Présentation de Sacher-Masoch. Le froid et le cruel*, Paris, Union Centrale d'Editions, '10/18', 1967, Deleuze shows that the transfer of the law by the (male) subject on to the all-powerful oral mother of the pregenital stage constitutes the rites of a fantasy rebirth, of the Greek, both virile and feminine, dephallicised and polymorphous. The coldness of the 'severe mother' should therefore be seen as a 'transumation of cruelty' (p. 9). Deleuze, who does not see masochism as the simple reversal of sadism, emphasises the formal and juridical aspects of masochism in the form of the contract and the law. Masochism's contract of violence works to negate paternal power by means of a two-fold disavowal: a positive, idealising disavowal of the mother (who is identified with the law) and an invalidating disavowal of the father (who is expelled from the symbolic order). Deleuze argues that exaggerated masochistic suffering is like a masquerade of passive submission put on for the benefit of the superego, which the masochist had already expelled when he split the ego into narcissistic and ideal halves. This show of pain disguises the masochist's complicity in the contracted alliance with his female torturer who, like Duras with Depardieu, ensures careful timing, suspense, delayed consummations, role-playing and surprise gestures of both cruelty and tenderness.

14 For a faithful application of Deleuze's theory of masochism to film, see Gaylyn Studlar's study of the self-consciously illusionistic collaborations of Von Sternberg and Dietrich, *In the realm of pleasure. Von Sternberg, Dietrich, and the Masochistic Aesthetic*, Urbana, University of Illinois Press, 1988. Going beyond the traditional view of cinematic visual pleasure as one produced by castration fear, Oedipal desire and sadistic voyeurism (a process set in train by Laura Mulvey's influential 1975 article, 'Visual Pleasure and Narrative Cinema'), Studlar takes the primal scene as a guiding metaphor for cinematic looking and concludes that the spectator passively surrenders to the filmic object of desire. The cinematic apparatus (e.g. slow lap-dissolves) creates 'identificatory positions for male and female spectators that reintegrate psychic bisexuality, offer the sensual pleasures of polymorphous sexuality, and make the male and female one in their identification with, and for, the pre-Oedipal mother' (p. 192).

15 See 'Contrasts' in *When the lights go down*, London, Boyars, 1980, pp. 291–95, where Kael states that Duras's is possibly the most sadomasochistic of all director relationships with the audience: 'Her [Duras's] battle with the audience reaches a new

stage in *The Truck*, in which the split between her artistry and what the public wants is pointed up and turned against the audience. She brings it off, but she's doing herself in, too. And so it isn't a simple prank.'

16 See 'Denial and Fetishism' in Christian Metz, *The Imaginary Signifier. Psychoanalysis and Cinema*, trans. Celia Britton, Annwyl Williams, Ben Brewster and Alfred Guzzetti, London, Macmillan, 1982, pp. 69–81; pp. 74–75.

17 See Julia Kristeva, *Powers of Horror. An essay on Abjection* [1980], trans. Léon Roudiez, New York, Columbia University Press, 1982, where Kristeva shows how the abject and sublime are equally devoid of an object. 'The sublime object dissolves in raptures of a bottomless memory', she writes (pp. 11–12). Kristeva defines sublimation here as 'the possibility of naming the pre-nominal, the pre-objectal'.

18 Using Freud's 1915 essay, 'Instincts and their Vicissitudes', Bersani and Dutoit trace the evolution of the Freudian difference between 'original', i.e. non-sexual, sadism and derived, sexual sadism. See *The Forms of Violence*, pp. 24–39.

19 'Je peux dire maintenant à partir de ce film que du point de vue politique, la peur m'a quittée. Vous savez, comme on dit qu'on s'est libéré de la foi' (p. 112). This contrasts somewhat with Duras's statement in Grant and Frenais, 'Un acte contre tout pouvoir', that *Camion*'s lack of representation renders impossible a 'catharsis of what is evoked' p. 127).

20 'Il laisse derrière lui un froissement de buissons d'épineux. C'est la force du vent remué par le passage de la masse du camion qui fait crisser les plantes mortes de l'été.'

21 Claire Devarrieux, 'La voie du gai désespoir' (interview with Marguerite Duras), *Le Monde*, 16 June 1977, reprinted in Barat and Farges, *Duras*, pp. 111–17; p. 117. All subsequent references to this interview will refer to the reprinted version.

22 'C'est par elle que je vois. Par elle que je prends l'extérieur et que je l'engouffre en moi.'

23 Devarrieux, 'La voie du gai désespoir', p. 113.

24 Grant and Frenais, 'Un acte contre tout pouvoir', p. 126.

25 Ibid.

26 See Youssef Ishaghpour, *D'une image à l'autre: La nouvelle modernité au cinéma*, Paris, Denoël/Gonthier, 1981, pp. 256–67.

27 See Daniel Gunn, *Psychoanalysis and Fiction: an exploration of literary and psychoanalytical borders*, Cambridge, New York, Cambridge University Press, 1988, in particular, 'For to end yet again', pp. 124–32.

28 See Madeleine Alleins, *Marguerite Duras, médium du réel*, Paris, L'Age d'homme, 1984, in particular the chapters 'L'amour est dépassement de soi' (pp. 99–110) and 'L'amour perdu et retrouvé' (pp. 155–70).

29 See 'Acinema' in *The Lyotard Reader*, ed. Andrew Benjamin, Oxford, Blackwell, 1989, pp. 169–80.

30 Bersani and Dutoit, *The Forms of Violence*, p. 116. Bersani and Dutoit show how narrative in Assyrian sculpture (in one sense, the simplest model of linear, non-transgressive story-telling) is constantly undermined because it produces a narrative movement from centres and climaxes of violence to supplemental non-narrative points of interest, thus offering a way to resist the seductive power of historical violence. The Assyrians are practitioners of a desiring fantasy understood not only as

mimetic (i.e.: it seeks to capture and replay images) but also as an 'approximation' that disturbs the self's equilibrium. Unlike insistently narrative sexuality, Assyrian art is a lesson in 'interstitial sensuality'. See 'Narrativity and violence', pp. 40–56.

31 Duras remarks in Aubenas, 'Entretien', that if any control intervenes in her work, it is at the moment of rewriting and montage (p. 13).

32 Bénichou and Le Masson, 'Duras tout entière', p. 61.

33 'Le livre avance et tandis qu'il avance il n'est rien que de la vie en puissance d'exister et comme la vie il a besoin de toutes les contraintes, d'étouffement, de douleur, de lenteur, de souffrances, d'entraves de toutes sortes, de silence et de nuit. Il en passe d'abord par le dégoût de naître, l'horreur de grandir, de voir le jour . . . Il faut subir ce voyage avec le livre, le bagne, tout le temps de l'écrit. On prend goût à ce malheur merveilleux.'

34 'En général, il y a la projection sur la page et la préhension de l'écrit par un tiers. C'est le spectacle. Là, ça n'existe pas. On ne descend pas vers l'éclatement du texte' (Devarrieux, 'La voie du gai désespoir', p. 111).

35 One might also claim that Duras played God in the very way that she treated Depardieu during the making of the film. In the 'Dossier de presse du *Camion*' (Cannes, 1977), Depardieu explains how Duras picked him up by car in the morning, briefly described her idea, and then began filming immediately. He adds that his experience of extreme passivity was an act of listening, love, regression and child-like happiness, and it allowed Duras 'to go to the limit'.

36 Grant and Frenais, 'Un acte contre tout pouvoir', p. 129.

37 See Kristeva, *Powers of Horror*, pp. 207–10. For Duras's own view of the sacred and erotic nature of puncturing, see *Parleuses* where she states that since a child she always thought that the first noise to be heard on earth was the bursting of a bubble against the surface of a huge, inert marsh which caused a reverberation to 'infinity' (p. 239). She never took this to be the work of God, however, who was merely the stale air inside the bubble.

38 See Grant and Frenais, 'Un acte contre tout pouvoir', pp. 119–21.

39 'S'il y avait eu un homme à la place de la visiteuse, le fait qu'ils s'évitent comme elles le font, ça serait inscrit directement dans le clivage d'un désir à venir, un rapport positif . . . Moi, sans un homme qui regarde, je n'arrive pas à voir le corps de Véra Baxter' (Grant and Frenais, 'Un acte contre tout pouvoir', pp. 120–21).

40 'J'ai cru que je pouvais transgresser l'homosexualité, cet interdit, cette espèce de différence. Comme quoi il ne faut jamais aller contre soi' (Grant and Frenais, 'Un acte contre tout pouvoir', p. 119).

41 'C'est fait. Elle sort. S'extrait des Colonnades . . . La chose s'est faite insensiblement, elle n'a pas dû s'apercevoir qu'elle sortait' (*Véra Baxter*, p. 110).

42 See Judith Roof, 'Marguerite Duras and the Question of a Feminist Theater', *Feminism and Psychoanalysis*, ed. Richard Feldstein and Judith Roof, Ithaca, London, Cornell University Press, 1989, pp. 323–40. By simply fusing 'the exterior turbulence' with the witch-like figure of Véra Baxter and her refusal of the Stranger's offer of identification, Roof reads *Véra Baxter* idealistically as an exposure of 'the prostitution economy of theater and psychoanalysis' (p. 339).

43 Witness Depardieu's own experience of acting in *Nathalie Granger*: 'I felt more of a woman [*plus femme*] than those three men looking at me' ('La classe de la violence').

44 For a more positive view of the film as a demonstration of female community, see 'Silence as female resistance in Duras's *Nathalie Granger*', in E. Ann Kaplan, *Women and film. Both sides of the camera*, London, New York, Methuen, 1983, pp. 91–103. A remarkably concrete version of Kristeva's 'choric' fantasy of the grand-mother/mother/child *'enceinte'* can be found in Duras's description in 'La classe de la violence' of an 'eternal moment': Isabelle Granger looks at her daughter Nathalie who looks at her sister Laurence on the water with the unnamed Friend. We have to wait until the publication of the screen-play, however, to appreciate all the film's ambiguities and ironies (for example, that it is Lawrence rather than Nathalie, problem child of the bourgeoisie, who is played by Nathalie Bourgeois).

45 Only one critic, Sue Ellen Case, has actually 'come out' and identified the Voices' desire as lesbian. See her 'From Split Subject to Split Britches: The metonymically displaced subject', *Feminine focus: the new women playwrights*, ed. Enoch Brater, Oxford, Oxford University Press, 1989, pp. 129–46.

46 See 'Motherhood according to Bellini', in Julia Kristeva, *Desire in Language: A semiotic approach to Literature and Art*, ed. Léon Roudiez, trans. Thomas Gora, Alice Jardine and Léon Roudiez, Oxford, Blackwell, 1980, pp. 237–70; pp. 241–42. Significantly, Kristeva relates the subjectless *jouissance* of maternity and its strange form of split symbolisation to the language of art itself. The (male) artist, working at the intersection of sign and rhythm, of representation and light, of the symbolic and the semiotic, 'delineates' what, in the mother, is a 'body rejoicing' (*jouissant*). 'This means', Kristeva concludes, 'that through and across secondary repression (the founding of signs), aesthetic practice touches upon primal repression (founding biological series and the laws of the species)' (pp. 242–43).

47 For a comprehensive account of the cinematic screen as a site of horror and mourning in Duras's literary work, see Borgomano's *L'écriture filmique de Marguerite Duras*, in particular 'Les métamorphoses de l'écriture'.

48 In *Homosexual Desire* [1972], trans. Danielle Dangoor, London, Allison and Busby, 1978, Guy Hocquenghem proposes homosexual desire as the return of what has been repressed and sublimated both in Freudian theory and Western society, i.e. anality, which, if pursued promiscuously, provides a guarantee of uncodifiable difference in the dominant culture of the Same.

49 Marguerite Duras, 'Baxter, Véra Baxter', in Barat and Farges, *Duras*, pp. 103–05; p. 105. Duras speaks here rather sardonically of the 'ruling theoretical freedom'.

50 For a helpful overview of this genre, see Danièle Dubroux, 'Il n'y aurait plus qu'une seule image', *Cahiers du Cinéma*, Nos. 279–80 (August–September 1977), pp. 38–43.

51 This point is successfully argued by Jean Narboni in his probing article on the visceral nature of Ackerman's film, 'La quatrième personne du singulier', *Cahiers du Cinéma*, No. 276 (May 1977), pp. 5–14.

52 For a clear analysis of the precarious Ackerman frame, see 'Le flux et le cadre', in Youssef Ishaghpour, *Le cinéma contemporain: de ce côté du miroir*, Paris, Différence, 1986, pp. 256–66.

53 See Prédal, 'Entretien', where Duras declares that she wants to distance herself from any idea of a specifically feminine language. She explains that no such thing exists, only a 'free' language (p. 20). For a powerful account of the dangers of a blindly essentialist theory of the cinematic apparatus, see Jacqueline Rose, *Sexuality*

in the Field of Vision, London, Verso, 1986, in particular, 'The Cinematic Apparatus—Problems in Current Theory' (pp. 119–214).

54 Erika Lennard, *Les femmes, les soeurs*, Paris, Editions des Femmes, 1978, with a postface by Marguerite Duras. Lennard's sister, Elizabeth, provided the photographs.

55 '[C]'est une sorte d'injonction interne. Je ne veux pas dire: du corps, parce que c'est fini . . . Les femmes parlent de leurs corps comme ça, tout le temps, je n'en veux plus, en entendre parler, du tout.' See also in this vein Duras's interview with Michèle Manceaux, 'Le désir est bradé, saccagé. On libère le corps et on le massacre, dit Marguerite Duras', *Marie-Claire*, No. 297 (May 1977).

56 In the notes to *Parleuses*, Duras clarifies her position: although she considers female nudity more beautiful, it is only with men that she really feels the necessary, 'hygienic' *jouissance* of passion (p. 225). This is a view that Gauthier finds herself unable automatically to endorse. Earlier in *Parleuses* Duras had emphasised that orgasm did not take place in *Gange* (p. 121). For a useful account of the considerable impact of *Parleuses* both on the women's movement in France and Duras's own popularity, see Katharine A. Jensen's Afterword to her translation of the text, *Woman to Woman*, Lincoln and London, University of Nebraska Press, 1987, pp. 181–95.

57 Absis, 'Ça me touche là où je crie' (interview with Marguerite Duras), *Sorcières*, No. 4 (1976), p. 59.

58 Leslie Hill is one critic persuaded by the over-dubbed sound-track of *Camion* and by Duras's remark that the sea is nearby. See 'Marguerite Duras: Sexual difference and tales of apocalypse', *Modern Language Review*, No. 84 (1989), pp. 601–14; p. 602.

59 Grant and Frenais, 'Un acte contre tout pouvoir', p. 130.

60 *La gaya scienza*, which also treats of nature and women although misogynistically, is framed by a prelude (German rhymes) and an epilogue (nine 'substantial' Songs), similar to *Camion* where, by means of Beethoven, the end folds over on to its beginning.

61 See George Bauer, 'Le Gai Savoir noir', *Contemporary French Civilization*, Vol. 16, No. 2 ('Discourses and Sex') (Summer–Fall 1992), pp. 194–213, where Bauer's summary opposition between Duras and Nietzsche hinges on making Duras's use of the word '*gai*' 'gay' (pp. 211–12).

Notes to Chapter 3

pp. 47–65

1 See Gilles Deleuze, *Cinéma 2: L'image-temps*, Paris, Minuit, 1985, pp. 334–40, where Deleuze highlights Duras's use of 'the grey of day', the 'alternation of the solar and the lunar', and the 'perception of liquidity'.

2 See, for example, Carol Murphy, 'New Narrative Regions: The Role of Desire in the Films and Novels of Marguerite Duras', *Literature/Film Quarterly*, Vol. 12, No. 2 (1984), pp. 122–28, and Dean McWilliams, 'Aesthetic Tripling: Marguerite Duras's *Le Navire Night*', *Literature/Film Quarterly*, Vol. 14, No. 1 (1988), pp. 17–21.

3 Leslie Hill, 'Marguerite Duras and the limits of fiction', *Paragraph*, Vol. 12, No. 1 (1989), pp. 1–22; p. 19.

4 See Ginette Vincendeau, 'Family Plots. The father and daughter of French cinema', *Sight and Sound*, Vol. 3, No. 4 (March 1992), pp. 14–17, for a helpful history of this persistent trope.

5 See Marcelle Marini, 'L'autre corps', in Bajomée and Heyndels, *Ecrire, dit-elle*, pp. 21–48.

6 'Quand le son se retire, et qu'on parle de la lumière sombre des yeux, des cheveux, du corps dans la glace, qu'on parle d'image voilée et de la beauté qu'elle se decouvre, cela sur le noir des grands blocs de granit contre lesquels son image peut se blesser, se déchirer, je ne suis pas au cinéma seulement mais tout à coup ailleurs, ailleurs encore, dans la zone indifférenciée de moi-même où je reconnais sans comprendre. Ici, tout se rejoint, se fond, la blessure, le tranchant glacé de la pierre noire et la tiède douceur de l'image menacée. Le bonheur de la coïncidence entre l'image et la parole me comble ici d'évidence, de jouissance.'

7 Youssef Ishaghpour, 'La voix et le miroir', in Bajomée and Heyndels (eds), *Ecrire, dit-elle*, pp. 99–108; p. 107.

8 Dominique Noguez, *Trente ans de cinéma expérimental en France (1950–80)*, Paris, ARCEF, 1982, p. 72.

9 '[I]l ne trouve pas son signe, son nom: il est coupant et atterrit cependant dans une zone vague de moi-même; il est aigu et étouffé, il crie en silence. Bizarre contradiction, c'est un éclair qui flotte' (Roland Barthes, *La chambre claire. Note sur la photographie*, Paris, L'Etoile, 1980, p. 87).

10 Ibid., p. 81.

11 See Terence Cave, 'Recognition and the reader', *Comparative Criticism*, No. 2 (1980), pp. 49–69.

12 'Il voit ce noir comme un passage par un non-penser, un stade où la pensée basculerait, s'effacerait. Il voit que cet effacement rejoindrait le noir de l'orgasme . . . Ici, dans mes films, il ne déchiffre pas, il se laisse faire et cette ouverture qui se produit en lui fait place à quelque chose de nouveau dans le lien qui le lie au film et qui serait de l'ordre du désir.'

13 Pierre Fedida, 'Entre les voix et l'image', in Barat and Farges, *Duras*, pp. 157–60; 160.

14 See Hill, 'The limits of fiction', p. 18.

15 Jacques Lacan, *Encore (Séminaire XX)*, Paris, Seuil, 1975, p. 85.

16 Jean Mascolo and Jérôme Beaujour, *Duras Filme* (1981) (video, 50', colour). In fact, *Agatha* generates more obvious ironies due to its counterpointing of Duras's (*elle*'s) intimate, low voice with Andréa's (*lui*'s) meticulously theatrical, high-pitched intensity, both set against the silent, ghost-like images of Bulle Ogier and Andréa, visibly different in age yet equally lost and consumed by some far-off, indefinable desire. This configuration of opposites confounds the close-ups of sand (both real and painted on canvas), the long-shots of sea and sky, and vistas of deserted roads and villas (a reference perhaps to Luchino Visconti's 1965 film about incestuous desire, *Vaghe stelle dell'orsa* [aka *Sandra*]).

17 Maurice Lemaître, *Pour en finir avec cet escroc plagiaire et généralisée*, Paris, Centre de Créativité, 1979, p. 35.

18 We can compare the effects between sound and image in Duras's cinema with those between word and word in her writing, as analysed by Alazet in 'Une écriture du soupir' (in Vircondelet, *Marguerite Duras: Rencontres de Cerisy*, pp. 83–98). Alazet suggests that Duras's loosening of syntax through ellipsis, syncope, and parataxis is a dissonant, non-linguistic moment, a 'sigh', which reinstates the presence of a remainder or an emotion. It is immediately followed by a 'return to life', i.e. the re-establishing of the act of breathing and the demands of speech.

19 Marie-Pierre Fernandes, *Travailler avec Marguerite Duras. La Musica Deuxième*, Paris, Gallimard, 1986, p. 189.

20 See Deleuze, *Cinéma 2*, p. 341.

21 This equation has been proposed by Jean-Jacques Lecercle in his critique of Walter Benjamin's 'logocentric' dismissal of the 'talking picture'. See 'To Do or Not to Do Without the Word. Ecstasy and Discourse in the Cinema', *New Formations*, No. 16 (Spring 1992), pp. 80–90.

22 *Erotisme noir* has been linked with Duras but only in connection with her literary work, notably *Douleur* and *Homme assis*. See Nancy Huston's devastating article on post-War French literature, 'Erotic Literature in Postwar France', *Raritan*, Vol. 12, No. 1 (Summer 1992), pp. 29–45, which argues that *érotisme noir* was a sublimating tradition that served to transfigure and exorcise the horror of war, replaying it as transgression but without the annihilation of the will.

23 See Madeleine Cottenet-Hage and Robert P. Kolker, 'The Cinema of Duras in Search of an Ideal Image', *French Review*, Vol. 63, No. 1 (1989), pp. 87–98; p. 94.

24 Ibid., p. 96.

25 Jean-Luc Godard, 'Conférence-débat à la Fémis du 26 avril 1989', *Confrontations* (1990), pp. 15–23; p. 18.

26 Stephen Heath, 'Repetition Time: Notes around "Structuralist/Materialist Films" ', *Wide Angle*, Vol. 2, No. 3 (1978), pp. 4–11; p. 9.

27 Bersani argues in *The Freudian body* that '[m]asochism as a solution to the dysfunctional sequences of human maturation would then be repeated as a dysfunctional choice—a choice, this time, for extinction, rather than for survival' (p. 41).

28 Aubenas, 'Entretien', p. 14. In 'Masochism and Subjectivity', Silverman argues very differently that Cavani's film dramatises the lure of negation, passivity, and loss for both male and female subjects, thus demonstrating the 'autonomy of the subjugating Gaze'.

29 Kristeva, *Soleil noir*, p. 237.

30 'Je suis au cinéma. Elle y est. Une fois elle s'est trouvée sur le quai de la Seine. C'était à deux heures de l'après-midi un jour d'été et on l'a embrassée et on lui a dit qu'on l'aimait.'

31 Hill, 'The limits of fiction', p. 14.

32 '[E]lle y était, elle le sait encore. Tout porte un nom: c'était le jour où elle a décidé de vivre avec un homme.'

33 Cited in *The Radio Times*, 23–29 September 1978, pp. 77–79.

34 See Elie Wiesel, *Night* [1958], trans. Stella Rodway, New York, Bantam Books, 1989, pp. 60–62 and pp. 105–06.

35 See François Gère, 'La mesure de l'homme', *Cahiers du Cinéma*, No. 315 (September 1980), pp. 36–42. Gère explains that a non-racist cinema is one that marks both 'camps' with 'difficult, risked connections, never completely won, but always possible' (p. 42). He ends with a plea for 'indifference'. In an interview on *Holocaust* entitled 'La fiction de la dernière fois', *Cahiers du Cinéma*, No. 301 (June 1979), pp. 17–24, Sibony argues that the Nazis wished to close up the gaps of the Symbolic in the Real and make the Jews function as its 'arrested parts'. Judaism, he adds, involves the 'montage' of writing where the Jews invent for themselves a god that they call the Name. According to Sibony, hatred of the Jews is thus a refusal of language.

36 For Steiner's view of Plath's 'subtle larceny', see 'Dying is an Art', *The Art of Sylvia Plath*, ed. Charles Newman, Bloomington, London, Indiana University Press, 1970. For a discussion of the outrage provoked by Plath's apparent identification with the Jewish victims of the Holocaust, see Jacqueline Rose's *The Haunting of Sylvia Plath*, Cambridge, MA, Harvard University Press, 1992, in particular ' "Daddy" ' (pp. 205–38), which concludes significantly with a reference to the torture scene of 'Albert des Capitales' in *Douleur*. Rose argues that the loss of metaphor, a condition noted in the children of Holocaust survivors, is also the loss of recognition of aggression in fantasy, due to a too literal understanding of the body or 'repetition compulsion'. Aurélia appears to defy this by staging and restaging an act of naming and metaphor through the sexual penetration of her own body. (Another link, of course, between Duras and Plath is the name 'Aurélia' which identifies Plath's mother with whom she wrote what later came to be published as *Letters Home. Correspondence 1950–1963* [1975]).

37 Leo Bersani and Ulysse Dutoit, 'Sadism and Film: Freud and Resnais', *Qui Parle*, Vol. 6, No. 1 (Fall–Winter 1992), pp. 1–34; p. 23.

38 See Christine Bange, *Die zurückgewiesene Faszination: Zeit, Tod und Gedächtnis als Erfahrungskategorien bei Baudelaire, Benjamin und Duras*, Weinheim, Beltz, 1987, in particular 'Das erinnerte Vergessen. Die Gedächtnis-Aufassung bei Marguerite Duras', and 'Dinge, Korper, Orte. Ihre "historischen Schatten" '.

39 Borgomano, for example, has proposed that *Enfants* represents a 'new turn' in Duras's cinema. See 'Cinéma-écriture', *L'Arc*, No. 98 (1984), pp. 76–80; p. 79. Yet *Enfants* appears more like an empty shell of spent, ironic forms. Witness, for example, the way it opposes an exaggerated, *India Song*-style immobility with the final, highly staged tracking-shot out of the house in the manner of *Camion*. In addition, the use of the actor, Daniel Gélin, recalls *Détruire*, the revolutionary message of which is echoed in Duras's brief voice-over dedicated to youth. Moreover,

the formal qualities of Durasian cinema have now been translated directly into the film's mise en scène: once enframed by the camera after stealing potatoes for his mother, Ernesto—half-boy and half-man—becomes a figure of controlled madness like Johannes in Dreyer's *Ordet*. He thus embodies in himself the founding, ironic split of Duras's sacred practice of montage. So self-absorbed, in fact, is *Enfants* that it enacts its refrain taken from Ecclesiastes, 'Tout est vanité'.

40 Catherine Portuges, who accepts Duras's claim of an 'open', formless image, regards this moment very differently as an unironic instance of metonymy. The barge marks 'the light reflecting off the water in a metonymy of desire'. She suggests that overall the film, 'a paradoxical configuration of desire-demand-lack, can be imagined as a countertransferential text' (p. 44). See 'Love and Mourning in Duras's *Aurélia Steiner*', *L'Esprit Créateur*, Vol. 30, No. 1 (Spring 1990), pp. 40–46; p 42.

41 Lucie Roy has pursued the slippage between Latin and French in terms of town and character in 'Marguerite Duras, scénariste exilée', *Etudes Littéraires*, Vol. 26, No. 2 (Autumn 1993), pp. 67–75. In a related article on *Vancouver*, 'Les réticences discursives à l'écran ou les voix négatives' (in Vircondelet, *Marguerite Duras: Rencontres de Cerisy*, pp. 151–69), she argues that the 'coming forth' of an image which is figuratively emptied out, or '*off*', serves to actualise the 'virtualities' of the text [p. 163]).

42 Louis Aragon, *Aurélien* [1944], Paris, Gallimard, 'Folio', 1972. For a pertinent discussion of both the phantasmatic role of Bérénice and the chiastic configurations in *Aurélien*, see Lionel Follet's study, *Aragon, le fantasme et l'histoire*, Paris, Français Réunis, 1980, which also considers the homosexual implications of Aurélien's character (pp. 73–74). At the time Duras wrote her attack on Aragon he was being celebrated on French television by a series of major interviews to which she in fact refers.

43 Racine, *Bérénice*, Act I, Scene IV, l. 235.

44 'Pour le film seulement je sais, je sais qu'aucune image, plus une seule, ne pourrait le prolonger.'

45 Alain Philippon, 'Filmer la mort du cinéma', *Cahiers du Cinéma*, No. 331 (1982), pp. 47–48; p. 48.

46 'Personne, personne d'autre au monde que vous ne pourra faire ce que vous allez faire maintenant: passer ici pour la deuxième fois aujourd'hui, par moi seule ordonné, devant Dieu.'

47 See Yann Andréa, 'The Atlantic man', *Film International*, No. 11 (1982).

48 Marguerite Duras, 'Le noir Atlantique', *Des femmes en mouvement (hebdo)*, No. 57, 11–18 September 1981, reprinted in *Monde*, pp. 14–17; p. 16.

49 For a theoretical account of this recent experiment in women's film-making, see 'Disembodying the Female Voice. Irigaray, Experimental Feminist Cinema and Femininity', and 'The Female Authorial Voice', in Silverman, *The Acoustic Mirror*.

50 René Payant, 'L'impossible voix', in Lamy and Roy, *Duras à Montréal*, pp. 157–69; p. 168.

51 See Bernheim, *Marguerite Duras tourne un film*, pp. 146–47.

52 'De cela je / sais seulement ceci : que je n'ai / plus rien à faire qu'à subir cette / exaltation à propos de quelqu'un / qui était là, quelqu'un qui ne / savait pas qu'il vivait et dont moi / je savais qu'il vivait, / de quelqu'un qui ne savait / pas vivre, je vous disais, et / de moi qui le savais et qui / ne savais pas quoi faire de / ça, de cette

connaissance / de la vie qu'il vivait, et qui / ne savais non plus quoi / faire de moi.'

53 '[C'est ainsi que] vous vous tenez face à moi, dans la douceur, dans une provocation constante, innocente, impénétrable. / Vous l'ignorez.'

54 Grant and Frenais, 'Un acte contre tout pouvoir', p. 125.

55 Colette Mazabrard, 'Marguerite Duras: "J'ai toujours désespérément filmé" ' (interview with Marguerite Duras), *Cahiers du Cinéma*, No. 421 (December 1989), pp. 62–65; p. 65.

Notes to Chapter 4
pp. 67–92

1 'Dans la chambre noire, je vous ai à votre tour enfermé. Dans l'espace illimité de la mer, je vous ai enfermé avec l'enfant. C'est fait. Cette couleur noire de mes yeux fermés, ces coups au coeur, votre similitude définitive.'

2 'Tout à coup, cet affaissement de la durée, ces couloirs d'air, cette étrangeté qui filtre, impalpable, à travers les sables, la surface de la mer, le flux de la marée montante.'

3 'Vous dites: l'enfant avance. Vous dites: il est sur le point de disparaître. Vous dites: C'est fait. Je dis vous aimer.'

4 See *L'homme sans qualités*, trans. Philippe Jaccottet, Paris, Seuil, 'Points', 1956, Vol. 2, p. 834, for the French translation of this particular episode. We can be certain that this is the text being referred to due to extratextual evidence, notably in Lamy and Roy, *Duras à Montréal*, where Duras explains that she was still trying to work out her feelings towards the book after having just read it. In another account—'Une des plus grandes lectures que j'aie jamais faites', *La Quinzaine littéraire*, No. 302, 1–15 June 1981, pp. 15–16—she contrasts the constructive exasperation she felt with Musil's text ('written as if by no-one') with what she terms the 'simple charms' of Proust's *Sodome et Gomorrhe*, a book she had read only too effortlessly as a child.

5 'Que sont les soirées devenues, oisives et lentes de l'été, étirées jusqu'à la dernière lueur, jusqu'au vertige de l'amour même, de ses sanglots, de ses larmes? Soirées écrites, embaumées dans l'écrit, dorénavant lectures sans fin, sans fond. Albertine, Andrée, étaient leurs noms. Qui dansaient devant lui déjà atteint par la mort et qui cependant les regardait . . . écrivait déjà le livre de leur passé.'

6 We can link Duras's approach to Proust here with Silverman's reading of *A la recherche* in *Male Subjectivity at the Margins*, London and New York, Routledge, 1992, where she claims that Proust encourages the reader to conceive of Marcel's affair with Albertine as one between two women, an idea in line with the second version of homosexuality as same-sex sexual conjunction in *Sodome et Gomorrhe*. It is ony through lesbianism, she concludes, that we are finally able to locate the homosexuality which structures authorial subjectivity in *A la recherche* (p. 383).

7 In Lamy and Roy, *Duras à Montréal*, Duras explains that as she wrote *Eté* she experienced the madness of nondifferentiation ('I held myself in an undifferentiated love [*amour indifférencié*]'), a crisis that was finally rewarded with the 'exaltation' of success (p. 22).

8 'Je veux emmener avec moi Hélène Lagonelle là où chaque soir, les yeux clos, je me fais donner la jouissance qui fait crier. Je voudrais donner Hélène Lagonelle à cet homme qui fait ça sur moi pour qu'il le fasse à son tour sur elle. Ceci en ma présence, qu'elle le fasse selon mon désir, qu'elle se donne là où moi je me donne. Ce serait par la traversée de son corps que la jouissance m'arriverait de lui, alors définitive. De quoi en mourir.'

9 See, for example, Leah D. Hewitt's *Autobiographical Tightropes: Simone de*

182   The Erotics of Passage

Beauvoir, Nathalie Sarraute, Marguerite Duras, Monique Wittig, and Maryse Condé, Lincoln, London, University of Nebraska Press, 1990, in particular Chapter 3, 'Re-writing Her Story, from Passive to Active: Substitutions in Marguerite Duras's *The Lover*' (pp. 93–126), and Peter Brooks's *Body Work: Objects of Desire in Modern Narrative*, Cambridge, MA and London, Harvard University Press, 1993, in particular Chapter 9, 'Transgressive Bodies' (pp. 257–86). Brooks considers that this scene, equivalent in its grammatical transformation of positions to Freud's essay, 'A Child is Being Beaten', portrays the 'intellection of desire', i.e. of desire becoming visual, erotic knowledge in order to be definitive.

10 See Ninette Bailey, 'Oublieuse Mémoire', *La Chouette*, No. 15 (January 1986), pp. 7–25; p. 24.

11 See Elizabeth A. Meese, *Ex(tensions): Refiguring the Other*, Urbana, IL, University of Illinois Press, 1990, in particular Chapter 4, 'Re:writing "The Other" in Marguerite Duras's *The Lover*' (pp. 78–79).

12 'Hélène Lagonelle donne envie de la tuer, elle fait se lever le songe merveilleux de la mettre à mort de ses propres mains . . . Je suis exténuée du désir d'Hélène Lagonelle. Je suis exténuée de désir.'

13 'Je n'avais jamais vu de film avec ces Indiennes qui portent ces mêmes chapeaux à bord plat et des tresses par le devant de leur corps . . . J'ai deux longues tresses par le devant de mon corps comme ces femmes du cinéma que je n'ai jamais vues mais ce sont des tresses d'enfant.'

14 *Yeux*, p. 65. Later in the same text Duras reveals her attraction for the film's animal violence and shots of the Ganges (p. 247).

15 See *Yeux*, p. 65, where Duras concludes that love is over-played in Renoir and 'desire replaced by display'.

16 'Puis le jour est arrivé où ça a dû être possible. Celui, justement, où le désir de la petite blanche devait être tel, intenable à un tel point, qu'il aurait pu en retrouver son image entière comme dans une grande et forte fièvre et pénétrer l'autre femme de ce désir d'elle, l'enfant blanche.'

17 'Sur le quai, quelqu'un a crié . . . Le bac avance vers le pétrolier. Le pétrolier continue d'avancer aussi vers le bac . . . Le bac a doublé l'avant du pétrolier, il a disparu derrière lui. Le pétrolier continue d'avancer. Le bac réapparaît dans le sillage du pétrolier . . . Le danger a disparu.'

18 Colette Fellous, 'Duras dans les régions claires de l'écriture' (interview with Marguerite Duras), *Le Journal littéraire*, No. 2 (December 1987–January 1988), pp. 120–21; p. 121.

19 '[C]e n'était pas assez non plus d'écrire comme ça, de faire accroire que c'était sans pensée aucune, guidé seulement par la main, de même que c'était trop d'écrire avec seulement la pensée en tête qui surveille l'activité de la folie. C'est trop peu la pensée et la morale et aussi les cas les plus fréquents de l'être humain, les chiens par exemple, c'est trop peu et c'est mal reçu par le corps qui lit et qui veut connaître l'histoire depuis les origines, et à chaque lecture ignorer toujours plus avant que ce qu'il ignore déjà.'

20 'Je vous ai dit qu'il fallait écrire sans correction. . . jeter l'écriture au-dehors, la maltraiter presque . . . ne rien enlever de sa masse inutile.'

21 See Carol J. Murphy, 'Duras's "Beast in the Jungle": Writing Fear (or Fear of Writing) in *Emily L.*', *Neophilologus*, No. 75 (1991), pp. 539–47.

22 Here is the poem in its entirety:
There's a certain Slant of light,
Winter Afternoons—
That oppresses, like the Heft
Of Cathedral Tunes—

Heavenly Hurt it gives us—
We can find no scar,
But internal difference,
Where the meanings, are—

None may teach it—Any—
'Tis the Seal Despair—
An imperial affliction
Sent us of the Air—

When it comes, the Landscape listens—
Shadows—hold their breath—
When it goes, 'tis like the Distance
On the look of Death—

'There's a certain Slant of light' is listed as No. 258 in *The Complete Poems of Emily Dickinson*, ed. Thomas H. Johnson, Boston, Toronto, Little, Brown and Company, 1951. The numbers given henceforth to Dickinson's poems correspond to those of Johnson.

23 For more positive interpretations of Emily L.'s masochism, see Raylene Ramsay, 'Through a Textual Glass, Darkly: The masochistic feminine self and Marguerite Duras's *Emily L.*', *Atlantis*, Vol 17, No. 1 (1991), pp. 91–104, and Raylene O'Callaghan, *Robbe-Grillet and Modernity*, Gainesville, Florida University Press, 1992, p. 160.

24 Referring to his 1987 film, *The Dead*, Duras states in *Monde* that Huston's 'cinematographic madness' makes all other cinema look played out ('Paris, 26 janvier 1992', p. 222).

25 See Tennessee Williams, *The Night of the Iguana*, New York, New Directions, 1962, which also includes as a post-script a Nazi marching song, to be linked, possibly, with the ambulant band of fascistic-looking 'Koreans' in *Emily*. (Williams, it should be noted, was not responsible for the script of Huston's film.)

26 See Vicki Mistacco, '*Plus ça change . . .*: The critical reception to *Emily L.*', *The French Review*, Vol. 66, No. 1 (October 1992), pp. 77–88.

27 In 'Murderous Poetics: Dickinson, the Father, and the Text', *Daughters and Fathers*, ed. Lynda E. Boose and Betty S. Flowers, Baltimore, Johns Hopkins University Press, 1989, pp. 326–43, Joanne Feit Diehl brilliantly analyses the oscillating nature of Dickinson's quest for the *patria potestas*. See also Camille Paglia's *Sexual Personae. Art and Decadence from Nefertiti to Emily Dickinson* [1990], New York, Vintage, 1991, in particular 'Emily Dickinson: Amherst's Madame de Sade', where Paglia proposes that Dickinson be viewed in the context of Baudelaire and Sade as a decadent male genius, or 'visionary sadist' (p. 673).

28 See Sandra M. Gilbert and Susan Gubar's *The Madwoman in the Attic*, New Haven, London, Yale University Press, 1979, in particular 'A Woman—White: Emily

Dickinson's Yarn of Pearl' (pp. 581–650), where Gilbert and Gubar outline the battle between Dickinson as a childlike Nobody and the male Other who resembles Blake's tyrannical God, creator of 'the old Anything'.

29 I am borrowing this term from Murray Cox and Alice Theilgaard who, in *Mutative Metaphors in Psychotherapy: The Aeolian Mode*, London, New York, Tavistock Publications, 1987, consider the possibilities of metaphor and *poiesis* as a therapeutic resource. Dickinson is one of their major sources of reference.

30 Cited in Caws, *A Metapoetics of the Passage*, pp. vi–vii.

31 Compare this with Lyotard's definition of the critical work as one where poetic forms will be reflected as play and unbound energy in a process of condensation and displacement (i.e. primary process). See Jean-François Lyotard, *Discours, figure*, Paris, Klincksieck, 1971, p. 322.

32 See Borgomano's '*L'Amant*: une hypertextualité illimitée', *Revue des Sciences Humaines*, Vol. 73, No. 202 (April–June 1986), pp. 67–77, which argues that Durasian hypertextuality, even 'auto-hypertextuality', cannot simply be reduced to 'transtextuality' (p. 68).

33 See ' "Ignorance" and Textuality' in Cohen, *Women and Discourse*, where Cohen argues that Duras's pluralising textuality is due to the absence of any verifiable 'givens'.

34 See Gérard Genette, *Introduction à l'architexte*, Paris, Seuil, 1979, p. 87.

35 The lovers' ability in *Agatha* to live their love 'by delegation' effectively negates *The Man Without Qualities* which is figured in the text as the mother and her quoted prophecy of doom: ' "you will have the chance to live an untouchable love as you will one day have that of dying from it" ' (p. 66). In fact, Duras's text, where the only named source (Balzac) is non-performative (p. 43), reprises and reinvents some of Musil's key themes and scenes, including the question of indifference (sexual now, rather than political), the forging of the dead father's will (here the mother's cited speech), images of danger (the shared memory of Ulrich entering the water) (p. 15). More specifically, the text's Germanicising of the name Agathe to Agatha (which affects even 'the villa Agatha'), and that character's reversion to the name Diotima in the throes of passion, highlights Duras's inversion of Musil's triangle of desire (Agatha, Ulrich, Diotima). This reworking of Musil is naturally rethematised and ironised in the narrative by an 'error', that of *elle*'s watch being an hour in advance. This error is left uncorrected by *lui* as a source of temporal confusion (pp. 53–54) and resolved only by the particular use of '*avant*' in *elle*'s last speech: 'it was a summer stronger than us . . . more deep [*plus avant*] than our beauty' (p. 67). In Duras's new symposium on love and sublimation which aims to attain a 'new stage in the nature of love' (Lamy and Roy, *Duras à Montréal*, p. 49), the author herself is Diotima, ironic phallus of spiritual *jouissance*, beautifully inverting and transcending her Father-text as surely as the original Diotima procreated the Platonic concept of love. At the same time, of course, the Law of the Father has been kept lovingly intact ('faire cette interdiction plus interdite encore').

36 See 'Le monde moderne n'est pas bavard', *Rendez-vous avec le théâtre*, No. 19 (1984), where Duras explains that although she cannot make Chekhov's characters change, they will at least complain less!

37 See Harold Bloom, *A map of misreading*, Oxford and New York, Oxford University Press, 1975, p. 84, where, in his presentation of a dialectic of revisionism,

Bloom charts the links between image, rhetorical trope, psychic defence and revisionary ratios, including the struggle of individual authors to attain maturity by swerving away from their precursors (*clinamen*), completing them (*tessera*), mythifying them (*daemonisation*), purging all links with them (*askesis*), even assuming their place (*apophrades*).

38 See Eribon, 'Comme une messe de mariage', where Duras states that the father's knowledge of Dickinson, 'that woman who opened the way to modern poetry in English', is crucial for Emily L.'s future formation as a poet. Another potentially fertile avenue of intertextual investigation in *Emily* concerns the Captain, who can be compared with the paternal figure dubbed the 'Captain' in Colette's *Sido* (1929). Struck down by an invisible wound, Colette's Captain is given new capacities after his death by the ghost-writing work of his daughter.

39 See Laurent Jenny, 'La stratégie de la forme', *Poétique*, No. 27 (1976), pp. 258–81. Although Jenny sees transitive intertextuality as an ideological re-activating of meaning, he does not explore or consider the implications of *perturbation*.

40 The term is proposed by Sean Hand in his study of citationality in the work of Edmond Jabès. See 'Double Indemnity: The Ends of Citation in Edmond Jabès', *Romance Studies*, No. 12 (Summer 1986), pp. 77–86.

41 'Nous possédons notre amant comme lui nous possède. Nous nous possédons. Le lieu de cette possession est le lieu de la subjectivité absolue.'

42 Marguerite Duras, 'L'homme assis dans le couloir', *L'Arc*, No. 20 (October 1962), pp. 70–77. This short text is a tale of consuming passion which ended with the arrival of 'non-sense', or (literally) 'the inversion of a vertiginous adequation'. Even if it writes over its earlier, suspended and fractured form, *Homme assis* draws on no other intertextual memory to offset its scenes of graphic abjection and is thus locked in an imaginary, specular relation with its former self. Indeed, it does no more than reverse the agent of destruction; where *lui* once did things by analogy ('he could have shouted the same'), *elle* does the same things 'differently' (p. 9). He said: 'it meant that, then, to love you [*c'était donc ça, t'aimer*]'; she now says: 'I love you'.

43 See Marini's 'La mort d'une érotique', *Les Cahiers Renaud-Barrault*, No. 106 (1983), pp. 37–57. See also Lydon, 'Translating Duras', pp. 264–65.

44 See Carl Plesch, 'The Self-Sufficient Text in Nietzsche and Kierkegaard', *Yale French Studies*, No. 66 (1987), pp. 160–87, where Plesch shows how Kierkegaard's late autobiographical and self-interpretive work, *The Point of View for my Work as an Author* (written in 1848 but not published until 1859), is one of autonomous, self-reflexive, self-deconstructing genius, where the author usurps the role of reader by acting out a Nietzschean fantasy to 'write a book and read it myself'. If Duras felt something similar with *Amant* (see Marianne Alphant, 'Duras à l'état sauvage' (interview with Marguerite Duras), *Libération*, 4 September 1984, pp. 28–29), she still needed the reader and an intertextual other to co-produce the work of 'violation'.

45 In 'La mort d'une erotique', Marini details the evolution of key ideas and phrases from the *Arc* version to *Maladie* via *Homme assis*. The phrase just cited, for example—'en le perdant avant qu'il soit advenu'—abstracts the last lines of 'L'homme assis', where the queen is described as 'défaite aussitôt qu'avenue' (p. 75) ('undone immediately she arrived'). In 'Marginal Canons: Rewriting the Erotic', *Yale French Studies*, No. 75 (1988), pp. 112–29, Lucienne Frappier-Mazur, while

emphasising that the narrator's attempt to introduce a distinction between herself and the woman is not sustained in *Homme assis*, conflates *Homme assis* with *Maladie* and thus concludes very differently that in both texts 'the ambiguity of voices suggests an inability on the part of the narrator to establish self-boundaries' (p. 126).

46 See Kierkegaard's *Diary of a Seducer* (included in *Either/Or*, trans. David F. Swensen and Lillian M. Swensen, Princeton, Princeton University Press, 1959), a work that in *De la séduction*, Paris, Galilée, 1970, Jean Baudrillard considers to be exemplary of the persuasive, antagonistic strategies and appearances of seduction (Cordelia is schooled by Johannes into the law of desire), as well as of a vertical, aesthetic irony which overcomes vulgar eroticism (pp. 135–64). This movement is similar to what we are finding in Duras although in reverse: her female narrator seduces the male other into playing the role of seducer.

47 In an important article, 'La fonction psychique du lecteur dans la poétique durassienne' (Vircondelet, *Marguerite Duras: Rencontres de Cerisy*, pp. 117–41), Jean-Marc Talpin proposes three modes of Duras's practice of 'aesthetic seduction', the third of which, relating to her work post-1980 and its establishing of an autobiographical pact with the reader, operates on the lines of narcissistic excitation, founded on idealisation and 'exacerbation'. Talpin's compelling psychoanalytic analysis of Duras's personal need to fill a perceived internal emptiness by seizing the reading subject through fusion, narcissism, narcissistic perversion, and the 'objectal' (the reader is manipulated as a narcissistic, textual object in order for Duras to avoid psychic recognition of the loss signified by the former's primary alterity [p. 132]), does not, however, acknowledge enough the reader's own pleasures, nor consider how Duras creates other formal and equally amenable instances of otherness (image, intertext, etc.).

48 For a discussion of the drive for knowledge as a sublimation of the sexual drive for mastery, see Laplanche's article, 'To Situate Sublimation', *October*, No. 28 (Spring 1984), pp. 7–26.

49 Hervé Le Masson, 'L'inconnue de la rue Catinat, par Marguerite Duras' (interview with Marguerite Duras), *Le Nouvel Observateur*, 28 September 1984, pp. 92–93; p. 93.

50 Eribon, 'Comme une messe de mariage', p. 61.

51 'L'écrit, lui, le texte, passe par un filtre qui le transforme. Il passe par une transgression que j'appelle le filtre. Cette modification définitive du filtre, c'est l'écrit. Ce que j'appelle l'écrit, c'est le filtre. Le filtre qui transforme, opère la modification. L'écrivain, c'est lui qui opère ce passage' (Lamy and Roy, *Duras à Montréal*, p. 58).

52 See Charles Bernheimer, 'A Shattered Globe: Narcissism and Masochism in Virginia Woolf's Life-Writing', *Psychoanalysis and . . .*, ed. Richard Feldstein and Henry Sussman, London, New York, Routledge, 1990, pp. 187–206, where Bernheimer, using Laplanche, claims that Woolf's text is at once an attempt at maternal recuperation and an opportunity for masochistic perturbation. On the one hand it moves towards an ecstasy of aesthetic impersonality, on the other towards a violent shattering of personality and illusion. Hence, if 'many readers feel an indefinably erotic quality in Woolf's novels, as if the sexuality that she often renounces on the narrative level returned as an effect of her style, this is because her writing repeats and extends the traumatic constitution of her sexuality' (p. 206).

53 'La vieille dame invente de chanter Moses . . . Le miracle est là. A mesure que le

chant se déroule le criminel se transforme. Une sorte de grâce à son tour—cette grâce étant le lieu commun de la vieille dame et des enfants—le chant remonte en lui, chemine en lui à travers sa mort . . . Le criminel et la vieille dame changent ensemble le retour à la vie, la dernière fête du père, et les enfants baignent dans ce chant jusqu'au matin . . . C'est à la fin de cette nuit-là que les enfants retrouvent leur père, dans ce criminel qu'ils retrouvent leur amour . . . Nuit des retrouvailles du criminel avec ses victimes, du père qui en même temps qu'il a créé de la vie a créé de la mort . . . A la fin de la nuit aussi, ce mal s'exhale du père . . . Ce transfert de leur tueur à ceux qui vont tuer leur tueur que voient les enfants—les enfants voient l'arrestation du père—est décisive. Ce père va mourir à cause d'eux. Il va mourir de ce qu'il voulait tant et tant les tuer. Ils sont cause de sa mort. La révélation est foudroyante. Comme la connaissance même. On pense à Moïse qui tant il était possédé par l'idée de Dieu ne pouvait pas parler, ne pouvait que crier. Les enfants crient et se livrent corps et âme au père, à leur tueur. Avec la violence entière de leur vie, ils se sauvent de la vieille dame et se donnent au père.'

54 See Lynda Zwinger, *Daughters, Fathers, and the Novel. The Sentimental Romance of Heterosexuality*, Madison, London, University of Wisconsin Press, 1991, in particular Chapter 6, 'A Child Never Banished from Home: The Daughter's Daughter'.

55 Although uncited, Fonda's last film, *On Golden Pond* (1981), about father-daughter reconciliation through the intermediary of the grandson, appears to be an inverted form of the grandmother/(grand)daughter bond of *Savannah*. The text reduces the suicidal waters of ravishment in its related tale by swallowing up 'the white rock' in a small intertextual pond of mastered irony, founded necessarily on the erratic breaking of a syntactical sequence. The verb form 'est', instead of being simply repeated as one would normally expect, is contracted into the similarly sounding preposition 'et': 'Madeleine: . . . How white the stone is [*Comme la pierre est blanche*]. Young girl: Like pain and long [*Comme la douleur et longue*]. Pause. How it changes. Pause. How it becomes' (pp. 127–28). In 'Child's Play: Repetition and Death in Duras's *Savannah Bay*', *Neophilologus*, No. 77 (1993), pp. 215–21, George Moskos argues very differently that the text privileges the metonymical because it refuses the metaphorisation of an end.

56 See Kristeva's 'Histoires d'amour', *ICA Documents*, No. 1 ('Desire'), London, ICA Publications, 1984, pp. 18–21; p. 21. For a very different view of Duras's Third, see Chapter 7 of Adèle King's *French women novelists: defining a female style*, New York, St Martin's Press, 1989, which, by reworking René Girard's theory of mimetic desire, argues that Durasian desire is mediated through the mother who represents not the rival but the body with which the lover desires erotic reunion (p. 159).

57 In *The Resistance to Theory*, Minneapolis, University of Minnesota Press, 1986, de Man identifies the moment of 'giving face', or *prosopopoeia*, as the move that enables the predicative and demonstrative function of language to take place. See 'Hypogram and Inscription'. For a pertinent account of the links between de Man's theory of defacement and Kristeva's theory of abjection, see Cynthia Chase, 'Primary Narcissism and the Giving of Figure: Kristeva with Hertz and de Man', *Abjection, Melancholia, and Love*, ed. Andrew Benjamin and John Fletcher, London, New York, Routledge, 1990, pp. 124–36.

58 See *Ma mère*, Paris, Jean-Jacques Pauvert, '10/18', 1966. For Kristeva's

account of the basic metaphorical workings of this text which, like *Homme assis*, also favours the conditional perfect tense, see her *Tales of Love* [1983], trans. Léon S. Roudiez, New York, Columbia University Press, 1987, in particular 'Bataille and the Sun, or the guilty text' (pp. 365–71).

59 See Sean Hand, 'Missing You: Intertextuality, transference and the language of love', *Intertextuality: theories and practices*, ed. Judith Still and Michael Worton, Manchester, Manchester University Press, 1990, pp. 79–91, for a Lacanian account of transference as an intertextual relation.

60 Kristeva, *Soleil Noir*, pp. 264–65.

Notes to Chapter 5
pp. 93–114

1 It is worth noting that while the revised 1987 edition of *Yeux* at last credits its photographic sources (p. 253), it actually modifies the running order of illustrations, even replacing the image of an unidentified woman with a 1960s photograph of Duras herself (p. 48).

2 Duras swung from an initially ecstatic opinion of Annaud's cinematic 'reduction' of *Amant* (see Pierette Rosset, 'Duras parle du nouveau Duras' (interview with Marguerite Duras), *Elle*, 15 January 1990, pp. 38–39) to a deeply hostile one (see Jean-Michel Frodon and Danièle Heymann, 'Duras Song. Vous faites une différence entre mes livres et mes films?' [interview with Marguerite Duras], *Le Monde*, 13 June 1991, pp. 17–19). For Duras's case against Lindon see her interview with Marianne Alphant, 'Duras dans le parc à amants', *Libération*, 13 June 1991, pp. 26–27, which is followed by Lindon's laconic reply.

3 No sooner is the topic of lesbian love raised ('more or less conscious, secretive compensations') than Duras steers the conversation back to the more familiar idea of self-flagellation as a sexual outlet. See 'Dialogue avec une carmélite', *Outside*, pp. 162–70.

4 '[Q]uand le dehors me submergeait, quand il y avait des choses qui me rendaient folle, *outside*.'

5 In *Jean-Luc Godard par Jean-Luc Godard*, ed. Alain Bergala, Paris, Cahiers du Cinéma/l'Etoile, 1985, Godard notes how Duras reacted with a 'beautiful smile' to his suggestion that she may be the 'true' daughter (p. 616) of three other writers who were also film-makers—Jean Cocteau, Marcel Pagnol, Sacha Guitry—and may thus figure in an exclusively male, in part homosexual, tradition of French cinema.

6 Duras's exposé of male exclusivity in 'Les hommes', in particular the fact that a man's true self ('l'homme numéro un') (*Vie mat.*, p. 45) can only be properly revealed in the company of other men, reverses such phrases as 'L'homme seul et nu est la vérité', articulated by Jouhandeau in *Bréviaire. Portrait de Don Juan. Amours*, Paris, Gallimard, 1981, p. 31. In fact, 'Les hommes' could be seen in general terms as a revision of classic French maxims on sexuality. 'Parler de l'amour, c'est faire l'amour' (p. 44), for example, is already an extension of Pascal's maxim, 'A force de parler, on devient amoureux'.

7 Duras is actually trying to wrest *Ah! Ernesto*, Boissy-St Léger, François Ruy-Vidal and Harlin Quist, 1971, from Jean-Marie Straub and Danielle Huillet who adapted it in 1983 into a black and white short entitled *En rachâchant* and which brought out superbly its anal humour (at one point Ernesto shouts out 'Merde'). Duras subsequently entered into litigation over the film rights. *Enfants* represents perhaps a second attempt by Duras to recover and rewrite *Ah! Ernesto*.

8 Marguerite Duras, 'L'exacte exactitude de Denis Belloc' (interview with Denis Belloc), *Libération*, 19–20 September 1987, pp. 32–33.

9 'Le livre est là, éclatant, magnifique, comme toujours la vérité. Et c'est ça, le

principal'; 'Il y a des pauvres qui n'ont pas fait les pissotières'; 'Il y a aussi les gens qui font les pissotières et qui n'ont pas fait votre livre. Il y a aussi des riches qui n'ont jamais fait ni les pissotières, ni votre livre.'

10 'Le réalisme est longtemps apparu comme un militantisme périmé, un suivisme démagogique aussi, un peu l'argot de gauche. Dans ton livre, il devient une position rigoureusement personnelle et inimitable, il est à toi, il est de toi. Et tu n'en es pas responsable, il te sort du corps, pas plus qu'avant le livre. Tout ce qu'on peut faire, c'est consigner certaines choses . . . Ce livre qu'on ne peut pas quitter une fois qu'on l'a commencé, et qui a l'air d'être sur ton histoire, en fait, il est sur tous les gens mais un par un dénombrés, sur tous ceux des minorités majeures et sur tous ceux des majorités mineures, mais un par un dénombrés.'

11 Marguerite Duras, 'Denis Belloc, la nuit sociale', *Libération*, 22 September 1988, p. viii.

12 It is significant that Duras did not promote Belloc's fourth novel, *Les aiguilles à tricoter*, Paris, Julliard, 1990, which treats explicitly of lesbian desire. As we would expect by now, the repression of *Néons* is a protracted affair. *Néons*, printed in August 1987, coincided with the publication of *Emily*, and, as Duras explained later to Colette Fellous in 'Duras dans les régions claires de l'écriture', the last three pages of *Emily* were only completed the night before the manuscript was sent to the printers on 21 September 1987, that is to say, two days after the appearance in *Libération* of 'L'exacte exactitude'. Everything leads us to suppose that the sublime 'apparition' on the last page of *Emily* has an inverted referent, or 'useless mass' (p. 153), i.e. Belloc, as though Duras needs a 'real', nameable ground of non-differentiation and inversion (sexual and linguistic) to ensure literary sublimation.

13 Gérard Meudal, 'Les outsiders de Marguerite Duras' (interview with Marguerite Duras), *Libération*, 26 May 1986, p. 16.

14 In Aubenas, 'Entretien', p. 12, Duras addresses the issue of imitation and plagiarism, declaring that those who 'do a Duras' are going to date (p. 12).

15 ' "Ils" ne pourront pas les détruire quoi qu' "ils" fassent. "Ils", c'est l'impondérable du mal, ce n'est pas la peine de donner des détails. Les gens qui en sont reconnaîtront tout de suite leur appartenance à cette microsociété qui macère dans l'amertume, le rétrécissement de l'âme, le rattrapage par la somme culturelle et l'exercice régulier de la jalousie méchante.'

16 Henri Choukroun, *Pour une nouvelle économie de la création*, Paris, 1985, with a preface by Marguerite Duras (pp. 9–17) (reprinted in *Monde*, pp. 149–56). Choukroun is a lawyer specialising in the defence of artists and writers.

17 For Duras's views on Handke's 1985 adaptation of *Maladie*, which, in effect, played her off against other writers such as René Char, see *Yeux*, pp. 232–34.

18 See 'Et clap! Passe-moi Lépanges: Les grands tournages de Gérard Lefort', *Libération*, 7 January 1987, p. xiv, a stinging, spoof account of the filming of 'Sublime'.

19 See Philippe Sollers, 'Duras Telle-Quelle', *Le Nouvel Observateur*, 12 January 1970. Duras's antipathy towards Sollers is a running theme in her interviews during the 1980s.

20 For Duras's views on Blanchot's negative reading of *Maladie* due to his failure to recognise the topos of homosexuality, see *Yeux*, pp. 232–33, a charge she repeats in *Au-delà des pages*. In fact, Blanchot does refer explicitly to homosexuality on p. 84

of 'La communauté des amants' (*La communauté inavouable*, Paris, Minuit, 1983) but only in parenthesis. His point is that homosexuality is not in itself the cause of 'the sickness of death' examined in *Maladie* and that all feelings of love and desire are universal.

21 Michel Tournier, 'The Faces of Marguerite Duras: The Lover', *Vanity Fair*, July 1985, pp. 64–67.

22 See Hocquenghem's *Lettre ouverte à ceux qui sont passés du col Mao au Rotary*, Paris, Albin Michel, 1986.

23 See Angelo Rinaldi, 'Marguerite D. comme détective', *Le Point*, 26 July 1985. The sentiment is mutual. Duras states in *Vie mat.* that she would just as well give up writing as write like Rinaldi (p. 118).

24 See 'Tir groupé' in Renaud Camus, *Les Chroniques Achriennes*, Paris, POL, 1984.

25 *Les Nuits Magnétiques*, 27–31 October 1980.

26 Marguerite Duras, 'La lecture dans le train', *L'Autre Journal (mensuel)*, No. 9 (November 1985), pp. 6–9 (reprinted in *Monde*, pp. 136–44; 142–43).

27 Brée, 'An interview with Marguerite Duras', p. 404.

28 See the stinging 'Grandes Laudes à Marguerite Duras' in *Chroniques Achriennes*, pp. 100–04, where Camus states that because Duras's demand of total admiration from her courtiers will never be satisfied, she therefore attacks them for their inability to love.

29 See Duras's eloquent lament for Daney, 'Le jeune Serge avec son feutre noir', *Cahiers du Cinéma*, No. 458 (July–August 1992), p. 26 (reprinted in *Monde*, pp. 207–09).

30 See 'Pascale (. . .)', *Libération*, 30 November 1984 (reprinted in *Monde*, pp. 18–19), a letter written one month after Ogier's death and in which Duras focuses on her grace which 'still invades everything'.

31 See Pierre Léon and Brigitte Ollier, 'Pour Duras, le plus beau c'est Hulot' (interview with Marguerite Duras), *Libération*, 27 November 1987.

32 See Duras's interviews with Platini, ' "Le stade de l'ange" ', *Libération*, 13 December 1987, and ' "Qu'est-ce que ce jeu-là? Démoniaque et divin" ', *Libération*, 14 December 1987, on the occasion of his 1987 book, *Ma vie comme un match*. Platini only half-heartedly accepts Duras's idea that his life is the vocation of a martyr.

33 See Duras's review of Lévy's *La société des femmes* (1987), 'Thierry Lévy ou la littérature évitée', *Le Matin*, 17 February 1987, 'Supplément livres', p. 3. Although Duras praises Lévy's 'angelic nature', she states that his work is a raw text of 'mutilated writing' and deficient: its title is tendentious and it ought to have been terminated on p. 189.

34 Ralph Gibson, *L'Histoire de France*, New York, Aperture, 1991, with an introduction by Marguerite Duras (reprinted in *Monde*, pp. 34–36).

35 *Yves Saint Laurent et la photographie de mode*, with a preface by Marguerite Duras ('Le Bruit et le Silence'), Paris, Albin Michel, 1988, pp. 9–15 (reprinted in *Monde*, pp. 164–68; p. 166).

36 Marguerite Duras, 'Les Amants', *Le Nouvel Observateur*, 28 June 1985, pp. 62–63; p. 63 (reprinted in *Monde*, pp. 207–09). The image chosen by Duras to illustrate 'Les Amants', a still from Charles Vidor's 1946 triangle of doomed passion,

192   *The Erotics of Passage*

Gilda, is important for what it reveals of Duras's own technique. It captures the 'femme fatale' Gilda (Rita Hayworth) towering over her supplicating husband, Johnny (Glenn Ford), as she performs a strip-tease designed to provoke him into hitting her. Her intention is that he becomes suitably inspired to make love to her and thus overcome his lingering feelings for another man, Ballen, the third part of the triangle. In Vidor, as in Duras, sadomasochistic, heterosexual violence is the privileged 'answer' to latent gay desire.

37 For a clear account of Lacan's theory of transsexuality, see Catherine Millot, *Horsexe. Essay on transsexuality*, trans. Kenneth Hylton [1983], New York, Autonomedia, 1990, p. 143. For an alternative literary and social view of androgyny germane to our discussion, see Kari Weil, *Androgyny and the Denial of Difference*, Charlottesville, London, University Press of Virginia, 1992, which argues that the androgyne is merely a patriarchal construction designed to establish the limits of sexual and aesthetic identity.

38 'Dans l'hétérosexualité il n'y a pas de solution. L'homme et la femme sont irréconciliables et c'est cette tentative impossible et à chaque amour renouvelée qui en fait la grandeur.'

39 In Horer and Socquet, 'Marguerite Duras', Duras suggests that Pascal proceeds from a 'certain androgyny', or 'darkness of a feminine nature' (p. 186).

40 This fact is discussed by Hocquenghem in the context of W. H. Gillespie and the 1965 Stockholm conference on homosexuality. See 'Anti-homosexual paranoia', *Homosexual desire* (p. 47).

41 See Rolland Thélu, 'DURAS: The Thing' (interview with Marguerite Duras), *Le Gai Pied*, No. 20 (November 1980), p. 16. On the question of misogyny, Duras declares that Barthes was 'submerged' only by the 'audacity' that the fact of being openly homosexual represented for him in his youth.

42 See, for example, Jane Gallop, 'The Perverse Body', in *Thinking through the Body*, New York, Columbia University Press, 1988, pp. 100–15, and Naomi Schor, 'Dreaming Dissymmetry: Barthes, Foucault, and Sexual Difference', *Men in Feminism*, ed. Alice Jardine and Paul Smith, London, New York, Methuen, 1987, pp. 98–110.

43 See *Roland Barthes par Roland Barthes*, Paris, Seuil, 1975, in particular, 'Les idées méconnues' (pp. 107–08). Barthes's point that Duras fails to recognise 'the third term' is most ironic in view of her absolute dependence on a third, intertextual instance.

44 Roland Barthes, *S/Z*, Paris, Seuil, 1970, p. 15.

45 Gregory Bredbeck, 'B/O—Barthes's Text/O'Hara's Trick', *PMLA*, Vol. 108, No. 2 (March 1993), pp. 268–82; p. 279.

46 I am following the delineation of irony and humour proposed by Candace Lang in *Irony/Humour*, Baltimore, Johns Hopkins University Press, 1988 where she opposes the notion of a post-modernist humour—baroque, horizontal, metonymical, and masochistic—to a vertical, and sadistic, Platonic-Kierkegaardian irony. As we are seeing, the poetic for Duras functions as ironic while the paradoxical is merely the parodic.

47 See Lamy and Roy, *Duras à Montréal*, pp. 69–70.

48 See Camus's *Notes Achriennes*, Paris, Hachette, 1982, p. 138, where Camus quotes at length Barthes's discussion of Proust's 'enantiology' of desire in 'Une idée de

recherche' (included in the collection *Le bruissement de la langue*, Paris, Seuil, 1982).

49 See Lee Edelman, *Transmemberment of Song. Hart Crane's Anatomies of Rhetoric and Desire*, Stanford, CA, Stanford University Press, 1987, in particular the conclusion, where Edelman offers a rhetorical reading of Crane's 'The Broken Vessel'. For a more explicitly gay re-evaluation of Crane's work, see Thomas E. Yingling's *Hart Crane and the Homosexual Text. New Thresholds, New Anatomies*, Chicago, University of Chicago Press, 1990, in particular Chapter 2, 'Homosexuality and the matter of style'.

50 In *Closet Writing/Gay Reading. The Case of Melville's 'Pierre'*, Chicago, Chicago University Press, 1993, Creech uses this term to characterise Barbara Johnson's essentially homophobic, rhetorical reading of Herman Melville's *Billy Budd* in her article, 'Melville's Fist: The Execution of *Billy Budd*' (*The Critical Difference*, Baltimore, Johns Hopkins University Press, 1980, pp. 79–109), which, with a 'rhetorical razzle-dazzle', uses the chiasmus as its master trope. He also claims that by choosing chiastic equivocality as a master cipher for *Billy Budd*, Johnson opts for an 'empty' modernist reading.

51 '[O]n n'*appartient* jamais dans l'homosexualité comme on appartient dans l'hétérosexualité. Cet enfer de ne pas pouvoir échapper au désir d'une personne, c'est là ce que j'appelle, quant à moi, la splendeur de l'hétérosexualité.'

52 'Le texte ne cesse de désigner les lois de son propre fonctionnement; c'est pour mieux, aussitôt formulées, les contredire. Ann-Mary Straighter n'est pas ébranlée par cette duplicité.' On the penultimate page of *Passage*, just after a reference to Indiana's song and to a couple locked in an eternal embrace (the vice-consul and Anne-Marie Stretter?), the narrator delivers what is possibly an attack on Duras in which author and work are confused. He asks why 'one should have to leave it [unspecified] up to the narratives of a jealous old lady, or to the conversations of the women on the chaises longues near the tennis courts' (p. 204).

53 *Passage* can be linked to Hocquenghem's Deleuzian treatise on gay desire, *L'après-mai des faunes: volutions*, Paris, Grasset, 1974, the final aims of which are, as Deleuze notes in the preface, the invention and reversibility of new sexual roles, or '*volutions*' (p. 15). The transvestite in particular is to be championed as a site of 'passage', or transmutation, from one universe to another (p. 15). We note in passing the opinion of Emily Apter that Camus represents, with Gide, the sexual component of Barthes's writing that Barthes could never inscribe himself (Emily S. Apter, *André Gide and the Codes of Homotextuality*, Saratoga, Anma Libri, 1987, p. 104). Barthes, of course, prefaced Camus's novel, *Tricks*, Paris, Persona, 1979, which he admired precisely for its 'passage' from sex to discourse.

54 See Bersani's controversial study of the privileged, symbolic power of anal sex in the AIDS era, 'Is the Rectum a Grave?', *October*, No. 43 (1987), pp. 197–222, which argues that male homosexuality 'proposes and dangerously represents *jouissance* as a mode of ascesis' (p. 222).

55 This is the conclusion reached by Bersani in his earlier analysis of the female homosexual desire between Anne and Claire in 'Jean de Berg''s *L'image* (1956). See *A Future for Astyanax: Character and Desire in Literature*, Boston, Toronto, Little, Brown and Company, 1976, pp. 306–07. It is significant in this regard that *Passage* also presents a crisis of authorship, forming as it does part of Camus's series entitled *Les Eglogues*, which includes *Echange* (1976), *Travers* (1978) and *Eté* (*Travers II*)

(1982), and which is written under the various names of Denis Duparc, Jean-Renaud Camus and Denis Duvert.

56 For a shrewd, theoretical analysis of this tradition, see Kevin Kopelson, *Love's Litany: The Writing of Modern Homoerotics*, Stanford, CA, Stanford University Press, 1994. Kopelson's focus is on four principal conceptions of romantic love: complementary merger; love as fatal union (*Liebestod*); the association of love with sadness; solitude and suicide ('Wertherism'); and Stendhalian 'crystallisation'.

57 See Naomi Schor, 'Reading Double: Sand's Difference', *The Poetics of Gender*, ed. Nancy K. Miller, New York, Columbia University Press, 1986, where Schor argues for Sand's subversion of sexual difference through such devices as incest (in *François le Champi*) and twinship (in *La petite Fadette*) and her recurring scenes of fetishistic eroticism and female travesty.

58 Duras stated in 'A propos de Georges Bataille' (*Outside*, pp. 34–36) that Bataille's abjection, contrary to that of Genet, delivers his characters of their singularity and allows them to emerge into their own indetermination. They are therefore no longer in the 'straitjacket' of an individual royalty but rather on the way to their own 'dissolution' and 'destruction' (pp. 35–36).

59 In 'The Homotext of Tournier's *Les météores*', *Sub-stance*, Vol. 58, No. 1 (1989), pp. 35–50, Lawrence R. Schehr examines the narrative's need for Alexandre and his 'homotext' to die. What Schehr attributes to homosexual desire and its connection with auto-textuality in Tournier I am attributing to Duras's ostensibly 'heterological' intertextuality, namely, that it seeks to bridge the gap of desire and difference and remake difference by closing the space between self and other (pp. 42–43).

60 See 'Et si je n'avais pas lu', *Roland Barthes*, p. 104.

61 See Lee Edelman, *Homographesis: essays in gay literary and cultural theory*, New York, London, Routledge, 1994, in particular Chapter 11, 'Imagining the Homosexual: *Laura* and the Other Face of Gender' (pp. 192–241), which offers a complex reading of Waldo's ambiguous male body in *Laura*. In order to show how the film positions Waldo as 'the other face of female sexuality', Edelman focuses on key scenes of figuration such as the portrait and the 'face' of the clock that Waldo strikes down at the end of the film.

62 'Yann Andréa, j'ai rencontré cet été quelqu'un que vous connaissez, Jean-Pierre Ceton, nous avons parlé de vous, je n'avais pas pu deviner que vous vous connaissiez.'

63 This is evident even at the level of the book's cover which, with its tricolore of blue, black and white, also has the look and feel of a Minuit text. Most unusually, however, the title in blue dominates the author in black: Duras's name is written in full at the top in pale-black lettering and in humble, italicised lower-case, while the title in blue-ultramarine stands in bolder and wider type. In addition (and this is an effect of the publisher's changing format), the POL logo located at the bottom of the cover—a seven-ball design by Jean-Pierre Reissner—has now been slightly altered, lacking a square frame in which to capture its four balls of blue and three of black. Finally, the surface texture of the cover is no longer shiny but coarse and tessellated.

64 Jean-Louis Ezine, 'Les nostalgies de l'amante Duras' (interview with Marguerite Duras), *Le Nouvel Observateur*, No. 1442, 25 June–1 July 1992, pp. 53–55; p. 54. The story of Théodora Kats is also related by Dionys Mascolo in *Autour d'un*

effort de mémoire: Sur une lettre de Robert Antelme, Paris, Maurice Nadeau, 1987.

65 '[J]'ai fait de mon mieux pour que le phénomène de la gare se reproduise . . . il s'est reproduit.'

66 '[J]e les ai ramenés comme je le fais de vous, de la mer et du vent, je les ai enfermés dans cette chambre noire égarée au-dessus du temps. Celle que j'appelle La Chambre des Juifs.'

Notes to Chapter 6
pp. 115–38

1 Serge July, 'La transgression de l'écriture', *Libération*, 17 July 1985, p. 4.

2 For a summary of responses to 'Sublime' see Benoîte Groult's series of interviews with (among others) Simone Signoret, Françoise Sagan and Michèle Perrein in *L'Evénement du Jeudi*, 25 July 1985. According to *Libération* of 25 July 1985, the only feminist on record as approving of the article was Edmonde Charles-Roux.

3 An extract of Delanoë's letter (originally published by *Libération* in December 1985) was released as 'Ascenseur pour l'échafaud', *Esprit*, No. 116 (July 1986), pp. 85–86.

4 Paul Thibaud, 'Marguerite Duras: Les Ambiguïtés de la Compassion', *Esprit*, No. 116 (July 1986), pp. 75–77.

5 (I) David Amar, 'A propos d'un article paru dans *Libération*', (II) Pierre Yana, 'Enonciation d'un crime', *Revue des sciences humaines*, Vol. 73, No. 202 (1986), pp. 154–66 and pp. 167–76 respectively.

6 See 'Dominici ou le triomphe de la Littérature', Roland Barthes, *Mythologies*, Paris, Seuil, 1957, pp. 51–53. Gaston Dominici was an illiterate peasant condemned to death for the murder in 1952 of Sir Jack Drummond, his wife and daughter. Although he was freed in 1960 on compassionate grounds, the case is still regarded as a probable miscarriage of justice.

7 'Du moment que ce crime, dans le cas précis où elle était d'avoir à le commettre personne n'aurait pu l'éviter, coupable elle n'a pas été.'

8 Amar, 'A propos', p. 161.

9 'Si elle criait je crois ce serait ceci: *"Que tout le monde meure autour de moi, ce nouvel enfant, mon mari et moi-même, mais coupable comme la justice le veut, je ne le serai jamais."* '

10 'Elle est encore seule dans la solitude, là où sont encore les femmes du fond de la terre, du noir, afin qu'elles restent telles qu'elles étaient avant, reléguées dans la matérialité de la matière. Christine V. est sublime. Forcément sublime.'

11 See, for example, Patricia Yaeger's article, 'Toward a Female Sublime', *Gender and Theory. Dialogues on Feminist Criticism*, ed. Linda Kauffman, Oxford, Blackwell, 1989, pp. 191–212, which studies Elizabeth Bishop's poem 'The Moose'.

12 See Neil Hertz, *The End of the Line. Essays on Psychoanalysis and the Sublime*, New York, Columbia University Press, 1985, pp. 40–60 and pp. 231–32, where Hertz takes up Kristeva's theory of abjection and primary narcissism.

13 'Le Bruit et le Silence', *Monde*, p. 166.

14 See Verena Andermatt Conley, ' "L'Affaire Grégory" and Duras's Textual Feminism', *L'Esprit Créateur*, Vol. 30, No. 1 (Spring 1990), pp. 101–10.

15 See *Parleuses*, p. 235, where Duras dismisses Bataille's notion of transgression as pure wish-fulfilment.

16 See Barbara Molinard, *Viens*, Paris, Mercure de France, 1969, with a preface by Marguerite Duras (reprinted in *Monde*, pp. 161–63).

17 See Annie Le Brun, 'Vagit-Prop', *Le Monde*, 6 December 1984.

18 While ostensibly admiring Issermann's film, Duras casts it in the most banal of terms, claiming it stages an 'equivalence' between the awful life of the body which lives the horror and the spirit which discerns it and defends the body from it (*Yeux*, p. 228). In an uncomfortable interview with Issermann in *L'Autre Journal* (*hebdo*), 11–17 June 1986, pp. 48–50, on the occasion of her new film, *L'amant magnifique*, Duras began typically by praising Issermann's sexually explicit work but then effectively nullified it on account of its attempt to show 'the coma of ecstasy' ('it is quite possible that the film we're watching is not the film you wanted to make').

19 See 'La petite fille de Brooklyn', *Le Nouvel Observateur*, 3–9 August 1987, pp. 64–65. See also the very strained first encounter between Duras and Kaplan in 1985 on the occasion of the publication by POL of Kaplan's *L'excès-L'usine*, entitled '*L'Excès-L'Usine*', *L'Autre Journal* (*mensuel*), No. 5 (May 1985) (later reprinted in L-excès-L'usine as 'Usine' [pp. 109–119]).

20 This phrase is the title of a short piece by Duras in *Le Monde*, 17–18 March 1985 (reprinted in *Monde,* pp. 66–67).

21 For a powerful analysis of the paranoid structures in Pynchon, whereby what is excluded from the text's Symbolic frame returns in the text's Real as its own paranoid construction, see Leo Bersani, 'Pynchon, Paranoia, and Literature', *Representations*, No. 25 (1989), pp. 99–118.

22 For Duras's earlier account of Sartre as father of her generation, see Brée, 'An interview with Marguerite Duras'.

23 See *L'effet-Godard*, ed. Carole Desbarates and Jean-Paul Gorace, Toulouse, Editions Milan, 1989, where, in a short note originally written in 1984, Duras explained that whereas Godard passes directly to cinema and is 'in cinema', she writes books (p. 12).

24 See Anne de Gasperi, 'Je vais faire un film avec Godard' (interview with Marguerite Duras), *Le Quotidien de Paris*, 3 February 1981.

25 See, for example, 'Work and Words' (*EVC*), where Duras claimed to detest the word '*rêve*' above all others. Duras is characteristically inverting a real event here: the shocking murder of Malik Oussekine by supporters of le Pen in December 1986.

26 Jean-Louis Barrault, 'Un enfant obstiné', *L'Arc*, No. 98 (1985), pp. 56–57; p. 57.

27 See Freud's 1927 paper, 'Fetishism', *The Standard Edition*, Vol. 21, pp. 149–57, where Freud proposes that the fetish, a 'token of triumph over the threat of castration and a protection against it', also saves the (male) fetishist from being homosexual 'by endowing women with the characteristic which makes them tolerable as sexual objects' (p. 154).

28 See 'Viva Callas' in *Monde*, pp. 125–26, an article from 1965 which, significantly, is also included (in English) in *Outside* (pp. 250–51). For Duras, Callas is both a Gorgon and a Medusa.

29 See Frodon and Heymann, 'Vous faites une différence entre mes livres et mes films?'. Duras is talking here about making her own screen version of *Chine*.

30 See Berkeley Kaite's discussion of pornography and the phallic woman, 'The Pornographer's Body Double: Transgression is the Law', *Body Invaders: Panic Sex in*

America, ed. Arthur and Marilouise Kroker, New York, St Martin's Press, 1987, which claims that such masochistic pleasure for the spectator is possible whether the phallus is 'literal' (as in transvestism) or vestiary (the so-called 'real girl') (p. 158).

31 In *The Madwoman in the Attic*, Gilbert and Gubar give a comprehensive analysis of the 'uniforms of snow' that Dickinson often donned alone in her father's house, and show how this relates to a poetic persona of both fragile and virile *'virginity'* (pp. 645–46).

32 It is perhaps significant in view of the direction of our discussion that the one hundred and sixty 'negative hands' found in a cave at Gargas were probably not connected with love at all but hunting. Furthermore, Duras admits in 'La caverne noire' that the text is founded on a formal error: it was not, as stated in the prologue, the area of the hands which was coloured blue but rather the trace of their outline.

33 See Panivong Norindr, ' "Errances" and Memories in Marguerite Duras's Colonial Cities', *Differences*, Vol. 5, No. 3 (1993), pp. 52–78. Norindr refers to Barthes's concept of a 'city of Drift', i.e. a site of sexual *errance* and amorous *jouissance*.

34 See Christine Holmlund, 'Displacing Limits of Difference: Gender, Race, and Colonialism in Edward Said and Homi Bhabha's Theoretical Models and Marguerite Duras's Experimental Films', *Quarterly Review of Film and Video*, Vol. 13, Nos 1–3 (1991), pp. 1–22; p. 15. Holmlund provides no actual detailed analysis of the film itself to support this statement.

35 'Dire non pas tout crûment sa vision, mais, par un *transfert* instantané, constant, l'écho de sa présence' (cited in James Clifford, *The Predicament of Culture: Twentieth-Century Ethnography, Literature, and Art*, Cambridge, MA, Harvard University Press, 1988, p. 152).

36 See 'Le Mélodrame de la Différence' in Baudrillard's *La transparence du mal: essai sur les phénomènes extrêmes*, Paris, Galilée, 1990, which refers to Segalen's *Essai sur l'exotisme*. One of Baudrillard's humanist bêtes noires, Tzvetan Todorov, has carefully noted in his own study how Segalen stumbles on a problem shared by other relativists, namely that all realities are relative except their own. See 'Segalen', *Nous et les autres. La réflexion française sur la diversité humaine*, Paris, Seuil, 1989, pp. 357–72. It should be pointed out that Duras's play with the concept of undifferentiation never strikes the cynical note of Baudrillard's abstractions. She did, for example, fear the possibility of 'real' chaos after the collapse in 1989 of the wall separating East and West Germany. See Jean-Marcel Bouguereau, 'Duras 89–90' (interview with Marguerite Duras), *L'Evénement du Jeudi*, 1–7 February 1990, pp. 84–87.

37 See Homi K. Bhabha, 'The Other Question—the Stereotype and Colonial Discourse', *Screen*, Vol. 24, No. 6 (1983), pp. 18–36; p. 33.

38 For an analysis of these techniques in the case of the colonization of the Ilongots, see Renato Rosaldo, 'The Rhetoric of Control: Ilongots viewed as Natural Bandits and Wild Indians', *The Reversible World: Symbolic Inversion in Art and Society*, ed. Barbara A. Babcock, Ithaca, Cornell University Press, 1978, pp. 240–57.

39 'Vous ne m'importez plus . . . Je vous ai abandonné . . . Mais, voyez-vous, je vous appelle cependant . . . La distance qui nous sépare est justement celle de la mort. C'est une seule et même distance pour vous et pour moi. De la même façon que vous, vous voulez la garder pure entre nous, de la même façon, moi, je la recouvre de mes

cris et de mes appels. Comme vous, je sais que cette distance est infranchissable, impossible à couvrir. La différence entre vous et moi c'est que pour moi cette impossibilité est un inconvénient négligeable. Alors voyez, nous sommes pareils, nous nous tenons tous les deux pareillement dans nos cases respectives, dans nos territoires brûlés incalculablement narcissiques, mais moi je crie *vers* les déserts, de préférence dans la direction des déserts.'

40 See Gilles Costaz, 'Demain, les hommes' (interview with Marguerite Duras), *Le Matin*, 3 October 1985, p. 6 (reprinted in *Monde*, pp. 102–03), where Duras states that the art of intelligence is to take genius out of oneself and put it on to the canvas or into the book.

41 'Moi', *L'Autre Journal*, No. 10, 30 April 1986 (reprinted in *Monde*, pp. 74–75). 'Moi' might usefully be compared with Segalen's *Essai sur soi-même*, Montpellier, Fata Morgana, 1986, a small text of equally brief statements about the self and dedicated to Segalen's inner demon.

42 This is one of the twelve captions in Duras's article, 'L'année 90: Les 12 photos émotion', *France-Soir*, 29 December 1990.

43 'Je crois que les juifs, ce trouble pour moi si fort, et que je vois en toute lumière, devant quoi je me tiens dans une clairvoyance tuante, ça rejoint l'écrit. Ecrire, c'est aller chercher hors de soi ce qui est déjà au-dedans de soi' (*Yeux*, p. 176).

44 See Marguerite Duras and François Mitterrand, 'Africa, Africa', *L'Autre Journal (hebdo)*, No. 4, 19–25 March 1986, where Duras states not only that the West is Jewish but also that the faculty of European man to be simultaneously the other and oneself is specifically Jewish (p. 31). For Duras's account of Chaplin as the physical embodiment of 'passage', see 'Chaplin, oui' in *Yeux* (p. 87).

45 'Le seul avantage d'être sortie de moi-même, d'être allée dehors, "outside", comme je l'ai fait pendant 10 ans de militante, c'est que les raisons que j'aurai eues de mourir étaient extérieures à moi. Comme le sort fait au juif, la douleur de voir les gens torturés . . . ce sont des raisons extérieures à ma vie' (Aubenas, 'Entretien', p. 15).

46 See Marilyn Schuster's 1967 interview with Duras, 'Entretien avec Marguerite Duras', reprinted in Vircondelet, *Marguerite Duras ou le temps de détruire*, pp. 171–84; p. 179.

47 Aubenas, 'Entretien', p. 14.

48 See *Yeux*, pp. 15–16. Duras expounded further on the sheer enormity of her visceral 'politics' of loss in 'A propos de Reagan', *L'Autre Journal (hebdo)*, No. 12, 14–21 May 1986 (reprinted in *Monde*, pp. 76–77). She states there that if she belonged to anything 'instinctively' and 'organically', it would be to American freedom which is infinite. She clarifies this as her poetic and political desire for the long, slow and certain decay of America.

49 Marguerite Duras, 'La perte de la vérité', *L'Autre Journal (mensuel)*, No. 8, 1985, pp. 6–9; p. 9 (reprinted in *Monde*, pp. 81–90).

50 'La gauche, c'est aussi jouer. C'est le plaisir, très fort. C'est partir dans l'écoute de l'autre, fût-il un ennemi, ne pas pouvoir faire autrement. C'est savoir et ignorer dans le même temps' ('La perte de la vérité', p. 9).

51 See Baudrillard's *La gauche divine. Chronique des années 1977–1984*, Paris, Grasset, 1985, which gives the high period of 'the divine left' as September 1983.

52 'Elle n'a pas de fonction policière. Là où elle est inaugurale, c'est ailleurs, c'est qu'elle met l'homme "appelé" devant sa responsabilité essentielle: sa souveraineté.

Elle demande a l'homme "appelé" de se connaître, mais ici à partir de ce qu'il sait de lui, de son vouloir, de son refus et de la violence criminelle qui l'habite et dont il découvre qu'elle est le lot de l'humanité entière . . . Seul le rapport d'une réciprocité fondamentale entre l'homme et l'homme, entre tous et tous, et cela, de seul à seul avec soi-même toujours, est la référence unique de la Déclaration des 121' ('Texte écrit pour tous les temps, tous les carêmes', *L'Autre Journal [mensuel]*, No. 9 [November 1985], p. 73 [reprinted in *Monde*, pp. 78–80]). Duras's article in *L'Autre Journal* accompanies the publication in facsimile of the document as well as a text by Mascolo.

53 It should be emphasised that the nationalistic and patriotic aims of this book were perfectly in keeping with the policies of the Minister for the Colonies at the time, Georges Mandel, who sought to counter French defeatism in the face of Hitler by promoting the idea that France was still a major world power.

54 See Pierre Assouline, 'Mes Amours c'est à moi' (interview with Marguerite Duras), *Lire*, No. 193 (October 1991), pp. 58–59.

55 'La perte de la vérité', p. 8. For an excellent theoretical account of the implications of this murky chapter of French politics, see Andrew J. McKenna, *Violence and Difference: Girard, Derrida, and Deconstruction*, Urbana, IL, University of Illinois Press, 1992, in particular Chapter 5, 'State Secrets' (pp. 143–72).

56 'Je crois que Greenpeace ne dispose que d'une explication absurde. Etre de gauche c'est savoir ce que je dis là. Si Greenpeace ne le sait pas ce n'est plus la peine qu'il s'occupe de la terre' ('La perte de la vérité', p. 9). As simplistic as they are, Duras's views on foreign policy can sometimes, however, get all tangled up. For example, in 'Lettre au Président Pham Van Dong à propos de Nguyên Sy Tê (Paris, le 19 mars 1986)', *L'Autre Journal (hebdo)*, No. 5, 26 March–2 April 1986, pp. 8–9 (reprinted in *Monde*, pp. 98–99), Duras first argues that an innocent man has been wrongly imprisoned for ten years, then insists that she is not 'begging' for him to be released. This is because, according to the 'rule of political criminals', and by means of a 'permanent and superb inversion', Sy Tê is already assured of joining the 'universal list of heroes'. As if that was what mattered the most!

57 One example of the cloying self-admiration shared by Duras and Mitterrand during their five interviews is Duras's statement in 'Le dernier pays avant la mer' that all Mitterrand says is true and 'incomparable'. The stage-play resulting from the interviews, *Marguerite et Le Président*, had a short Paris run from December 1992 to January 1993.

58 Sanford S. Ames, 'Dead Letters, Impossible Witness', in Ames, *Remains to be Seen*, pp. 279–85; p. 284.

59 Leo Bersani and Ulysse Dutoit, *Arts of Impoverishment*, Cambridge, MA, Harvard University Press, 1993, p. 189.

60 See Barbara Probst Solomon, 'Indochina mon amour', *The New Republic*, No. 3686, 9 September 1985, pp. 29–35, which argues that the lover's return to Paris at the end of *Amant* may stand for Duras's dream that France's lost Indochina be restored and that France renounce its marriage to 'the other Chinese woman'.

61 In 'Learn to Read, She Said', *October*, No. 41 (1987), pp. 49–60, Ann Smock argues that the torture scene in *Douleur* is set up in such a way 'as to allow the thought that the determination to expose a human being as not-human really lay

elsewhere—actually lay deeper—than the history of racism and oppression to which it is in fact absolutely central' (p. 60).

62 See Marguerite Duras, 'Tapie-Duras: quand Bibi Fricotin découvre la femme de sa vie' (interview with Bernard Tapie), *Globe*, 28 July–3 August 1993, pp. 10–15.

63 Duras, 'L'année 90: Les 12 photos émotion'.

64 See 'Drug', *Globe*, October 1989 (reprinted in *Monde*, pp. 100–01).

65 See Bouguereau, 'Duras 89–90', where Duras declared her vehement opposition to the unjust idea of prison. This was a constant of Duras's public life, as evidenced by her support of Max-Ernest Vandapuy, in her view a man wrongly condemned in 1982 for the attempted murder of a police officer.

66 See Claire Devarrieux, 'La dernière idole parfaite', *Le Monde*, 1 November 1984, p. 11, which celebrates Duras's 'risk' of freedom and universal love.

67 Jean-François Josselin, 'Ecrire sous la pluie', *Le Nouvel Observateur*, 11–17 January 1990, p. 75 (a review of *Pluie*).

68 See René Girard, *Violence and the Sacred*, trans. Patrick Gregory, Baltimore, Johns Hopkins University Press, 1978, p. 49.

69 See, for example, Gilles Costaz, 'Tchernobyl, la mort géniale' (interview with Marguerite Duras), *Le Matin*, 4 June 1986, and Costaz, 'Demain, les hommes' where Duras fantasizes that the year 2050 and its inevitable lack of belief in 'God'—a word opening up 'the fabulous void'—will signal the end of writing, i.e. the end of the 'doubling' of life by an 'eternity of passage'.

70 See Mikkel Borch-Jacobsen, *The Freudian Subject*, trans. François Roustang, Stanford, Stanford University Press, 1988, p. 86.

71 Duras discusses this process in Fernandes, *Travailler avec Duras*, p. 138, a text which documents the gradual erasing of the Third in Duras's 1985 play, *La musica deuxième*.

72 Villemin's attempt to use a new provision in the Code Civil dating from 4 January 1993 in order to claim damages of one million francs was dismissed on 26 January 1994, on the grounds that 'Sublime' was 'an exercise in style' rather than a legal column.

Notes to Chapter 7
pp. 139–59

1 'Nous avons fait fi de tous les compromis, de tous les arrangements habituels entre les gens, nous avons affronté l'impossibilité de cet amour, nous n'avons pas reculé, nous ne nous sommes pas sauvés . . . nous nous moquions, nous ne le reconnaissions pas et nous l'avons vécu comme il se présentait, impossibile, vraiment, et sans intervenir, sans rien faire pour moins en souffrir, sans le fuir, sans le massacrer ni partir. Et ça n'a pas été suffisant.'

2 Jean Montalberti, like many others, compares *Yeux* unfavourably with *Amant*, claiming that there is no 'symbolic opening of sense', only the scattered, pedestrian remorse of a broken music-box ('Le faux amant de l'Atlantique', *Magazine littéraire*, No. 237 [January 1987], p. 77). For Costaz, however, to whom Duras granted a full interview, the novel purifies everything to its most essential by 'entering into the unknown regions of human matter, breaking our molecules' ('Au-delà de l'audace'), *Le Matin*, 14 November 1986, p. 25. A representative example of the novel's often tortuous style is the following: 'Il doit le faire, l'aimer avec sa bouche, l'aimer comme elle aime, elle, elle aime qui la fait jouir, elle crie qu'elle l'aime, de le faire, qu'il est pour elle n'importe qui, comme elle pour lui' (pp. 56–57) ('He must do it, love her with his mouth, love her as she loves, she who loves whoever gives her pleasure. She shouts that she loves it, to do it, that he is anybody for her, as she is for him').

3 'C'était elle qui l'avait pris, elle s'était fait pénétrer elle-même par lui, tandis que sous elle il était mort de douleur d'avoir à la quitter. Et c'était là qu'il l'avait appelée de son propre nom, celui de l'Orient par elle déformé.'

4 Hugo Marsan's 'La maladie de l'amour' (*Le Gai Pied Hebdo*, No. 46, 29 November, 1986, pp. 39–41), Dominique Fisher's ' "L'écrit", le jeu de la lecture et la mise en voix de l'écriture dans *La Vie matérielle* et dans *Les Yeux bleus cheveux noirs*' (*L'Esprit Créateur*, Vol. 30, No. 1 [Spring 1990], pp. 76–85, and Gabrielle Cody's 'Duras's Theater of Emptied Space and Impossible Performances' (*Theater*, Vol. 25, No. 2 [1994], pp. 56–66), all choose to conflate the main narrative with the interspersed, hypothetical theatrical directions, rather than consider the differences between these two distinct, textual entities.

5 Marcel Proust, *A l'ombre des jeunes filles en fleurs*, Paris, Gallimard, 'Folio', 1987, Vol. 2, pp. 104–06.

6 Lange's *Les cabines de bain*, Paris, Gallimard, 1984, is the story—complete with a space of outside crossings—of one sick woman's successful attempt to regain her self-identity through erotic encounters with an old, blue-eyed man in a similar French coast location (Roscoff in Brittany). Roche's *Maladie Mélodie*, Paris, Seuil, 1980, is a series of witty restagings (nine plays and six divertimenti) of a final act which leads ironically to a delicious, musical reconciliation with death, or 'HAPPY END' (p. 136). Compare, for example: 'L'on compose un chant avec l'agonie. Est-ce la douleur qui s'en va, ou moi qui m'y habitue?' (*Maladie Mélodie*), with: 'elle croit que oui, que [la mort] c'est la chose à laquelle on s'habitue le mieux' (*Yeux bleus*, p. 81),

and: 'pour tenter de retenir la vie qui s'en va' (*Maladie Mélodie*), with: 'cette envie de retenir ce temps qui passe' (*Yeux bleus*, p. 75 ['One composes a song with the throes of death. Is it pain withdrawing, or me getting used to it?'/'She thinks that yes, that it [death] is the thing one gets used to the best'; '. . . to try to retain the life which is slipping away'/'. . . that wish to retain this time which is passing']).

7 *L'homme blessé*, co-scripted by Guibert and published by Minuit in 1983, is a heavy-handed, tragic tale of casual gay sex centred around a Paris railway station, the inspiration perhaps for *elle*'s fear in *Yeux bleus* of being killed in a station hotel after the often fantasised (but never realised) night of separation (p. 144).

8 Eribon, ' "C'est fou c'que j'peux t'aimer" ', p. 22.

9 It is notable that when he is not committing 'sadistic acts' Kristeva's gay 'soulosexual' shares the same depressive economy as her melancholic. See 'Manic Eros, Sublime Eros: On male sexuality', in *Tales of Love*, pp. 59–82; pp. 78–80. In fact, according to Kristeva, the 'delightfully melancholy' gay man (*Soleil Noir*) is exemplary in his introjection of the maternal image which is the condition of melancholia. (The homophobic implications of this theory demand a full and separate study.) It could be argued, of course, that the consumer-minded gay man of *Yeux bleus*, steeped in 'silent images' and 'drunk with the desire to recover a lost object, as well as to buy one that he still has not got' (p. 65), represents only a jaded version of the Barthesian lover whom Duras castigates and yet who, although obsessed with his own image and hungry for maternal warmth, could also stage (at least until *Chambre*) his unconscious as an imaginary discourse.

10 Kristeva, *Soleil Noir*, p. 256.

11 Marsan goes so far as to claim that, by reconciling herself with *elle*, Duras is able to understand the 'grandeur' of homosexual (self)destruction ('La maladie de l'amour', p. 41). In an interview with André Rolland ('Au peigne fin: Marguerite Duras', *Lire*, No. 136 [January 1987], pp. 97–99), Duras argues that the situation of gay men not knowing or desiring women is a 'common disability' shared by 'us' and 'them', and similar to not believing in God. Duras adds that there exists a 'conjugation' of detesting in the novel which allows the couple to love each other: she feels detested by men, he detests women. This rather forced juxtaposition is somewhat undermined by the fact that Duras describes the male protagonist in terms of repression: he is 'our' repressed other, 'the world's outside', looking at 'us'.

12 Costaz, ' "La littérature est illégale" ', p. 24.

13 Aliette Armel, 'J'ai vécu le réel comme un mythe' (interview with Marguerite Duras), *Magazine littéraire*, No. 278 (June 1990), pp. 18–24; p. 24.

14 At the beginning of *L'Agent double. Sur Duras, Gracq, Kundera etc*, Paris, Complexe, 1989, Pierre Mertens describes the Afterword as an outdated literary form although he never actually relates it to his own account in the same book of Duras's later work.

15 'Lisez le livre. Dans tous les cas, même dans celui d'une détestation de principe, lisez-le. Nous n'avons plus rien à perdre, ni moi de vous, ni vous de moi. Lisez tout . . . Continuez à lire et tout à coup l'histoire elle-même, vous l'aurez traversée, ses rires, son agonie, ses déserts. Sincèrement vôtre.'

16 'Je l'ai complètement séparé de ses paroles, comme s'il les avait attrapées sans le savoir, et qu'il en était tombé malade.'

204   *The Erotics of Passage*

17 'A la fin, ça a pu commencer à être lisible. On était arrivés quelque part dans un lieu où la vie n'était pas complètement absente.'

18 'Tous les sens se rejoignaient en lui à la fin des journées . . . Il y avait les marées aussi, et puis Quilleboeuf, qu'on sait être loin, partout à la fois, comme Yann.'

19 Proust, *A la recherche*, Vol. 2, p. 614.

20 See Eve Kosofsky Sedgwick, *Epistemology of the Closet*, Berkeley, Los Angeles, London, University of California Press, 1991, in particular, 'The Beast in the Closet. James and the Writing of Homosexual Panic', pp. 182–212, for a discussion of the topos of the omnipotent, unknowing mother in recent 'high' gay male culture.

21 *La bête dans la jungle* (included in *Théâtre III*), had, by means of a short epilogue, already banished any homoerotic suggestion of graveyard cruising between Marcher and the stranger which might exist in the original. No exploration is ever made by Duras of Marcher's identification with the 'scarred', incised face of passion of the other man, his *'analogue inoubliable'*, and it is significant that she chooses never to entertain the idea of Marcher's homosexuality, despite comments made to that effect by Samy Frey who played the character in her 1981 Paris production at the Théâtre du Rond-Point (see Fernandes, *Travailler avec Duras*, p. 171). Instead, in an article entitled 'Le Château de Weatherend' (*L'Arc*, No. 89 [October 1983], pp. 100–12) (reprinted in *Monde*, pp. 119–24), Duras explained that Marcher was really innocent because, in his attitude to the female sex, he was simply representing the views of all men of 'ancient-recent times'. Compare this with Silverman's analysis of visual masochism in James's story, 'Too Early/Too Late. Subjectivity and the Primal Scene in Henry James', *Novel*, Vol. 21, Nos 2–3 (Winter/Spring 1988), pp. 147–73, which emphasises the 'whining wound' of pain and passion that is displaceable between the two men, and which forms in Marcher a 'pederastic identification with the phantasmatic father'.

22 'C'était en deçà du raisonnable de la raison, ou du déraisonnable de la même raison. C'était comme un but: tuer ça.'

23 'Ici, les lecteurs vont dire: Qu'est-ce qu'il lui prend? Rien ne s'est passé, puisque rien n'arrive. Alors que ce qui est arrivé ce qui s'est passé. Et, quand plus rien n'arrive, l'histoire est vraiment hors de portée de l'écriture et de la lecture.'

24 Armel, 'J'ai vécu le réel', p. 24.

25 'Vous êtes ma préférence absolue, désormais inévitable'; 'Vous dites: Ecrire, c'est savoir résister à l'écriture.'

26 'Vous dites: Je ne comprends pas comment on peut vivre comme vous le faites, d'une manière aussi veule. Mieux voudrait vous tuer. Je ne réponds pas, j'évite à peine les larmes.'

27 *Maladie*: 'Vous continuez à parler, seul au monde, comme vous le désirez'/ *M.D.*: 'Je suis le seul au monde'. *Maladie*: 'ton sexe dressé dans la nuit . . . appelle où se mettre, où se débarrasser des pleurs qui le remplissent'/*M.D.*: 'Je ne pleure pas, je ne veux pas pleurer. Les larmes restent dans mes yeux.'

28 See Christiane P. Makward, 'For a Stylistics of Marguerite Duras', *L'Esprit Créateur*, Vol. 30, No. 1 (Spring 1990), pp. 28–39; p. 32.

29 In his review of *M.D.* in *Masques*, No. 20 (1983), René de Ceccatty writes that the degree of 'non-concerted osmosis' existing between Duras and Andréa and which extends even into their writing, has never been seen before and is probably unrepeatable. Similarly, in 'La cure d'amour de Marguerite', *Libération*, 12

September 1983, Françoise Xénakis recognises in *M.D.* 'an extraordinary act of love', adding that Andréa has become Duras in terms of his writing and also his way of seeing and understanding the world. Our analysis centres on just how 'non-concerted' *M.D.*'s 'osmosis' and M.D.'s 'cure of love' really are.

30 'Toujours, ce tremblement à peine visible de la vie, la blessure irréparable, le dommage fait à votre corps transi, cette splendeur revenue du plus loin, ce ratage merveilleux, vous.'

31 'Et moi, je veux mourir de vous savoir morte . . . C'est ce que vous voulez, que je sois mort, que le monde disparaisse.'

32 See Robert J. Stoller, 'Sexual Excitement', *Archives of General Psychiatry*, No. 33 (1976), pp. 899–909, where Stoller proposes that sexual and non-sexual excitement involves quick switches between fantasised danger, repetition of prior trauma, and fantasised triumph and revenge. See also Stoller's *Perversion: the erotic form of hatred*, New York, Pantheon, 1975.

33 In Manceaux's *Brèves*, Andréa is quoted as saying that his relationship with Duras has two faces: love as worship ('l'amour adoré') and death as loathing ('la mort abhorée') (p. 198). Manceaux adds at one point that listening to Duras and Andréa was like hearing the refrain from *Hiroshima*, 'Tu me tues, tu me fais du bien'.

34 See Leopoldina Pallotta Della Torre, *Marguerite Duras. La passione sospesa*, Milan, La Tartaruga, 1989, p. 110.

35 See Lois W. Banner, *In Full Flower: Aging Women, Power, and Sexuality*, New York, Vintage Books, 1993, in particular Chapter 6, 'The Eroticized Young Male and Women's Response', pp. 198–231.

36 See Peter Novick, *The Resistance Versus Vichy: The Purge of Collaborators in Liberated France*, New York, Columbia University Press, 1968, pp. 68–69. As regards her former collaborator, Resnais, it is notable that Duras later took great pleasure in, as she put it, 'speaking ill of him' (*Au-delà des pages*). One critic has even suggested that her mocking use in *Enfants* of a Resnais regular, Pierre Arditi, was an implied attack on his continuing influence. See Charles Tesson, 'Des journées entières dans les classes', *Cahiers du Cinéma*, No. 370 (April 1985), pp. 54–56.

37 See *As Fine as Melanctha. The unpublished writings of Gertrude Stein*, ed. Carl Van Vechten, New Haven, Yale University Press, 1954, Vol. 4 (1914–1930) p. 11.

38 For an introduction to this predominantly heterosexual tradition, see Joseph Barry, *French Lovers: From Heloise and Abelard to Beauvoir and Sartre*, New York, Arbor House, 1987.

39 Personal reference. In 'Marguerite Duras à corps perdu', *Etudes Littéraires*, Vol. 22, No. 2 (Autumn 1989), pp. 123–36, Chantal Théry argues with much bitterness that by virtue of his name, '*IAnn AndréA*', Andréa has usurped the radical potential of Duras's play with transvestism. An indication of the fictional status of Andréa's name is Duras's passing reference to him in *Duras Filme* as 'Yann Le May-Andréa'.

40 See Wayne Koestenbaum, *Double Talk. The erotics of male literary collaboration*, London, Routledge, 1990, in particular Chapter 4, '*The Wasteland*: T. S. Eliot and Ezra Pound. Collaboration in Hysteria'.

41 The full history of *Histoire d'O* has been uncovered by John de St Jorre in 'The Unmasking of O', *New Yorker*, 1 August 1994, pp. 42–50. He reveals how Paulhan, almost twenty-five years Aury's senior and one of the supposed authors of the book,

did not respond in kind to her '*lettre d'amour*', although he did edit the book and even wrote a preface to the first edition.

42 Personal reference.

43 See Toril Moi's entry, 'transference/countertransference', in Wright, *Feminism and Psychoanalysis*, pp. 430–35.

44 The charge made against de Beauvoir of '*captation d'héritage*', as well as of voyeurism and almost necrophagia, was published in 1982 in *Magazine littéraire*. Recent research is showing, in fact, how it was Sartre, not de Beauvoir, who appropriated the other's work. In *Simone de Beauvoir and Jean-Paul Sartre: The Remaking of a Twentieth Century Legend*, Hemel Hempstead, Harvester Wheat-sheaf, 1993, Edward and Kate Fullbrook argue compellingly that Beauvoir's *L'invitée* (1943) is essentially a philosophical text that Sartre used to produce his philosophical system of existentialism in *L'être et le néant* (1943), a fact that de Beauvoir herself conspired to conceal.

45 See Deirdre Bair, *Simone de Beauvoir: A Biography*, New York, Summit, 1990, pp. 197–211.

46 See Part II of Simone de Beauvoir, *La Vieillesse*, Paris, Gallimard, 1970.

47 Costaz, ' "La littérature est illégale" ', p. 25.

48 Thélu, 'DURAS: The Thing', p. 16.

49 Costaz, ' "La littérature est illégale" ', p. 25.

50 See ' "Ecce Ego" ' in Borch-Jacobsen, *The Freudian Subject*, for an analysis of the fluctuating fortunes of homosexuality as 'homosociality' in Freud's work. In his exegesis of 'On Narcissism' and 'Psycho-Analytic Notes on an Autobiographical Account of a case of Paranoia (Dementia Paranoides)', Borch-Jacobsen shows how homosexuality, which can be erotic and non-erotic, libidinal and non-libidinal, is actually sublimation's target of choice (p. 87) and the very eroticisation of the social bond (p. 83) because less sexual than heterosexuality (in one sense it is already desexualised). Compared with the narcissistic phase, homosexuality is an opening up of the possibility of object-choice, although, as Borch-Jacobsen remarks, narcissistic a-sociality, homosexual archisociality and egoic sociality are at one stage in Freud 'all the Same'.

51 'Tout a été écrit par toi, par ce corps que tu as. / Je vais arrêter là ce texte pour en prendre un autre de toi, fait pour toi, fait à ta place.'

52 'Vous n'écrivez pas parce que vous savez tout sur cette chose-là, cette chose tragique, d'écrire, de le faire ou de ne pas le faire, de ne pas écrire, de ne pas pouvoir le faire, vous savez tout. Vous, c'est parce que vous êtes un écrivain que vous n'écrivez pas.'

53 See, for example, Eribon, ' "C'est fou c'que j'peux t'aimer" ', where Andréa stands in for Eribon as the silent interlocutor.

54 Proust, *A la recherche*, Vol. 2, p. 861.

55 This is to be compared with the attitude of M. Andesmas to his ageing body in *Andesmas*, which Kathleen Woodward has described, a touch optimistically, as one of companionship and relative mobility. See her book, *Aging and its Discontents. Freud and other fictions*, Bloomington, IN, Indiana University Press, 1991, pp. 171–77.

56 'Je trouve que ça ressemble à du cinéma. Et j'aime beaucoup ça. A un certain

cinéma. Il me regarde vraiment. Et je regarde à côté' (Marguerite Duras, 'Une journée à Trouville', *Vogue* [November 1993], pp. 158–67; p. 160).

57 '[I]l y en a un, c'est le chef . . . il a un corps de nain avec une queue de cochon de lait, poilue, il la prend tout le temps dans sa bouche comme s'il fumait. Les premiers temps, ça me fait peur, vomir. Et puis, je me suis aperçue qu'il me gardait contre l'invasion des autres animaux.'

58 Pallotta Della Torre, *Marguerite Duras*, p. 108.

59 Aubenas, 'Entretien', p. 15.

Bibliography

(N.B.: With the exception of sections one and two, this bibliography aims to provide a complete list of Duras's work only for the period directly covered by the book, i.e. post-1976. For a more comprehensive record of Duras's interviews, articles, etc. prior to this period, consult Leslie Hill's *Marguerite Duras: Apocalyptic Desires*, London and New York, Routledge, 1993.)

(1) Novels, Essays, Plays and Translations

L'Empire français. Avec trois cartes (with Philippe Roques), Paris, Gallimard, 1940.
Les impudents, Paris, Plon, 1943.
La vie tranquille, Paris, Gallimard, 'Folio', 1944.
Un barrage contre le Pacifique, Paris, Gallimard, 'Folio', 1950.
Le marin de Gibraltar, Paris, Gallimard, 'Folio', 1952.
Les petits chevaux de Tarquinia, Paris, Gallimard, 'Folio', 1953.
Des journées entières dans les arbres; Le boa; Madame Dodin; Les chantiers, Paris, Gallimard, 1954.
Le square, Paris, Gallimard, 1955.
Moderato cantabile, Paris, Gallimard, 1958.
Les Viaducs de la Seine-et-Oise, Paris, Gallimard, 1960.
Dix heures et demie du soir en été, Paris, Gallimard, 1960.
Hiroshima mon amour (scénario et dialogues), Paris, Gallimard, 'Folio', 1960.
Une aussi longue absence (scénario et dialogues) (with Gérard Jarlot), Paris, Gallimard, 1961.
L'après-midi de Monsieur Andesmas, Paris, Gallimard, 1962.
Miracle en Alabama, Paris, L'Avant-Scène, 1963, translation and adaptation of *Miracle in Alabama* by William Gibson, in collaboration with Gérard Jarlot.
Le ravissement de Lol V. Stein, Paris, Gallimard, 'Folio', 1964.
Théâtre I: Les eaux et forêts [1965]; *Le square* [1965]; *La musica* [1965], Paris, Gallimard, 1965.
Le vice-consul, Paris, Gallimard, 1965.
L'amante anglaise (roman), Paris, Gallimard, 1967.
L'amante anglaise (théâtre), Paris, Cahiers du Théâtre National Populaire, 1968.
Théâtre II: Suzanna Andler [1968]; *Des journées entières dans les arbres* [1965]; *Yes, peut-être* [1968]; *Le Shaga* [1968]; *Un homme est venu me voir* [1968], Paris, Gallimard, 1968.
Détruire, dit-elle, Paris, Gallimard, 1969.
Abahn, Sabana, David, Paris, Gallimard, 1970.
Les papiers d'Aspern, Paris, Editions Paris-Théâtre, 1970.
L'amour, Paris, Gallimard, 1971.
Ah! Ernesto, Boissy-St Léger, François Ruy-Vidal et Harlin-Quist, 1971, with illustrations by Bernard Bonhomme.

Home, by David Storey, trans. Marguerite Duras, Paris, Gallimard, 1973.

Nathalie Granger, suivi de La femme du Gange, Paris, Gallimard, 1973.

India Song (texte–théâtre–film), Paris, Gallimard, 1973.

Les parleuses, in collaboration with Xavière Gauthier, Paris, Editions de Minuit, 1974.

Adoracíon, by Eduardo Chillida, trans. Marguerite Duras, Paris, 1977.

Les lieux de Marguerite Duras, in collaboration with Michelle Porte, Paris, Editions de Minuit, 1977.

Le camion, suivi de Entretien avec Michelle Porte, Paris, Editions de Minuit, 1977.

L'Eden cinéma, Paris, Mercure de France, 1977.

'Le navire night', *Minuit*, No. 29, May 1978, pp. 2–14.

Le navire Night; Césarée; Les mains négatives; Aurélia Steiner; Aurélia Steiner; Aurélia Steiner, Paris, Mercure de France, 1979.

Véra Baxter ou les plages de l'Atlantique, Paris, Albatros, 1980.

L'homme assis dans le couloir, Paris, Editions de Minuit, 1980.

'Les yeux verts', *Cahiers du Cinéma*, Nos 312–13, June–July 1980.

L'été 80, Paris, Editions de Minuit, 1980.

Outside. Papiers d'un jour, Paris, Albin Michel, 1981 (republished by POL in 1984).

Agatha, Paris, Editions de Minuit, 1981.

L'homme atlantique, Paris, Editions de Minuit, 1982.

Savannah Bay, Paris, Editions de Minuit, 1982.

La maladie de la mort, Paris, Editions de Minuit, 1982.

Savannah Bay (nouvelle édition augmentée), Paris, Editions de Minuit, 1983.

Théâtre III: La Bête dans la Jungle [1962] by Henry James, adaptation by James Lord and Marguerite Duras; *Les papiers d'Aspern* [1961] by Henry James, adaptation by Marguerite Duras and Robert Antelme; *La danse de Mort* [1970] by August Strindberg, adaptation by Marguerite Duras, Paris, Gallimard, 1984.

L'amant, Paris, Editions de Minuit, 1984.

La douleur, Paris, POL, 1985.

La musica deuxième, Paris, Gallimard, 1985.

La mouette de Tchékov, Paris, Gallimard, 1985.

Les yeux bleus cheveux noirs, Paris, Editions de Minuit, 1986.

La pute de la côte normande, Paris, Editions de Minuit, 1986.

Les yeux verts (nouvelle édition augmentée), Paris, Cahiers du Cinéma, 1987.

La Vie matérielle, Paris, POL, 1987.

Emily L. (roman), Paris, Editions de Minuit, 1987.

Eden Cinéma (nouvelle version scénique) (texte bilingue français-anglais), Paris, Actes Sud–Papiers, 1988.

La pluie d'été, Paris, POL, 1990.

L'amant de la Chine du Nord, Paris, Gallimard, 1991.

Yann Andréa Steiner, Paris, POL, 1992.

Ecrire, Paris, Gallimard, 1993.

Le Monde extérieur. Outside II, Paris, POL, 1993.

C'est tout, Paris, POL, 1995.

La mer écrite, Paris, Editions Marval, 1996, with photographs by Hélène Bamberger.

(2) Filmography

La musica (1966), b/w, 80', co-dir. by Paul Seban, prod. Les Films RP, distr. Les Artistes Associés.

Détruire, dit-elle (1969), b/w, 90', prod. Ancinex, Madeleine Films, distr. SNA.

Jaune le soleil (1971), b/w, 80', prod. Albina productions (never distributed).

Nathalie Granger (1972), b/w, 83', prod. Luc Moullet Films et Cie, distr. Les Films Molière.

La femme du Gange (1972–73), colour, 90', prod. Service de la Recherche de l'ORTF and Sunchild, distr. Olympic.

India Song (1975), colour, 120', co-prod. S. Damiani, A. Valio-Cavaglione, Sunchild, Les Films Armorial, Antenne 2, SFP, distr. Josepha Productions.

Son nom de Venise dans Calcutta désert (1976), 120', co-prod. Cinéma 9, PIPA, Editions Albatros, distr. Benoît Jacob, Cinéma 9 Ursulines.

Des journées entières dans les arbres (1976), colour, 95', prod. Jean Baudot (Théâtre d'Orsay), distr. Gaumont.

Baxter, Véra Baxter (1976–77), colour, 90', prod. Stella Quef (Sunchild), INA, distr. Sunchild.

Le camion (1977), colour, 80', prod. Pierre et François Barat for Cinéma 9 and Auditel, distr. Les Films Molière.

Le navire Night (1978), b/w, 20' (never distributed).

Le navire Night (1978), colour, 94', prod. MK2, Gaumont, Les Films du Losange, distr. Les Films du Losange.

Césarée (1979), colour, 11', prod. Les Films du Losange, Paris-Audiovisuel.

Les mains négatives (1979), colour, 18', prod. Les Films du Losange, Paris-Audiovisuel.

Aurélia Steiner (Melbourne) (1979), colour, 35', prod. Films Paris-Audiovisuel.

Aurélia Steiner (Vancouver) (1979), b/w, 48', prod. Les Films du Losange, Paris-Audiovisuel.

Agatha et les lectures illimitées (1981), colour, 90', prod. Les Berthemont, INA, Des Femmes Filment, distr. Hors Champ Diffusion.

L'homme atlantique (1981), colour, 42', prod. Les Berthemont, INA, Des Femmes Filment, distr. Hors Champ Diffusion.

Dialogo di Roma (1982), colour, 62', prod. Lunga Gittata, RAI.

Les enfants (1985), colour, 90', co. dir. by Jean Mascolo, Jean-Marc Turine, prod. Les Berthemont, distr. Films sans Frontières.

(3) Discography

La jeune fille et l'enfant (1981), cassette, adaptation of *L'été 80* by Yann Andréa, prod. and distr. Editions des Femmes, 'La Bibliothèque des voix'.

(4) Television, Radio and Video Work

Television:

Les lieux de Marguerite Duras, colour, 120', dir. Michelle Porte, prod. INA, TF1, 3 and 17 May 1976.

Savannah Bay, c'est toi, colour, 66', dir. Michelle Porte, prod. INA, Antenne 2, 2 April 1984.

'Carte blanche à une 1ère A' (discussion including Marguerite Duras), prod. Jean-Pierre Janiaud, dir. Valérie Mannel, Antenne 2, 3 September 1994.

'Marguerite Duras' (interview with Bernard Pivot), *Apostrophes,* prod. Jean Cazenave, dir. J.-L. Léridon, Antenne 2, 28 September 1984 (available on video as *Apostrophes: Bernard Pivot rencontre Marguerite Duras*, Paris, Editions du Seuil, 'Vision Seuil', 1990).

'Marguerite Duras', *The South Bank Show,* dir. Daniel Wiles, prod. Hilary Chadwick, LWT, 17 November 1985.

'Deux ou trois choses qu'ils se sont dites' (interview with Jean-Luc Godard), *Océaniques,* prod. Colette Fellous and Pierre-André Boutang, dir. Jean-Didier Verhaeghe (recorded 2 December 1987), FR3, 28 December 1987 (text published in part in *Magazine littéraire,* No. 278 [June 1990], pp. 46–48).

'Au-delà des pages' (series of four interviews with Luce Perrot recorded in February–March 1988), prod. Guy Lopez, TF1, 26 June–17 July 1988.

Interview with Patrick Poivre d'Arvor, *Ex-Libris*, TF1, 15 February 1990.

Interview with Bernard Rapp, *Caractères*, Antenne 2, 5 July 1991.

Interview, *Cinéma de Poche*, FR3, 1 February 1992.

Interview with Pierre Dumayet (recorded 1992), *Lire et Ecrire*, Arte, 29 January 1993.

Radio:

'Interview de Marguerite Duras' (interview with Jacques Duchateau), Jacques Floran, and Michel Chapuis, *Le Pont des Arts,* France-Culture, 26 January 1980.

'Entretiens avec Marguerite Duras' (interviews with Jean-Pierre Ceton), *Les Nuits Magnetiques,* France-Culture, 27–31 October 1980.

Quelque part ailleurs en étant là: Le bon plaisir de Marguerite Duras, prod. Marianne Alphant, with Jean Daniel, Denis Roche, Gérard Desarthe, Nicole Hiss, Catherine Sellers, France-Culture, 20 October 1984.

Interview with Pierre Assouline and others, *Inter-lire*, France-Inter, 5 July 1987.

Interview with Alain Veinstein, *Les Nuits magnétiques*, France-Culture, 25 November 1987.

'Du jour au lendemain' (interview with Alain Veinstein), France-Culture, 16 March 1990.

Interview with Patricia Martin and Gérard Courchelle, *Inter 13/14*, France-Inter, 29 June 1991.

Interview with Jean-Christophe Marty, *Discothèques privées*, France-Musique, 5–9 August 1991.

Video:

Duras Filme (1981), colour, 50', dir. Jean Mascolo and Jérôme Beaujour.

Les oeuvres cinématographiques de Marguerite Duras. Edition Vidéographique Critique, Paris, Ministère des Relations extérieures, 1983, prod. Pascal Gallet, dir. Jean Mascolo and Jérôme Beaujour. A five-part box set of Duras's films including post-face interviews with Marguerite Duras by Dominique Noguez:

   'La classe de la violence' (on *Nathalie Granger*), 48' (with Gérard Depardieu);
   'La couleur des mots' (on *India Song*), 63' (with Delphine Seyrig, Carlos d'Alessio and Michael Lonsdale);

'Le cimetière anglais' (on *Son nom de Venise dans Calcutta désert*), 48' (with
Delphine Seyrig, Michael Lonsdale and Bruno Nuytten);
'La dame des Yvelines' (on *Le camion*), 59' (with Dominique Auvray, Gérard
Depardieu and Bruno Nuytten);
'La caverne noire' (on *Césarée, Les mains négatives, Aurélia Steiner [Mel-
bourne], Aurélia Steiner [Vancouver]*), 57', followed by 'Work and Words' (a
video Afterword by Duras).

(5) Articles, reviews and prefaces by Marguerite Duras not included in her own
collections (*Outside. Papiers d'un jour, Les yeux verts [nouvelle version augmen-
tée], Le Monde extérieur. Outside II*)

'L'homme assis dans le couloir', *L'Arc*, No. 20 (October 1962), pp. 70–77.
Le Cinéma ouvert', *Le Quotidien de Paris*, 3 June 1976.
Erika Lennard, *Les femmes, les soeurs*, Paris, Editions des femmes, 1976, text by
Elisabeth Lennard, with a post-face by Marguerite Duras.
'Mothers', *Le Monde*, 10 February 1977 (reprinted in François Barat and Joël Farges
[eds], *Marguerite Duras* [1975], Paris, Editions Albatros, 1979, pp. 99–101).
' "Il y a en lui un doute fondamental" ' (on François Mitterrand), *Le Quotidien
de Paris*, 7 October 1977, p. 5.
'Le cinéma de Lol V. Stein', *Art Press International*, No. 24, January 1979.
'*Agatha* est le premier film que j'écris sur le bonheur', *Cahiers du Cinéma*, Nos 322–
24 (May 1981), pp. 4–5.
'Un Pays du Nord', *Des femmes en mouvements (hebdo)*, No. 48, 3–10 July 1981.
'*Agatha, ou les lectures illimitées*', *Des femmes en mouvements (hebdo)*, No. 57, 11–
18 September 1981.
'Je n'ai rien à justifier', *Le Quotidien de Paris*, 8 October 1981.
'Les Rendez-vous manqués: après 1936 et 1956, 1981?' (petition organised by
Michel Foucault and signed by Marguerite Duras and nine others), *Libération*,
15 December 1981.
'Le monde moderne n'est pas bavard', *Rendez-vous avec le théâtre*, No. 19 (1984).
'Pourquoi écrivez-vous?' (response to a questionnaire by Marguerite Duras), *Libér-
ation*, hors-série, March 1985.
'La Chair des Mots', *Autrement*, No. 70, May 1985, p. 210.
'Duras: "Les journalistes, me dit-on . . ." ' (with Jean-Marc Turine and Jean
Mascolo), *Libération*, 12 June 1985, p. 35.
'Marguerite Duras: Sublime, forcément sublime Christine V.', *Libération*, 17 July
1985, pp. 5–7.
'Réponses de Marguerite Duras', *Libération*, 23 July 1985.
'Le scandale de la vérité', *Cahiers du Cinéma*, No. 374 (July–August 1985), p. 13.
'Elle a sorti la France de ses gonds' (on the death of Simone Signoret), *Le Quotidien de
Paris*, 1 October 1985.
'Recevez chers amis, nos salutations mystiques et polyflores' (on Baby Doc Duvalier)
(with René Depestre), *L'Autre Journal*, No. 1, 26 February–4 March 1986.
'Le Prix Ritz-Hemingway 1986 à Marguerite Duras', with a brief statement by the
author, *Le Monde*, 19 April 1986.

'La pute de la côte normande', *Libération*, 14 November 1986 (reprinted in 1986 by Editions de Minuit as *La pute de la côte normande*).

'Le livre, un plaisir partagé' (a questionnaire by Pierrette Rosset and Françoise Ducout, with responses from Marguerite Duras and others), *Elle*, 23 March 1987.

'Ceux qui veulent continuer à nous lire, de gauche à droite', with a contribution by Marguerite Duras, *Le Matin*, 13–14 June 1987.

'La lecture: un bonheur sans mélange' (questionnaire by Pierrette Rosset with responses from Marguerite Duras and others), *Elle*, 31 August 1987.

'Remarques générales sur "Les Juifs" de *Jaune de Soleil* (1971) et note de tournage sur *Jaune le soleil*', *Cahiers du Cinéma*, No. 400 (October 1987), pp. 20–21.

'L'internationalisme de l'idée française', *Globe*, No. 23 (December 1987).

'Thierry Lévy, ou la littérature évitée', *Le Matin*, 17 February 1988, 'Supplément livres', p. 3.

'La Cigarette dans le couple: un ménage à trois' (a questionnaire by Christine Bravo and Patricia Gandin, with responses from Marguerite Duras and others), *Elle*, 11 July 1988.

'Denis Belloc, la nuit sociale', *Libération*, 22 September 1988, p. 8.

'Marguerite Duras, Ecrivain (et cinéaste) (Paris, 19 décembre 1984)', *L'effet-Godard*, ed. Carole Desbarates and Jean-Paul Gorace, Toulouse, Editions Milan, 1989, p. 112.

'L'année 90: Les 12 photos émotion', *France-Soir*, 29 December 1990.

'Trouville, le 10 septembre 1992', *Marguerite Duras*, Paris, Milan, Cinémathèque française and Nuove edizioni Gabriele Mazzotta, 1992.

'Une journée à Trouville' (with Yann Andréa), *Vogue*, November 1993, pp. 158–67.

Prologue to *Maisons d'Ecrivains*, ed. Francesca Premoli-Droulers, with photographs by Erica Lennard, Paris, Editions du Chêne, 1994, pp. 8–17.

(6) Interviews with Marguerite Duras

Jean Schuster, 'Entretien avec Marguerite Duras', *L'Archibras*, No. 2 (October 1967), pp. 11–15.

Jacques Rivette and Jean Narboni, 'La destruction, la parole', *Cahiers du Cinéma*, No. 217 (November 1969), pp. 45–57.

Bettina Knapp, 'Interviews with Marguerite Duras and Gabriel Cousin', *The French Review*, Vol. 44, No. 4 (1971), pp. 653–64.

Germaine Brée, 'An interview with Marguerite Duras', *Contemporary Literature*, No. 13 (August 1972), pp. 401–22.

Suzanne Horer and Jeanne Socquet, 'Marguerite Duras. Interview', *La Création étouffée*, Paris, Editions Pierre Horay, 1973, pp. 172–87.

'Marguerite Duras: "Ce que parler ne veut pas dire . . ." ' (interview with Jean-Louis Ezine), *Les Nouvelles littéraires*, 15 April 1974, p. 3.

Susan Husserl-Kapit, 'An interview with Marguerite Duras', *Signs: Journal of Women in Culture and Society*, No. 1 (Winter 1975), pp. 423–34.

Absis, 'Ça me touche là où je crie' (interview with Marguerite Duras), *Sorcières*, No. 4 (1976), p. 59.

Simone Benmussa, 'Rencontre des Cahiers Renaud-Barrault', with Marguerite

Duras, Madeleine Renaud and Jean-Louis Barrault etc., *Cahiers Renaud-Barrault*, No. 91 (1976), pp. 3–26.

'Je ne me laisserai pas récupérer' (interview with Anne de Gasperi), *Les Nouvelles littéraires*, 25 November–1 December 1976.

'Renaud-Duras: une profonde connivence' (interview with Anne de Gasperi), *Le Quotidien de Paris*, 9 February 1977.

'Le feu d'artifice de Marguerite Duras' (interview with Jack Gousseland), *Le Point*, No. 230, 14 February 1977.

'Irrésistible et jalouse, Madeleine' (interview with Anne de Gasperi), *Les Nouvelles littéraires*, 17 February 1977.

'Le désir est bradé, saccagé. On libère le corps et on le massacre, dit Marguerite Duras' (interview with Michèle Manceaux), *Marie-Claire*, No. 297, May 1977.

'Marguerite Duras explique sa vision politique' (interview with Anne de Gasperi), *Le Quotidien de Paris*, 26 May 1977.

'Marguerite Duras au Quotidien: "Je hais la narration au cinéma" ' (interview with Henry Chapier), *Le Quotidien de Paris*, 8 June 1977.

'Un acte contre tout pouvoir' (interview with Jacques Grant and Jacques Fresnais), *Cinéma 77*, No. 223 (July 1977), pp. 48–58 (reprinted in Barat and Farges [eds], *Marguerite Duras*, pp. 119–30).

G. Lenoir and M. Young, 'Entretien avec Marguerite Duras', *Rouge Combat*, 1977, pp. 10–13.

René Prédal, 'Entretien avec Marguerite Duras', *Jeune Cinéma*, No. 104 (July–August 1977), pp. 16–21.

'Marguerite Duras' (interview with Jean-Claude Bonnet and Jacques Fieschi), *Cinématographe*, No. 32 (November 1977), pp. 25–28.

'L'état sauvage du désir' (interview with Anne de Gasperi), *Le Quotidien de Paris*, 27 June 1978.

'La Nuit sur le navire de Marguerite Duras' (interview with Pierre Montaigne), *Le Figaro*, 2 August 1978.

Catherine Francblin: 'Interview', *Art Press International*, 24 January 1979.

'En effeuillant la marguerite' (interview with Patrick Duval), *Libération*, 22 March 1979.

'*Le Navire Night* ou l'embarcation du désir' (interview with Anne de Gasperi), *Les Nouvelles littéraires*, 22–29 March 1979.

'The Thing' (interview with Rolland Thélu), *Le Gai Pied*, No. 20 (November 1980), p. 16.

'Je vais faire un film avec Godard' (interview with Anne de Gasperi), *Le Quotidien de Paris*, 3 February 1981.

'Voter Giscard, c'est voter contre Lech Walesa' (interview with Jane Hervé), *Les Nouvelles littéraires*, 7–14 May 1981.

'Ecrire c'est tout' (interview with Jean Roger), *Le Devoir*, 13 June 1981 (reprinted in Jean Roger, *Ecrivains Contemporains*, Montreal, L'Hexagone, 1985, pp. 248–52).

Jacques Rivette, 'Sur le pont du Nord un bal est donné: dialogue avec Marguerite Duras', *Le Monde*, 25 March 1982, pp. 15–16.

Andrea Gunert, 'Den Ton des schwarzen Bildes betrachten. Ein Interview mit Marguerite Duras. Paris 14–12–81', *Film Faust*, No. 26 (1982), pp. 20–31.

Didier Eribon, 'Marguerite Duras: "C'est fou c'que j'peux t'aimer" ' (interview with Marguerite Duras and Yann Andréa), *Libération*, 4 January 1983, pp. 22–23.

Jacqueline Aubenas, 'Entretien avec Marguerite Duras', *Alternatives théâtrales*, No. 14 (March 1983), pp. 11–15.

'Marguerite Duras: "Il n'y a sans doute rien de plus difficile que de décrire un amour' (interview with Gilles Costaz), *Le Matin*, 29 September 1983, pp. 12–13.

Roberto Plate, 'Entretien avec Marguerite Duras', *Cahiers Renaud-Barrault*, No. 106 (September 1983), pp. 7–12.

'Au Théâtre du Rond-Point Marguerite Duras met en scène sa dernière pièce, *Savannah Bay*, écrite pour Madeleine Renaud et Bulle Ogier' (interview with Armelle Heliot), *Le Quotidien de Paris*, 30 September 1983.

'Marguerite Duras à l'état sauvage' (interview with Marianne Alphant), *Libération*, 4 September 1984, pp. 28–29.

'Marguerite Duras: "Ce qui arrive tous les jours n'arrive qu'une seule fois" ' (interview with Gilles Costaz), *Le Matin*, 28 September 1984.

'L'inconnue de la rue Catinat, par Marguerite Duras' (interview with Hervé Le Masson), *Le Nouvel Observateur*, 28 September 1984, pp. 92–93.

'Ils ne m'ont pas trouvé de raisons de me le refuser' (interview with Marianne Alphant), *Libération*, 13 November 1984.

'L'amour est impossible à décrire' (interview with Michel Vial), *Le Gai Pied (hebdo)*, Nos 149–50 (22 December 1984), pp. 58–59.

'L'insomnie creuse l'intelligence' (interview with Michèle Manceaux [20 November 1983]), in Michèle Manceaux, *Eloge de l'insomnie*, Paris, Hachette, 1985, pp. 31–44.

'Comment ne pas être effrayée par cette masse fabuleuse de lecteurs?' (interview with Pierre Assouline), *Lire*, January 1985.

'A Vintage Year for Duras', including an interview with Mary Blume, *The International Herald Tribune*, 22 March 1985. 'Musica Duras, Acte II' (interview with Gilles Costaz), *Le Matin*, 25 March 1985.

'Avril 45: nuit et Duras' (interview with Marianne Alphant), *Libération*, 17 April 1985, p. 37.

'L'excès-l'usine' (interview with Leslie Kaplan), *L'Autre Journal (mensuel)*, No. 5 (May 1985) (reprinted and retitled as 'Usine', a post-face interview in Leslie Kaplan, *L'excès-l'usine*, Paris, POL, 1987, pp. 109–19).

'Marguerite Duras. Demain les hommes' (interview with Gilles Costaz), *Le Matin*, 2 October 1985, p. 16.

'Le bureau de poste de la rue Dupin' (interview with François Mitterrand), *L'Autre Journal (hebdo)*, No. 1, 26 February 1986.

'Le dernier pays avant la mer' (interview with François Mitterrand), *L'Autre Journal (hebdo)*, No. 2, 5 March 1986.

'Le ciel et la terre' (interview with François Mitterrand), *L'Autre Journal (hebdo)*, No. 3 (12 March 1986), pp. 33–41.

'L'innocence infernale de Knobelspiess' (interview with Thierry Lévy), *L'Autre Journal (hebdo)*, No. 3 (12–18 March 1986), pp. 79–85.

'Afrique, Afrique' (interview with François Mitterrand), *L'Autre Journal (hebdo)*, No. 4 (19 March 1986), pp. 24–33.

'Parler des ôtages ou ne pas parler des ôtages' (interview with Joëlle Kauffmann), *L'Autre Journal (hebdo)*, No. 5, 26 March–2 April 1986.

'La nouvelle Angoûleme' (interview with François Mitterrand), *L'Autre Journal (hebdo)*, No. 11, 7–13 May 1986.

'Jean-Marie Tjibaou, kanak' (interview with Jean-Marie Tjibaou), *L'Autre Journal (hebdo)*, No. 13, 22 May 1986.

'Les outsiders de Marguerite Duras' (interview with Gérard Meudal), *Libération*, 26 May 1986, p. 18.

'Tchernobyl, la mort géniale' (interview with Gilles Costaz), *Le Matin*, 4 June 1986.

'L'Amant Magnifique' (interview with Aline Issermann), *L'Autre Journal (hebdo)*, No. 16 (11–17 June 1986), pp. 48–50.

'Marguerite Duras: "La littérature est illégale ou elle n'est pas" ' (interview with Gilles Costaz), *Le Matin*, 14 November 1986, pp. 24–25.

'Duras tout entière. Entretien avec un écrivain au-dessus de tout Goncourt' (interview with Pierre Bénichou and Hervé Le Masson), *Libération*, 14–20 November 1986, pp. 56–59.

'Marguerite Duras par Anne Sinclair' (interview with Anne Sinclair), *Elle*, 8 December 1986.

'Au peigne fin: Marguerite Duras' (interview with André Rolland), *Lire*, No. 136 (January 1987), pp. 97–99.

Michel Bergain, 'Duras, de gauche complètement', *Globe*, No. 13 (January 1987).

'Marguerite Duras: la vera scrittura e un soffio' (interview with Leopoldina Pallotta della Torre), *La Stampa (Tuttilibri)*, 20 June 1987, pp. 4–5.

'A tort et à travers *Le Matin*' (interview with Gilles Costaz, Sophie Fontanel and J.P. Iommi-Amunategui), *Le Matin*, 23 June 1987.

'La petite fille de Brooklyn' (interview with Leslie Kaplan), *Le Nouvel Observateur*, 3–4 August 1987, pp. 4–5.

'L'exacte exactitude de Denis Belloc' (interview with Denis Belloc), *Libération*, 19–20 September 1987, pp. 32–33.

'Comme une messe de mariage' (interview with Didier Eribon), *Le Nouvel Observateur*, 16–22 October 1987, pp. 60–61. '*Emily L.* ou le procès de l'homme' (interview with Françoise Ducout and Pierrette Rosset), *Elle*, 9 November 1987.

'Pour Duras, le plus beau c'est Hulot' (interview with Pierre Léon and Brigitte Ollier), *Libération*, 27 November 1987, p. 53.

'Qu'est-ce que c'est ce jeu-là? Démoniaque et divin' (interview with Michel Platini), *Libération*, 14 December 1987.

'Duras-Platini: Le stade de l'ange' (interview with Michel Platini), *Libération*, 15 December 1987.

'Duras dans les régions claires de l'écriture' (interview with Colette Fellous), *Le Journal littéraire*, No. 2 (December 1987–January 1988), pp. 126–27.

'La letteratura é femmina' (interview with Paolo Tortonese), *Corriere della sera*, 24 January 1988.

'Marguerite Duras: "Je suis muette devant le théâtre que j'écris" ' (interview with Gilles Costaz), *Le Matin*, 3 June 1988, p. 38.

'Parler, dit-elle' (interview with Jean-Claude Raspiengeas), *Télérama*, 22 June 1988.

'Intervista a Marguerite Duras' (interview with Flavia Celotto), *Micromégas*, Vol. 15, Nos. 41–42 (June–August 1988), pp. 55–60.

'Duras est SEXY!' (interview with Pierre Bergé), *Globe*, No. 30 (July–August 1988), pp. 79–83.

Alice Jardine and Anne M. Menke, 'Interview with Marguerite Duras', trans. Heidi Gilpin, in 'Exploding the Issue: "French" "Women" "Writers" and "The Canon"?; Fourteen Interviews', *Yale French Studies*, No. 75 ('The Politics of Tradition: Placing Women in French Literature') (1988), pp. 229–58; pp. 238–40.

'Le coupeur d'eau' (interview with Michel Marcus), *Autrement*, No. 104 ('Obsession, Sécurité') (February 1989), pp. 17–21.

'J'ai toujours désespérément filmé . . .' (interview with Colette Mazabrard), *Cahiers du Cinéma*, No. 426 (December 1989), pp. 62–65.

'Vitry-ma-ville' (interview with Marianne Alphant), *Libération*, 11 January 1990.

'Duras parle du nouveau Duras' (interview with Pierrette Rosset), *Elle*, 15 January 1990, pp. 38–39.

'Duras: un mondo di paura' (interview with Ulderico Munzi), *Corriere della sera*, 25 January 1990.

'Duras 89–90' (interview with Jean-Marcel Bouguereau), *L'Evénement du Jeudi*, 1–7 February 1990, pp. 84–87.

'Des années entières dans les livres' (interview with Renaud Monfourny), *Les Inrockuptibles*, No. 21 (February–March 1990), pp. 111–15.

'Duras and Her Thoughts of Love' (interview with Alan Riding), *The New York Times*, 26 March 1990, Supplement C, pp. 1–16.

'Marguerite retrouvée' (interview with Frédérique Lebelley), *Le Nouvel Observateur*, 24–30 May 1990, pp. 59–63.

'J'ai vécu le réel comme un mythe' (interview with Aliette Armel), *Magazine littéraire*, No. 278 (June 1990), pp. 18–24.

'La lanterne magique de Marguerite Duras' (interview with Gilbert Guez), *Le Figaro*, 7 February 1991.

'Duras dans le parc à amants' (interview with Marianne Alphant), *Libération*, 13 June 1991, pp. 26–27.

'Vous faites une différence entre mes livres et mes films?' (interview with Jean-Michel Frodon and Danièle Heymann), *Le Monde*, 13 June 1991.

'Je suis pour les femmes de plus en plus' (interview with Jean-Claude Lamy), *France-Soir*, 20 June 1991.

'The Life and Loves of Marguerite Duras' (interview with Leslie Garis), *The New York Times Magazine*, 20 October 1991, pp. 45–60.

'Mes Amours c'est à moi' (interview with Pierre Assouline), *Lire*, No. 193 (October 1991), pp. 58–59.

'La Brune de la Dordogne' (interview with Marianne Alphant), *Libération*, 27 February 1992.

'Vive Cresson et la lutte des classes!' (interview with Jean-Louis Ezine), *Le Nouvel Observateur*, 2–8 April 1992.

'Les nostalgies de l'amante Duras' (interview with Jean-Louis Ezine), *Le Nouvel Observateur*, 25 June–1 July 1992, pp. 53–55.

'Appelez-moi Marguerite Duras de Trouville' (interview with Roland Godefroy), *Ouest-France*, 3 August 1992.

'L'enfer, nous dit Marguerite Duras' (interview with Maurice Najman), *Globe Hebdo*, 24–30 March 1993, pp. 8–9.

'Marguerite Duras' (interview with Susan Husserl-Kapit), *Visions Magazine*, Spring 1993, pp. 8–12.

'Jacquot filme Duras' (interview with Benoît Jacquot), *Cahiers du Cinéma*, Nos 467–68 (1993), pp. 9–11 (partial transcription of *Ecrire* [1983] and *La mort du jeune aviateur anglais* [1983] by Benoît Jacquot).

'Tapie-Duras: quand Bibi Fricotin découvre la femme de sa vie' (interview with Bernard Tapie), *Globe*, 28 July–3 August 1993, pp. 10–15.

'Je ne mens pas sauf aux hommes' (interview with Alix de Saint-André), *Elle*, 4 October 1993, pp. 94–97.

Ana María Moix, 'An interview with M. Duras', *Two by Duras*, trans. Alberto Manguel, Toronto, Coach House Press, 1993, pp. 59–86.

List of Works Cited

1. Critical Works on Marguerite Duras

Bernard Alazet, 'Je m'appelle Aurélia Steiner', *Didascalies*, No. 3 ('Aurélia Steiner') (April 1982), pp. 111–23.

——, 'Une écriture du soupir', in Vircondelet, *Marguerite Duras: Rencontres de Cerisy*, pp. 83–96.

Madeleine Alleins, *Marguerite Duras: Médium du Réel*, Paris, L'Age d'homme, 1980.

Liesbeth Korthals Altes, 'L'ironie ou le savoir de l'amour et de la mort: lecture de quatre oeuvres de Marguerite Duras', *Revue des sciences humaines*, Vol. 73, No. 202 (April–June 1986), pp. 39–52.

David Amar, 'Sublime, forcément sublime: A propos d'un article paru dans *Libération*', *Revue des sciences humaines*, Vol. 73, No. 202 (April–June 1986), pp. 155–66.

Yann Andréa, 'The Atlantic Man', *Film International*, No. 11 (1982).

——, *M.D.*, Paris, Editions de Minuit, 1983.

Anon. *Le dossier de presse du 'Camion'*, Cannes, May 1977.

Aliette Armel, *Marguerite Duras et l'autobiographie*, Paris, Le Castor Astral, 1990.

Ninette Bailey, 'Oublieuse Mémoire', *La Chouette*, No. 6 (January 1986), pp. 7–25.

Danielle Bajomée, *Duras ou la douleur*, Paris, Editions Universitaires, 1989.

—— and Ralph Heyndels (eds), *Ecrire, dit-elle: Imaginaires de Marguerite Duras*, Brussels, Editions de l'Université de Bruxelles, 1985.

Christine Bange, *Die zurückgewiesene Faszination: Zeit, Tod und Gedäctnis als Erfahrungskategorien bei Baudelaire, Benjamin and Duras*, Wienheim, Beltz, 1987.

François Barat and Joël Farges (eds), *Marguerite Duras* [1975], Paris, Editions Albatros, 1979, with Maurice Blanchot, Marguerite Duras, Jacques Lacan, et al.

Jean-Louis Barrault, 'Un enfant obstiné', *L'Arc*, No. 98 (1985), pp. 56–57.

Nicole Lise Bernheim, *Marguerite Duras tourne un film* (India Song), Paris, Albatros, 1975.

Maurice Blanchot, *La communauté inavouable*, Paris, Editions de Minuit, 1983, pp. 50–93.

——, *Le Livre à venir*, Paris, Gallimard, 'Idées', 1958, pp. 207–09.

Christaine Blot-Labarrère, *Marguerite Duras*, Paris, Seuil, 'Les contemporains' 14, 1992.

Madeleine Borgomano, '*L'Amant*: Une hypertextualité illimitée', *Revue des Sciences humaines*, Vol. 73, No. 202 (April–June 1986), pp. 67–77.

——, *L'écriture filmique de Marguerite Duras*, Paris, Editions Albatros, 1984.

——, *Duras. Une lecture des fantasmes*, Brussels, Cistre, 1985.

Jean-Louis Bory, 'Ecrire sous la pluie', *Le Nouvel Observateur*, 11–17 January 1990, p. 75.

Germaine Brée, 'A singular adventure: The writings of Marguerite Duras', *L'Esprit Créateur*, Vol. 30, No. 1 (Spring 1990), pp. 8–14.

Peter Brooks, *Body Work: Objects of Desire in Modern Narrative*, Cambridge, MA, Harvard University Press, pp. 257–86.

Maurice Cagnon, 'Marguerite Duras: Willed Imagination as Release and Obstacle', *Nottingham French Studies*, Vol. 16, No. 1 (May 1977), pp. 55–64.

Sue-Ellen Case, 'From Split Subject to Split Britches. The metonymically displaced subject', *Feminine Focus: the new women playwrights*, ed. Enoch Brater, Oxford, Oxford University Press, 1989, pp. 134–41.

Claire Cerasi, *Marguerite Duras: de Lahore à Auschwitz*, Paris, Geneva, Champion-Slatkine, 1993.

Hélène Cixous and Michel Foucault, 'A propos de Marguerite Duras', *Cahiers Renaud-Barrault*, No. 89 (October 1975), pp. 8–22.

Gabrielle Cody, 'Duras's Theater of Emptied Space and Impossible Performances', *Theater*, Vol. 25, No. 2 (1994), pp. 56–66.

Susan D. Cohen, 'La présence de rien', *Cahiers Renaud-Barrault*, No. 106 (1983), pp. 17–36.

———, *Women and Discourse in the Fiction of Marguerite Duras: Love, Legends, Language*, Oxford, Macmillan, 1993.

Verena Andermatt Conley, ' "L'Affaire Grégory" and Duras's Textual Feminism', *L'Esprit Créateur*, Vol. 30, No. 1 (Spring 1990), pp. 69–75.

Joan Copjec, '*India Song/Son nom de Venise dans Calcutta désert*: the compulsion to repeat', *October*, No. 17 (1981), pp. 37–52.

Gilles Costaz, 'Au-delà de l'audace', *Le Matin*, 14 November 1986, p. 25.

Madeleine Cottenet-Hage and Robert P. Kolker, 'The Cinema of Duras in Search of an Ideal Image', *The French Review*, Vol. 63, No. 1 (1989), pp. 87–98.

René de Ceccatty, 'Yann Andréa: M.D.', *Masques*, No. 20 (Winter 1983).

Michel de Certeau, 'Marguerite Duras: On dit', in Bajomée and Heyndels, *Ecrire, dit-elle*, pp. 257–65.

Nelcya Delanoë, 'Ascenseur pour l'échafaud', *Esprit*, No. 116 (July 1986), pp. 85–86.

Claire Devarrieux, 'La dernière idole parfaite', *Le Monde*, 1 November 1984, p. 11.

Michèle Druon, 'Mise en scène et catharsis de l'amour dans *Le ravissement de Lol V. Stein* de Marguerite Duras', *The French Review*, Vol. 58, No. 3 (February 1985), pp. 382–90.

Danièle Dubroux, 'Il n'y aurait plus qu'une seule image', *Cahiers du Cinéma*, Nos 279–80 (August–September 1977), pp. 38–43.

Joël Farges and François Barat (eds), *Marguerite Duras* [1975], Paris, Editions Albatros, 1979, with Maurice Blanchot, Marguerite Duras, Jacques Lacan, et al.

Pierre Fedida, 'Entre les voix et l'image', in Barat and Farges, *Marguerite Duras*, pp. 157–60.

Patricia Fedkiw, 'Marguerite Duras: Feminine Field of Hysteria', *Enclitic*, Vol. 6, No. 2 (Fall 1982), pp. 78–86.

Marie-Pierre Fernandes, *Travailler avec Duras. La Musica Deuxième*, Paris, Gallimard, 1986.

Dominique Fisher, ' "L'écrit", le jeu de la lecture et la mise en voix de l'écriture dans

La Vie matérielle et dans *Les Yeux bleus cheveux noirs*', *L'Esprit Créateur*, Vol. 30, No. 1 (Spring 1990), pp. 76–85.

Jill Forbes, *The Cinema in France After the New Wave*, Bloomington, IN, Indiana University Press, 1992, pp. 94–102.

Michel Foucault and Hélène Cixous, 'A propos de Marguerite Duras', *Cahiers Renaud-Barrault*, No. 89 (October 1975), pp. 8–22.

Yvonne Guers-Villate, *Continuité/Discontinuité de l'oeuvre durassienne*, Brussels, Editions de l'Université de Bruxelles, 1985.

Daniel Gunn, *Psychoanalysis and Fiction: an exploration of literary and psychoanalytical borders*, Cambridge, Cambridge University Press, 1988, pp. 124–32.

Ralph Heyndels and Danielle Bajomée (eds), *Ecrire, dit-elle. Imaginaires de Marguerite Duras*, Brussels, Editions de l'Université de Bruxelles, 1985.

Leslie Hill, 'Marguerite Duras and the limits of fiction', *Paragraph*, Vol. 12, No. 1 (March 1989), pp. 1–22.

——, 'Marguerite Duras: Sexual Difference and Tales of Apocalypse', *Modern Language Review*, No. 84 (1989), pp. 601–14.

——, 'Lacan with Duras', *Journal of the Institute of Romance Studies*, No. 1 (1992), pp. 405–24.

——, *Marguerite Duras: Apocalyptic Desires*, New York, London, Routledge, 1993.

Marianne Hirsch, *The Mother/Daughter Plot. Narrative, Psychoanalysis, Feminism*, Boomington, IN, Indiana University Press, 1989, pp. 146–54.

Christine Holmlund, 'Displacing Limits of Difference: Gender, Race, and Colonialism in Edward Said and Homi Bhabha's Theoretical Models and Marguerite Duras's Experimental Films', *Quarterly Review of Film and Video*, Vol. 13, Nos 1–3 (1991), pp. 1–22.

Marie-Paule Ha, 'Duras on the Margins', *The Romanic Review*, Vol. 83, No. 3 (1993), pp. 299–320.

Kathleen Hulley, 'Contaminated Narratives: The Politics of Form and Subjectivity in Marguerite Duras's *The Lover*', *Discourse*, Vol. 15, No. 2 (Winter 1992–93), pp. 30–50.

Nancy Huston, 'Erotic Literature in Postwar France', *Raritan*, Vol. 12, No. 1 (Summer 1992), pp. 29–45.

Youssef Ishaghpour, *D'une image à l'autre. La nouvelle modernité au cinéma*, Paris, Denoël-Gonthier, 1982, pp. 225–98.

——, 'La voix et le miroir', in Bajomée and Heyndels, *Ecrire, dit-elle*, pp. 99–108.

Alice Jardine, *Gynesis: Configurations of woman and modernity*, Ithaca, London, Cornell University Press, 1985, pp. 159–77.

Katharine A. Jensen, Afterword to Marguerite Duras and Xavière Gauthier, *Woman to Woman*, trans. Katharine A. Jensen, Lincoln, London, University of Nebraska Press, 1987, pp. 181–95.

Pauline Kael, *When the lights go down*, London, Boyars, 1980, pp. 291–95.

E. Ann Kaplan, *Women and Film. Both Sides of the Camera*, London, New York, Routledge, 1983, pp. 91–103.

Adèle King, *French Women Novelists: defining a female style*, New York, St Martin's Press, 1989.

Julia Kristeva, *Soleil Noir: dépression et mélancolie*, Paris, Editions du Seuil, 1987, pp. 227–65.

Jacques Lacan, 'Hommage fait à Marguerite Duras du Ravissement de Lol V. Stein', *Cahiers Renaud-Barrault*, No. 52 (December 1965), pp. 7–15 (reprinted in Barat and Farges, *Marguerite Duras*, pp. 131–37).

Suzanne Lamy and André Roy (eds), *Marguerite Duras à Montréal*, Montreal, Editions Spirale, 1981.

Frédérique Lebelley, *Duras, ou le poids d'une plume*, Paris, Grasset, 1994.

Annie Le Brun, 'Vagit-Prop', *Le Monde*, 6 December 1984.

Gérard Lefort, 'Et clap! Passe-moi Lépanges', *Libération*, 7 January 1987, 'Supplément', p. xiv.

Susan H. Leger, 'Marguerite Duras's Cinematic Spaces', *Women and Literature*, ed. Janet Todd, New York, London, Holmes and Meier, 1988.

Maurice Lemaître, *Marguerite Duras. Pour en finir avec cet escroc et plagiaire généralisée*, Paris, Centre de Créativité, 1979.

Mary Lydon, 'Translating Duras: *The Seated Man in the Passage*', *Contemporary Literature*, No. 24 (Summer 1983), pp. 113–26.

——, 'The Forgetfulness of Memory: Jacques Lacan, Marguerite Duras and the Text', *Comparative Literature*, No. 29 (1988), pp. 351–68.

Elisabeth Lyon, 'The Cinema of Lol. V. Stein', *camera obscura*, No. 6 (1980), pp. 9–39.

Christiane P. Makward, 'For a stylistics of Marguerite Duras', *L'Esprit Créateur*, Vol. 30, No. 1 (Spring 1990), pp. 28–39.

Marcelle Marini, *Territoires du féminin. Avec Marguerite Duras*, Paris, Editions de Minuit, 1977.

——, 'La mort d'une érotique', *Cahiers Renaud-Barrault*, No. 106 (1983), pp. 37–57.

——, 'L'autre corps', in Bajomée and Heyndels, *Ecrire, dit-elle*, pp. 21–48.

Hugo Marsan, 'La maladie de l'amour', *Le Gai Pied (hebdo)*, 29 November 1986, pp. 39–41.

Dean McWilliams, 'Aesthetic Tripling: Marguerite Duras's *Le Navire Night*', *Literature/Film Quarterly*, Vol. 12, No. 2 (1984), pp. 122–28.

Elizabeth A. Meese, 'Re:writing "The Other" in Marguerite Duras's *The Lover*', in *Ex(tensions): Refiguring the Other*, Urbana, IL, University of Illinois Press, 1990, pp. 78–96.

Pierre Mertens, *L'agent double. Sur Duras, Gracq, Kundera etc.*, Paris, Editions Complexe, 1989.

Vicki Mistacco, '*Plus ça change. . .*: The Critical Reception to *Emily L.*', *The French Review*, Vol. 66, No. 1 (October 1992), pp. 77–88.

Jean A. Montalberti, 'Le faux amant de l'Atlantique', *Magazine littéraire*, No. 237 (January 1987), p. 77.

Michèle Montrelay, *L'Ombre et le nom. Sur la féminité*, Paris, Editions de Minuit, 1977, pp. 9–23.

George Moskos, 'Child's Play: Repetition and Death in Duras's *Savannah Bay*', *Neophilologus*, No. 77 (1993), pp. 215–21.

Carol J. Murphy, *Alienation and Absence in the Novels of Marguerite Duras*, Lexington, KY, French Forum Publishers, 1982.

————, 'New narrative regions: The role of desire in the films and novels of Marguerite Duras', *Literature/Film Quarterly*, Vol. 12, No. 2 (1984), pp. 122–28.

————, 'Duras's "Beast in the Jungle": Writing Fear (or Fear of Writing) in *Emily L.*', *Neophilologus*, No. 75 (1991), pp. 539–47.

Dominique Noguez, 'La gloire des mots', *L'Arc*, No. 98 (1985), pp. 25–39.

Panivong Norindr, ' "Errances" and Memories in Duras's Colonial Cities', *Differences*, Vol. 5, No. 3 (1993), pp. 52–78.

John O'Brien, 'Metaphor between Lacan and Duras: Narrative Knots and the Plot of Seeing', *Forum for Modern Language Studies*, Vol. 27, No. 3 (1993), pp. 59–70.

Raylene O'Callaghan, 'The art of the (im)possible', *Australian Journal of French Studies*, No. 25 (1988), pp. 71–90.

Leopoldina Pallotta Della Torre, *Marguerite Duras. La passione sospesa*, Milan, La Tartaruga, 1989.

Liliane Papin, *L'Autre Scène: Le Théâtre de Marguerite Duras*, Saratoga, Anma Libri, 1988.

————, 'Place of Writing, Place of Love', *Remains to be Seen. Essays on Marguerite Duras*, ed. Sanford S. Ames, New York, Peter Lang, 1988, pp. 81–94.

René Payant, 'L'impossible voix', in Lamy and Roy, *Duras à Montréal*, pp. 157–69.

Alain Philippon, 'Filmer la mort du cinéma', *Cahiers du Cinéma*, No. 331 (1982), pp. 47–48.

Catherine Portuges, 'Love and Mourning in Duras's *Aurélia Steiner*', *L'Esprit Créateur*, No. 30 (Spring 1990), pp. 28–39.

Patrick Rambaud, *Virginie Q. de Marguerite Duraille*, Paris, Balland, 1988.

Raylene Ramsay, 'Through a Textual Glass, Darkly: The masochistic feminine self in Marguerite Duras's *Emily L.*', *Atlantis*, Vol. 17, No. 1 (1991), pp. 91–104.

Janine Ricouart, *Ecriture féminine et violence. Une étude de Marguerite Duras*, Birmingham, AL, Summa Publications, 1991.

Angelo Rinaldi, 'Marguerite Duras comme détective', *Le Point,* 26 July 1985.

Catherine Rodgers, 'Sublime, forcément sublime: The body in Duras's Texts', *Romance Studies*, No. 20 (Summer 1992), pp. 45–57.

————, 'Déconstruction de la masculinité dans l'oeuvre durassienne', in Vircondelet, *Marguerite Duras: Rencontres de Cerisy*, pp. 47–68.

Judith Roof, 'Marguerite Duras and the Question of a Feminist Theater', *Feminism and Psychoanalysis,* ed. Richard Feldstein and Judith Roof, Ithaca, London, Cornell University Press, 1989, pp. 323–40.

Marie-Claire Ropars-Wuilleumier, 'The Disembodied Voice: *India Song*', *Yale French Studies*, No. 60 (1980), pp. 241–68.

————, 'How history begets meaning: Alain Resnais' *Hiroshima mon amour* (1959)', *French Film. Texts and Contexts*, ed. Susan Hayward and Ginette Vincendeau, London, Methuen, 1989, pp. 173–85.

Lucie Roy, 'Marguerite Duras, scénariste exilée', *Etudes Littéraires*, Vol. 26, No. 2 (Autumn 1993), pp. 67–75.

————, 'Les réticences discursives à l'écran ou les voix négatives', in Vircondelet, *Marguerite Duras: Rencontres de Cerisy*, pp. 151–70.

Trista Selous, 'A Triumph of the Will', *Free Associations*, No. 9 (August 1987), pp. 97–101.

———, *The Other Woman: Feminism and Femininity in the Work of Marguerite Duras*, New Haven, London, Yale University Press, 1988.

———, 'Marguerite and the Mountain', *Contemporary French Fiction by Women*, ed. Margaret Atack and Phil Powrie, Manchester, Manchester University Press, 1990, pp. 84–95.

Daniel Sibony, 'Repenser la déprime', *Magazine littéraire*, No. 244 ('Littérature et mélancolie') (July–August 1987), pp. 54–56.

Ann Smock, 'Learn to Read, She Said', *October*, No. 41 (Summer 1987), pp. 53–56.

Philippe Sollers, 'Duras Telle-Quelle', *Le Nouvel Observateur*, 12 January 1970, p. 36.

Barbara Probst Solomon, 'Indochina mon amour', *The New Republic*, No. 3686 (9 September 1985), pp. 29–35.

Jean-Louis Sous, 'M. Duras ou le ravissement du réel', *Littoral*, No. 14 (1984), pp. 59–70.

Susan Rubin Suleiman, 'Nadja, Dora, Lol V. Stein: Women, Madness, and Narrative', *Discourse in Psychoanalysis and Literature*, ed. Shlomith Rimmon-Kenan, New York, Methuen, 1988, pp. 124–51.

Jean-Marc Talpin, 'La fonction psychique du lecteur dans la poétique durassienne', in Vircondelet, *Marguerite Duras: Rencontres de Cerisy*, pp. 117–42.

Charles Tesson, 'Des journées entières dans les classes', *Cahiers du Cinéma*, No. 370 (April 1985), pp. 54–56.

Chantal Théry, 'Marguerite Duras à Corps Perdu: La vie au fil de l'écriture, entre Androgynie et Anoréxie', *Etudes Littéraires*, Vol. 22, No. 2 (Autumn 1989), pp. 123–36.

Micheline Tison-Braun, *Marguerite Duras*, Amsterdam, Rodopi, 1985.

Michel Tournier, 'Faces of Marguerite Duras: *The Lover*', *Vanity Fair* (July 1985), pp. 64–67.

Pamela Tytell, 'lacan, freud, et duras', *Magazine littéraire*, No. 158 (March 1980), pp. 14–15.

William F. Van Wert, 'The Cinema of Marguerite Duras: Sound and Voice in a Closed Room', *Literature/Film Quarterly*, Vol. 33, No. 1 (Fall 1979), pp. 22–29.

Alain Vircondelet, *Marguerite Duras ou le temps de détruire*, Paris, Editions Seghers, 1972.

———, *Duras: Biographie*, Paris, Editions François Bourin, 1991.

——— (ed.), *Marguerite Duras: Rencontres de Cerisy*, Paris, Ecriture, 1994.

Sharon Willis, *Writing on the Body*, Urbana, Chicago, University of Illinois Press, 1986.

Françoise Xénakis, 'La cure d'amour de Marguerite', *Le Matin*, 12 September 1983.

Pierre Yana, 'Enonciation d'un crime', *Revue des Sciences Humaines*, Vol. 73, No. 202 (April–June 1986), pp. 167–76.

2. Other Works Cited

Anon., *The Radio Times*, 23–29 September 1978, pp. 77–79.

Robert Antelme, *L'espèce humaine* , Paris, La Cité Universelle, 1947.

Emily S. Apter, *Andre Gide and the Codes of Homotextuality*, Saratoga, Anma Libri, 1987.

Louis Aragon, *Aurélien* [1944], Paris, Gallimard, 'Folio', 1972.

Dominique Aury (Pauline Réage), *Histoire d'O*, Paris, Jean-Jacques Pauvert, 1954.

Deirdre Bair, *Simone de Beauvoir. A Biography*, New York, Summit, 1990.

Lois W. Banner, *In Full Flower. Aging Women, Power, and Sexuality*, New York, Vintage Books, 1993.

Joseph Barry, *French Lovers. From Heloise and Abelard to Beauvoir and Sartre*, New York, Arbor House, 1987.

Roland Barthes, *S/Z* , Paris, Editions du Seuil, 1970.

——, *L'Empire des Signes*, Paris, Editions du Seuil, 1971.

——, *Le plaisir du texte*, Paris, Editions du Seuil, 1973.

——, *Roland Barthes par Roland Barthes*, Paris, Editions du Seuil, 1975.

——, *Les fragments d'un discours amoureux*, Paris, Editions du Seuil, 1977.

——, *Le bruissement de la langue*, Paris, Editions du Seuil, 1984.

Georges Bataille, *Ma mère*, Paris, Jean-Jacques Pauvert, '10/18', 1966.

Jean Baudrillard, *De la séduction*, Paris, Editions Galilée, 1979.

——, *La gauche divine. Chronique des années 1977–84*, Paris, Grasset, 1985.

——, *La transparence du mal: essai sur les phénomènes extrêmes*, Paris, Editions Galilée, 1990.

George H. Bauer, 'Le Gai Savoir noir', *Contemporary French Civilization*, Vol. 16, No. 2 ('Discourses and Sex') (Summer–Fall 1992), pp. 194–213.

Denis Belloc, *Néons*, Paris, Lieu Commun, 1987.

——, *Suzanne*, Paris, Lieu Commun, 1988.

Charles Bernheimer, 'A Shattered Globe: Narcissism and Masochism in Virginia Woolf's Life-Writing', *Psychoanalysis and . . .*, ed. Richard Feldstein and Henry Sussman, New York, London, Routledge, 1990, pp. 187–206.

Leo Bersani, *A Future for Astyanax. Character and Desire in Literature*, Boston, Toronto, Little, Brown and Company, 1976.

——, *The Freudian Body. Psychoanalysis and Art*, New York, Columbia University Press, 1986.

——, 'Is the Rectum a Grave?', *October*, No. 43 ('AIDS: Cultural Analysis, Cultural Activism') (Winter 1987), pp. 197–222.

——, 'Pynchon, Paranoia, and Literature', *Representations*, No. 25 (1989), pp. 98–118.

——, *The Culture of Redemption*, Cambridge, MA, Harvard University Press, 1990.

—— and Ulysse Dutoit, *The Forms of Violence: Narrative in Assyrian Art and Modern Culture*, New York, Schocken, 1983.

——, 'Sadism and Film: Freud and Resnais', *Qui Parle*, Vol. 6, No. 1 (Fall/Winter 1992), pp. 1–34.

——, *Arts of Impoverishment*, Cambridge, MA, Harvard University Press, 1993.

Homi K. Bhabha, 'The Other Question—the Stereotype and Colonial Discourse', *Screen*, Vol. 24, No. 6 (1983), pp. 18–36.

Harold Bloom, *A Map of Misreading*, Oxford, New York, Oxford University Press, 1975.

——, *Wallace Stevens: The poems of our climate*, Ithaca, NY, Cornell University Press, 1977.

Mikkel Borch-Jacobsen, *The Freudian Subject*, trans. Catherine Porter, with a foreword by François Roustang, Stanford, CA, Stanford University Press, 1988.

Gregory W. Bredbeck, 'B/O—Barthes's Text/O'Hara's Trick', *PMLA*, Vol. 108, No. 2 (March 1993), pp. 268–82.

Renaud Camus, *Passage*, Paris, Flammarion, 1975.

——, *Notes achriennes*, Paris, Hachette, 1982.

——, *Chroniques achriennes*, Paris, POL, 1984.

Raymonde Carasco, 'Vers une érotique fragmentaire. Le nouveau cinéma', *Revue de l'Esthétique (nouvelle série)*, No. 11 (1986), pp. 93–112.

Terence Cave, 'Recognition and the reader', *Comparative Criticism*, No. 2 (1980), pp. 49–69.

Mary Ann Caws, *A Metapoetics of the Passage. Architextures in Surrealism and After*, Hanover, London, University Press of New England, 1981.

Jean-Pierre Ceton, *Rauque la ville*, Paris, Editions de Minuit, 1980.

——, *Rapt d'amour*, Paris, POL, 1986.

Cynthia Chase, 'Primary Narcissism and the giving of Figure: Kristeva with Hertz and de Man', *Abjection, Melancholia and Love. The work of Julia Kristeva*, ed. Andrew Benjamin and John Fletcher, Warwick, Warwick University Press, 1990, pp. 124–36.

Robert Chazal, *Gérard Depardieu: L'Autodidacte inspiré*, Renens, 5 Continents, 1982.

Patrice Chéreau and Hervé Guibert, *L'Homme blessé (scénario et notes)*, Paris, Editions de Minuit, 1983.

Murray Cox and Alice Theilgaard, *Mutative Metaphors in Psychotherapy: The Aeolian Mode*, London, New York, Tavistock Publications, 1987.

Simone de Beauvoir, *La cérémonie des adieux*, Paris, Gallimard, 1981.

——, *La vieillesse*, Paris, Gallimard, 1970.

Madame de Lafayette, *La Princesse de Clèves* [1678], Paris, Flammarion, 1966.

Gilles Deleuze, *Présentation de Sacher Masoch. Le froid et le cruel*, Paris, Union Centrale d'Editions, '10/18', 1967.

——, *Différence et répétition*, Paris, Presses Universitaires de France, 1968.

——, *Cinéma 2: Image-temps*, Paris, Editions de Minuit, 1985.

Paul de Man, *Allegories of Reading*, New Haven, London, Yale University Press, 1979.

——, *The Resistance to Theory*, Manchester, Manchester University Press, 1986.

Catherine de Richaud, *Monsieur le Chevalier*, Paris, POL, 1986.

John de St Jorre, 'The Unmasking of O', *New Yorker*, 1 August 1994, pp. 42–50.

Emily Dickinson, *The Complete Poems of Emily Dickinson*, ed. Thomas H. Johnson, Boston, Toronto, Little, Brown and Company, 1951.

Lee Edelman, *Transmemberment of Song. Hart Crane's Anatomies of Rhetoric and Desire*, Stanford, CA, Stanford University Press, 1987.

——, *Homographesis: essays in gay literary and cultural theory*, New York, London, Routledge, 1991.

Joanne Feit Diehl, 'Murderous Poetics: Dickinson, the Father, and the Text', *Daughters and Fathers*, ed. Lynda E. Boose and Betty S. Flowers, Baltimore, Johns Hopkins University Press, 1989.

Lionel Follet, *Aragon, le fantasme et l'histoire*, Paris, Les Editeurs Français Réunis, 1980.

Sigmund Freud, *The Standard Edition of the Complete Psychological Works*, trans. and ed. James Strachey, in collaboration with Anna Freud, assisted by Alix Strachey and Alan Tyson, London, Hogarth Press and Institute of Psychoanalysis, 1953–73, 24 vols.

Edward Fullbrook and Kate Fullbrook, *Simone de Beauvoir and Jean-Paul Sartre: The Remaking of a Twentieth Century Legend*, Hemel Hempstead, Harvester Wheatsheaf, 1993.

Jane Gallop, *Thinking through the body*, New York, Columbia University Press, 1988.

Théophile Gautier, *Mademoiselle de Maupin* [1835], Paris, Garnier Flammarion, 1966.

Gérard Genette, *Introduction à l'architexte*, Paris, Editions du Seuil, 1979.

François Gère, 'La mesure de l'homme', *Cahiers du Cinéma*, No. 315 (September 1980), pp. 36–42.

Sandra M. Gilbert and Susan Gubar, *The Madwoman in the Attic*, New Haven, London, Yale University Press, 1979.

W. H. Gillespie, 'Homosexualité', *Revue française de psychanalyse* (July/August 1965).

René Girard, *Violence and The Sacred*, trans. Patrick Gregory, Baltimore, Johns Hopkins University Press, 1978.

Jean-Luc Godard, *Jean-Luc Godard par Jean-Luc Godard*, ed. Alain Bergala, Paris, Cahiers du Cinéma/Editions de L'Etoile, 1985.

———, 'Conférence-débat à la Fémis du 26 avril 1989', *Confrontations* (1990), pp. 15–23.

Hervé Guibert and Patrice Chéreau, *L'Homme blessé (scénario et notes)*, Paris, Editions de Minuit, 1983.

John Guillory, *Poetic Authority: Spenser, Milton, and Literary History*, New York, Columbia University Press, 1983.

Daniel Gunn, *Psychoanalysis and Fiction; an exploration of literary and psychoanalytic borders*, Cambridge, Cambridge University Press, 1988.

Sean Hand, 'Missing You: Intertextuality, transference and the language of love', *Intertextuality: Theories and practices*, ed. Judith Still and Michael Worton, Manchester, Manchester University Press, 1990.

———, 'Double Indemnity: The Ends of Citation in Edmond Jabès', *Romance Studies*, No. 12 (Summer 1986), pp. 77–86.

Stephen Heath, 'Repetition Time: Notes around "Structuralist/Materialist Films" ', *Wide Angle*, Vol. 2, No. 3 (1978), pp. 4–11.

Neil Hertz, *The End of the Line. Essays on Psychoanalysis and the Sublime*, New York, Columbia University Press, 1985.

Guy Hocquenghem, *Homosexual desire* [1972], trans. Daniella Dangoor, London, Allison and Busby, 1978.

———, *L'après-mai des faunes: volutions*, with a preface by Gilles Deleuze, Paris, Grasset, 1974.

———, *Lettre ouverte à ceux qui sont passés du col Mao au Rotary*, Paris, Albin Michel, 1986.

Luce Irigaray, *Ethique de la différence sexuelle*, Paris, Editions de Minuit, 1984.
Youssef Ishaghpour, *Cinéma contemporain: de ce côté du miroir*, Paris, Editions de la Différence, 1986.
Henry James, *The Jolly Corner and other tales*, ed. Roger Gard, Harmondsworth, Penguin, 1990.
'Jean de Berg', *L'Image*, Paris, Editions de Minuit, 1956.
Laurent Jenny, 'La stratégie de la forme', *Poétique*, No. 27 (1976), pp. 258–81.
Barbara Johnson, *The Critical Reference*, Baltimore, Johns Hopkins University Press, 1980.
Marcel Jouhandeau, *Bréviaire. Portrait de Don Juan. Amours*, Paris, Gallimard, 1981.
Berkeley Kaite, 'The Pornographer's Body Double: Transgression is the Law', *Body Invaders: Panic Sex in America*, ed. Arthur and Marilouise Kroker, New York, St Martin's Press, 1987.
E. Ann Kaplan, *Women and film. Both sides of the camera*, London, New York, Methuen, 1983.
Leslie Kaplan, *Le Pont de Brooklyn*, Paris, POL, 1987.
——, *L'excès-l'usine*, followed by 'Usine', an interview with Marguerite Duras, Paris, POL, 1987.
Sören Kierkegaard, *The Sickness unto Death* [1984], trans. Alistair Hannay, Harmondsworth, Penguin Books, 1989.
Wayne Koestenbaum, *Double Talk. The erotics of male literary collaboration*, New York, London, Routledge, 1989.
Kevin Kopelson, *Love's Litany: The Writing of Modern Homoerotics*, Stanford, CA, Stanford University Press, 1994.
Julia Kristeva, *Desire in Language: A semiotic approach to Literature and Art*, ed. Léon S. Roudiez, trans. Thomas Gora, Alice Jardine and Léon Roudiez, Oxford, Blackwell, 1980.
——, *Powers of Horror. An essay on abjection* [1980], trans. Léon S. Roudiez, New York, Columbia University Press, 1982.
——, 'Histoires d'amour—Love Stories', *ICA Documents*, No. 1 ('Desire'), London, Institute of Contemporary Arts, 1984, pp. 18–21.
——, *Tales of Love* [1983], trans. Léon S. Roudiez, New York, Columbia University Press, 1987.
Jacques Lacan, *Encore, Séminaire XX*, Paris, Editions du Seuil, 1975.
Candace Lang, *Irony/Humour*, Baltimore, Johns Hopkins University Press, 1988.
Monique Lange, *Les Cabines de bain*, Paris, Gallimard, 1984.
Jean Laplanche, *Life and Death in Psychoanalysis*, trans. Jeffrey Mehlman, Baltimore, Johns Hopkins University Press, 1976.
——, *Problématiques III: La Sublimation*, Paris, Presses Universitaires de France, 1980.
——, 'To situate sublimation', *October*, No. 28 (Spring 1984), pp. 7–26.
Jean-Jacques Lecercle, 'To Do or Not to Do Without the Word. Ecstasy and Discourse in the Cinema', *New Formations*, No. 16 (Spring 1992), pp. 80–90.
Emmanuel Levinas, *Totalité et infini: Essai sur l'extériorité* [1961], The Hague, Martinus Nijhoff, 1971.
Jack London, *Martin Eden* [1909], Harmondsworth, Penguin, 1985.

Jean-François Lyotard, *Discours, Figure*, Paris, Klincksieck, 1971.
——, *The Lyotard Reader*, ed. Andrew Benjamin, Oxford, Blackwell, 1989.
Juliet Flower MacCannell, *Figuring Lacan. Criticism and the Cultural Unconscious*, London and Sydney, Croom Helm, 1986.
Michèle Manceaux, *Brèves: Journal*, Paris, Editions du Seuil, 1984.
Dionys Mascolo, *Autour d'un effort de mémoire. Sur une lettre de Robert Antelme*, Paris, Maurice Nadeau, 1987.
Hans Mayer, *Outsiders. A study in Life and Letters*, trans. Denis M. Sweet, London, Cambridge, MA, The MIT Press, 1984.
Andrew J. McKenna, *Violence and Difference: Girard, Derrida, and Deconstruction*, Urbana, Chicago, University of Illinois Press, 1992.
Maurice Merleau-Ponty, *Le visible et l'invisible*, Paris, Gallimard, 1964.
Christian Metz, *The Imaginary Signifier. Psychoanalysis and Cinema*, trans. Celia Britton, Annwyl Williams, Ben Brewster, Alfred Guzzetti, London, Macmillan, 1982.
Catherine Millot, *Horsexe. Essay on transsexuality* [1983], trans. Kenneth Hylton, New York, Autonomedia, 1990.
Robert Musil, *L'homme sans qualités* [1952], trans. Philippe Jaccottet, Paris, Editions du Seuil, 'Points', 1956, 2 vols.
Dominique Noguez, *Sémiologie du parapluie et autres textes*, Paris, Editions de la Différence, 1990.
Peter Novick, *The Resistance versus Vichy: The Purge of Collaborators in Liberated France*, New York, Columbia University Press, 1968.
Raylene O'Callahan, *Robbe-Grillet and Modernity*, Gainesville, Florida University Press, 1992.
Camille Paglia, *Sexual Personae. Art and Decadence from Nefertiti to Emily Dickinson* [1990], New York, Vintage, 1991.
Constance Penley, *The Future of an Illusion: Film, Feminism and Psychoanalysis*, Minneapolis, University of Minnesota Press, 1989.
Carl Plesch, 'The Self-Sufficient Text in Nietzsche and Kierkegaard', *Yale French Studies*, No. 66 (1987), pp. 60–187.
Marcel Proust, *A la recherche du temps perdu*, Paris, Gallimard, 'Bibliothèque de la Pléiade', 1954, 3 vols.
——, *A l'ombre des jeunes filles en fleurs*, Paris, Gallimard, 1987, 2 vols.
Jean-Michel Ribetes, 'La troisième dimension du fantasme', in D. Anzieu et al., *Art et Fantasme*, Seyssel, Champ Vallon, 1984.
Michel Riffaterre, *The Semiotics of Poetry*, London, Methuen, 1978.
Maurice Roche, *Maladie, Mélodie*, Paris, Editions du Seuil, 1980.
Renato Rosaldo Jr, 'The Rhetoric of Control: Ilongots Viewed as Natural Bandits and Wild Indians', *The Reversible World*, ed. Barbara B. Babcock, Ithaca, London, Cornell University Press, 1978.
Jacqueline Rose, *The Haunting of Sylvia Plath*, Cambridge, MA, Harvard University Press, 1992.
George Sand, *Indiana* [1832], Paris, Garnier, 1989.
Lawrence R. Schehr, 'The homotext of Tournier's *Les Météores*', *Sub-stance*, Vol. 58, No. 1 (1989), pp. 35–50

Naomi Schor, 'Reading Double: Sand's Difference', *The Poetics of Gender*, ed. Nancy K. Miller, New York, Columbia University Press, 1986.

Eve Kosofsky Sedgwick, *Epistemology of the Closet*, Berkeley, Los Angeles, London, University of California Press, 1990.

Victor Segalen, *Essai sur l'exotisme: une esthétique du divers, etc*, Paris, Garnier-Flammarion, 1986.

——, *Voyage au pays du réel* [1915], Paris, Nouveau Commerce, 1980.

Daniel Sibony, 'La fiction de la dernière fois', *Cahiers du Cinéma*, No. 301 (June 1979), pp. 17–24.

Kaja Silverman, 'Masochism and Subjectivity', *Framework*, No. 12 (1980), pp. 2–9.

——, *The Subject of Semiotics*, Oxford, New York, Oxford University Press, 1983.

——, *The Acoustic Mirror. The Female Voice in Psychoanalysis and Cinema*, Bloomington, IN, Indiana University Press, 1988.

——, 'Too early/Too late: Subjectivity and the Primal Scene in Henry James', *Novel*, Vol. 21, Nos. 2–3 (Winter/Spring 1988), pp. 47–73.

——, *Male Subjectivity at the Margins*, New York, London, Routledge, 1992.

Gertrude Stein, *The Autobiography of Alice B. Toklas*, New York, Harcourt, Brace and Company, 1933.

——, *As Fine as Melanctha. The unpublished writings of Gertrude Stein*, New Haven, London, Yale University Press, 1954, Vol. 4 (1914–1930), ed. Carl Van Vechten, with an introduction by Nathalie Clifford Barney.

George Steiner, 'Dying is an Art', *The Art of Sylvia Plath*, ed. Charles Newman, Bloomington, London, Indiana University Press, 1970.

Judith Still, 'Literature', *Feminism and Psychoanalysis: A critical dictionary*, ed. Elizabeth Wright, Oxford, Blackwell, 1992.

Robert J. Stoller, 'Sexual Excitement', *Archives of General Psychiatry*, No. 33 (1976), pp. 899–909.

Gaylyn Studlar, *In the Realm of Pleasure. Von Sternberg, Dietrich and the Masochistic Aesthetic*, Urbana, IL, University of Illinois Press, 1988.

Alice Theilgaard and Murray Cox, *Mutative Metaphors in Psychotherapy: The Aeolian Mode*, London, New York, Tavistock Publications, 1987.

Tzvetan Todorov, *Nous et les autres. La réfléxion française sur la diversité humaine*, Paris, Editions du Seuil, 1989.

Michel Tournier, *Les météores*, Paris, Gallimard, 1975.

Ginette Vincendeau, 'Family Plots. The Father and Daughter of French cinema', *Sight and Sound*, Vol. 3, No. 4 (March 1992), pp. 14–17.

Kari Weil, *Androgyny and the Denial of Difference*, Charlottesville, London, University Press of Virginia, 1992.

Thomas Weiskel, *The Romantic Sublime: Studies in the Structure and the Psychology of Transcendence*, Baltimore, Johns Hopkins University Press, 1976.

Elie Wiesel, *Night* [1960], trans. Stella Rodway, New York, Bantam, 1989.

Tennessee Williams, *The Night of the Iguana*, New York, New Directions Books, 1962.

Kathleen Woodward, *Aging and its Discontents: Freud and Other Fictions*, Bloomington, IN, Indiana University Press, 1991.

Patricia Yaeger, 'Toward a Female Sublime', *Gender and Theory. Dialogues on Feminist Criticism*, ed. Linda Kauffman, Oxford, New York, Blackwell, 1989.

Thomas E. Yingling, *Hart Crane and the Homosexual Text. New Thresholds, New Anatomies*, Chicago, University of Chicago Press, 1990.

Slavoj Žižek, *Looking Awry. An introduction to Jacques Lacan through Popular Culture*, Cambridge, MA, The MIT Press, 1991.

Lynda Zwinger, *Daughters, Fathers, and the Novel. The Sentimental Romance of Heterosexuality*, Madison, University of Wisconsin Press, 1991.

Index